GENEALOGY

OF SOME DESCENDANTS OF

DR. SAMUEL FULLER

OF THE MAYFLOWER

COMPILED BY

WILLIAM HYSLOP FULLER

OF PALMER, MASS.

TO WHICH IS ADDED A SUPPLEMENT TO THE

GENEALOGY

OF SOME DESCENDANTS OF

EDWARD FULLER

OF THE MAYFLOWER
PUBLISHED IN 1908

PRINTED BY
C. B. FISKE & Co.
PALMER, MASS.
1910.

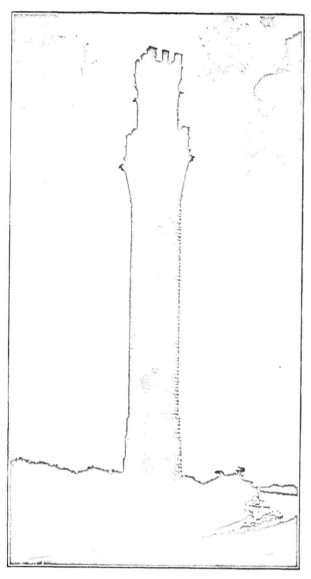

THE PILGRIM MEMORIAL
AT
PROVINCETOWN. MASS
DEDICATED AUGUST 5, 1910.

FREDERICK A. FULLER.

BOOKS

COMPILED, PUBLISHED AND FOR SALE BY

WILLIAM H. FULLER,   23 SCHOOL ST., PALMER, MASS.

Genealogy of Some Descendants of Edward Fuller of the Mayflower.
1 volume, 8 vo., cloth, 25 illustrations, 306 pp.
Price, postpaid, $5.00.

Genealogy of Some Descendants of Dr. Samuel Fuller of the Mayflower, with Supplement to the Edward Fuller volume.
1 volume, 8 vo., cloth, 31 illustrations, 263 pp.
Price, $5.00, postpaid.

CONTENTS.

PREFACE.

Nearly nine generations of Dr Samuel Fuller's descendants have passed away without any collection of their genealogical records having been made. Meanwhile old records have been fading, wearing out, being lost, neglected and burned, as for example, the list of towns whose documents have been destroyed by fire is quite extensive

While making a search for the records of descendants of Edward Fuller of the Mayflower, a brother of Dr Samuel, and since publishing (in 1908) the material obtained, I have been collecting information concerning this, another of the the ancestral American Fuller families, and herewith present the results thus far obtained.

Records of this kind will always be incomplete, and in this case it is my judgment that it is time, and the safest and most advisable course, to publish what I have already obtained rather than await the slow and uncertain process of accumulation of some of the data which will be found wanting.

In regard to the term "Ancestral Fuller families," it has seemed quite appropriate to speak of those American families as ancestral, whose emigrant ancestor settled in America prior to 1650.

These heads of families so far as I know were ten in number:

Edward Fuller, born in 1575, came to America in 1620.
Dr. Samuel, born in 1580, came to America in 1620. •
John of Lynn, born in ?, came to America in 1630.
John of Newton, born in 1611, came to America in 1635.
John of Ipswich, born in 1620, came to America in 1635.
Thomas of Woburn; born in ?, came to America in 1638.
Robert of Salem,·born in ?, came to America in 1638.
Robert of Dorchester, born in ?, came to America in 1640.
Captain Matthew, born in ?, came to America in 1640.
Thomas of Dedham, born in ?, came to America in 1642.

In this volume the extension of data concerning those descendants not bearing the name of Fuller, has been more restricted than in the first volume, in order to keep the cost of the work within the bounds suggested by previous experience. Beyond the names and dates of birth of children of Fuller daughters, who have married those having other names than Fuller, genealogical details have generally been left to the genealogist of the allied family.

The compiler has been especially aided in the records of the earlier generations by the work of the late Newton Fuller of New London, Ct., by the MSS of Prof. H. W. Brainard of Hartford, Ct., and by material furnished by F. A. Fuller of Buffalo, N. Y. and Charles M. Thatcher of Middleboro, Mass., all of whom are experienced genealogists.

Among correspondents, I have been favored by having many who were particularly interested in the work, as Mrs. L. A. Cobb, No. 148 of 1st Group, Mr. W. F. Fuller, No. 255 of 5th Group; the late Charles Richardson Smith, husband of Mrs. Nellie (Fuller) Smith, No. 319 of 5th Group; Miss Sarah M. Fuller, No. 143 of 5th Group, Mr. E. L. Philoon, descendant of No. 117 of 5th Group, Miss Mabel A, No 226, and Mr. Linus E. Fuller, No. 116 of 12th Group, and Mrs Anna (Fuller) Bennett, No. 69 of the 13th Group, and there are many others to whom thanks are due not only from the compiler, but also from the descendants.

Acknowledgements are also due to "The Mayflower Descendant" Magazine, the New England Historical and Genealogical Register, and the authors of numerous family genealogies for information taken from their pages.

Since it has seemed a most appropriate place, I have added to this volume a supplement containing additional information concerning the descendants of Edward Fuller of the Mayflower, and corrections of errors in Volume 1 that have been brought to my notice

These two volumes constitute what may be considered the "Mayflower Fuller Genealogy," and by Mayflower Fullers I mean those who came to America in 1620 on the ship Mayflower, and their descendants.

In conclusion I desire to thank the printers, C. B. Fiske & Company, of Palmer, Mass., for their care and attention; the photo-engravers, especially Mr McKinnon, of James B. McKinnon & Co., of Springfield, Mass., for his personal interest in the making of half-tone portraits, and the binder, Mr. W. J. Eldred of Springfield, for neat and substantial work on these volumes.

WM. H. FULLER.

Palmer, July, 1910.

ILLUSTRATIONS.

ABBREVIATIONS.

b., born , bapt., baptized

d , died.

G. S , Gravestone record.

m., married

Int. Pub., marriage intentions published.

? not sure of name or date.

In some cases the initials "H. W. B.", "F. A. F.", "N. F.", "C. M. T." and "L. E. F." have been used to indicate information obtained from H. W. Brainard, F. A. Fuller, Newton Fuller, Charles M. Thatcher, and Linus E. Fuller.

EXPLANATIONS.

In the arrangement of the genealogical record, each descendant bearing the surname Fuller has an individual number and also a family number.

The sign ‡ placed before the family number of a son indicates that his family record is given further on, in his group and generation, placed in order of seniority by his individual number.

In the case of daughters, it has been the intention to give immediately after their individual and family number and names, their individual genealogical record, and in case of marriage the date of the same, with name of husband, and if there are children their names and date and place of birth, their further genealogical record being generally left to the genealogist of the allied family. The explanation of the change from the record by generations to record by group and generation is given on page 22.

AMERICAN FULLER GENEALOGY.

DR. SAMUEL FULLER LINE.

SAMUEL[1] FULLER, born in England; baptized there Jan. 29, 1580; d. ———— 1633 in Plymouth, Mass.; m. 1, Alice Glascock; m. 2, April 24, 1613, Agnes Carpenter, who died ———— 1615 in Leyden, Holland; m. 3, May 27, 1617, Bridget Lee.

Samuel[1] Fuller was one of the band of Pilgrims, persecuted on account of religious convictions, who escaped from England to Holland in 1608, and settled in Leyden, Holland, in 1609.

In the results of Mr. Dexter's researches among the records of Holland, published in a volume entitled "The England and Holland of the Pilgrims," Samuel[1] Fuller is mentioned as a witness Oct. 7, 1611, to the betrothal of Degory Priest, and to that of William White Jan. 27, 1612.

As the widower of Alice Glascock, it is recorded he was betrothed to Agnes Carpenter March 15, 1613, and the witnesses were her father, Alexander Carpenter, Edward Southworth, William White, Roger Nelson, her sister, Alice Carpenter, and his sister, Anna or Susanna (Fuller) White.

Samuel[1] Fuller was also a witness May 7, 1613, to the betrothal of his sister-in-law, Alice Carpenter, to Edward Southworth, and that of Samuel Terry May 16, 1614. He buried his child June 29, 1615, and his wife Agnes July 3, 1615. Later he lived in Pieterskerkhof and was a witness Aug. 7, 1615, to the betrothal of Samuel Butler, and that of Edmond Jessup Sept. 16, 1615. He was betrothed to Bridget Lee, May 12, 1617, and as witnesses there were her mother, Josephine Lee, and her brother, Samuel Lee.

They took up their residence near Marepoort, and Samuel[1] Fuller witnessed the betrothal of John Goodman Sept. 16, 1619. He

joined with Isaac Allerton, Mr. Bradford and Mr. Winslow June 10,
1620, in a letter concerning the affairs of the Pilgrims, to their
associates, Mr. Carver and Mr. Cushman, then in England.

The Pilgrims left Holland for America about Aug. 1, 1620, by way
of Southampton, England, and Samuel[1] Fuller's name appears as
one of the signers of the "Compact" drawn up for the government
of the Colony at Cape Cod, in November, 1620, in the vicinity of
what is now Provincetown, Mass. Some days later the Pilgrims
made a permanent landing and settled at what is now Plymouth,
Mass.

Bridget (Lee) Fuller, third wife of Samuel[1] Fuller, came to
America in 1623 on the ship Anne. The date and place of her
death are not now known.

Anna, or Susanna (Fuller) White, sister of Samuel[1] Fuller, came
to America with the Pilgrims in 1620. She died in 1680. She
married for her first husband William White in Holland, who died
at Plymouth, March 3, 1621. She married second, Edward Winslow,
who became the third governor of the Colony. It was also his
second marriage. He died in 1655. By her first husband she had
Peregrine White, born on the Mayflower between Dec. 7 and 10,
1620, and Resolved White. It is stated that she had several
children by her second husband.

Alexander Carpenter, father of Samuel[1] Fuller's second wife, was
from Wrington in Somerset, England, and had five daughters, Agnes,
Alice, Juliana, Priscilla and Mary. The last four came to America.
Alice married first Edward Southworth; second, William Bradford.
Juliana married George Morton. Priscilla married William Wright.
Mary remained single.

It has been said that Samuel[1] Fuller was also from Wrington, but
from the researches of Mr. Francis H. Fuller in England, it appears
he was baptized in Redenhall Parish in Harleston, Norfolk County,
England, as a son of Robert Fuller. For extracts from the earliest
records of the Redenhall Parish Church, reference is made to the
55th volume of the New England Historical and Genealogical
Register. For a copy of the will of Robert Fuller, father of Samuel[1]
Fuller, see the volume on "Some Descendants of Edward Fuller of
the Mayflower," published by the compiler of this volume in
September, 1908.

Samuel[1] Fuller was a physician, and the biographical sketches

Redenhall Parish Church, Interior.

Redenhall Parish Church, Interior.

published mention him as eminent in his profession, devoutly pious, and wise in counsel in the affairs of the Massachusetts Bay Colony. His will, a copy of which is printed herewith, indicates that he was just, kind hearted and benevolent.

His children were:

	I.	A child that died in Holland.
2.	II.	A child born in Holland that died young in Plymouth, Mass.
3.	III.	Samuel², born about 1625 ; m. Elizabeth Brewster.
4.	IV.	Mary², b. ——, m. Ralph James.

Will of Dr. Samuel Fuller.

The first will entered in the first volume of Plymouth Colony Wills and Inventories is that of Dr. Samuel Fuller.

New Plymouth
1633
A true Coppy of the last will and Testm of Samuel ffuller the elder as it was proved in publick Court the 28th of Oct in the ninth yeare of the raigne of our Soveraign Lord Charles by the grace of God King of Engl Scott. ffr. & Irel. Defender of the ffaith &c

I Samuel ffuller the elder being sick & weake but by the mercie of God in perfect memory ordaine this my last will & Testmt And first of all I bequeath my soule to God & my body to the earth untill the resureccon Item I doe bequeath the educacon of my children to my Brother Will Wright & his wife, onely that my daughter Mercy be & remaine wthgoodwife Wallen so long as she will keepe her at a reasonable charge. But if it shall please God to recover my wife out of her weake estate of sickness then my children to be wth her and disposed by her. Also whereas there is a childe comitted to my charge called Sarah Converse, my wife dying as afore I desire my Brother Wright may have the bringing up of her. And if he refuse then I comend her to my loving Neighbour & brother in Christ Thomas Prence desiring that whosoever of them receive her pforme the duty of a step ffather unto her & bring her up in the ffear of God as their owne, wch was a charge laid upon me pr her sick ffather when he freely bestowed her upon me & wch I require of them. Item whereas Eliz Cowles was comitted to my educacon by her ffather & Mother still living at Charles Towne, my will is that she be conveniently apprelled & returne to her ffather or mother or either of them. And for George ffoster being placed wth me upon the same termes by his prents still living at Sago's (Lynn) my will is that he be restored to his Mother like wise

Item I give to Samuell my son my howse & lands at the Smeltriver to him & his heires for ever. Item (worn) will is that my Howse & garden at towne be sold & all my moveables there & at the Smeltriver (except my Cattle)

togeather wth the p^rnt Croppe of Corne there standing by my Overseers heer-after to be mencroned, except such as they shall thinke meet in the p^rnt educacon of my two children Samuell & Mercy my debts being first p^d out of them, the overplus to be disposed of towards the encrease of my stock of Cattle for their good at the discretion of my overseers   Item   I give two Acres of land that fell unto me by lott on the South side the Towne adjoyning to the Acres of m^r Isaack Allerton to Samuell my son   Also two other Acres of land wch were given me by Edward Bucher scituate & being at Strawberry hill if m^r Roger Williams refuse to accept of them as formerly he hath done   Also one other Acre by m^r Heeks his Acres neer the Reed pond All wch I give to the said Samuell and his heires forever. • It. my will is that my Cozen Samuell goe freely away wth his Stock of Cattle & Swine w^thout any further recconing which swine are the halfe of six sowes Six Hogges one boare & fowr shotes Also one Cow & one heyfer ˙ Item   my will is that not onely the other halfe afore menconed but also all other mine owne propr stock of Swine be sold wth other my moveables for the use before expressed except my best hogg wch I would have killed this winter for the p^rnt comfort of my children. It. whereas I have disposed of my children to my brother Will Wright & Prisilla his wife my will is that in case my wife die he enter upon my howse & land at the Smelt River & also my Cattle not disposed on together wth my two serv^ts Thomas Symons & Robt Cowles for the Remainder of their several termes to be employed for the good of my children he being allowed for their charg vizt my childrens what my Overseers shall thinke meet   But if in case my said brother Will Wright or Prisilla his wife die then my said Children Samuell & Mercy together wth the said joynt charge committed to the said Will & Prisilla be void except my Overseers (2) or the survivor of them shall think meet. To whos (worn) godly care in such case I leave them to be disposed of else where as the I aw shall direct them. My cattle not disposed on o to be employed for the good of my children I meane three Cowes & two steere calves Six old ewes & two ewe lambs two old wethers & three wether lambs together wth such overplus upon the sale of my goods before expressed as my Overseers shall adde heerunto. It. I give out of this stock of Cattle the first Cow calfe that my Browne Cow shall have to the Church of God at Plymouth to be employed by the Deacon or Deacons of the said Church for the good of the said Church at the oversight of the ruling Elders. Item   I give to my sister Alice Bradford twelve shillings to buy her a paire of gloves. Item   whatsoever is due unto me from Capt Standish I give unto his children. It. that a pr. of gloves of 5sh be bestowed on m^r Joh. Wynthrop Govr of the Massachusetts. It. I give unto my brother Wright aforesaid one cloath suit not yet fully finished lying in my trunk at Towne wch I give notw standing my wife survive. It. whereas Capt John Endecott oweth me two pownds of Beaver I give it to his sonne. It. my will is that when my children come to age of discretion that my Overseers make a full valuacon of that stock of Cattle & the increase thereof, & that it be equally devided between my children   And if any die in the meane time the whole to goe to the survivor or survivors It. my will is that they be ruled by my Overseers in marriage Also I would have them enjoy that smale porcon the Lord shall give them when my Overseers thinke them to be of fit discretion & not at any set time or appointm^t of yeares. It whereas my will is that my Overseers shall let out that stock of Cattle wch shall be bought wth the Overplus of my goods to halves to such as shall be as well carefull as honest men My will is that my brother Wright have the refusall of them It I give unto John Jenny & Joh. Wynslow each of them a paire of gloves of five shillings. It I give unto m^rs Heeks the full sum of twenty shillings. It. I give unto old m^r Brewster my best hat and band wch I h (worn) never wore. It my will is that if my children die that then my stock be thus distributed ffirst that what care or paines or charge hath been by any about my children be fully recompensed Next at the discretion of the Overseers I thus bequeath the rest vizt so as it may redownd to the Governing Elder or Elders of this Church at Plymouth aforesaid & towards the helping of such psons as are members of the same & are (illegible) as my Overseers shall thinke meet. It I give to Rebecca Prence 2sh 6d to buy her a paire of gloves . It my will is that in case my sonne Samuell & other my children die before such time as they are fitt to enter upon my land for inheritance that then my kinsman Sam ffuller now in the howse wth me enjoy w^tsoever lands I am now possessed of except my dwelling howse at town or whatsoever shall be due to me or them It. I give to him my Ruffet Cloake & my stuffe sute I now weare. It. I institute my son Samuell my Executor. and because he is young and tender I enjoyne him to be wholly ordered by Edw Wynslow m^r Will Bradford & m^r Tho Prence whom I make his Overseers & the Overseers of this my last will & Testm^t so often menconed before in the same. And for their paines I give to each of them twenty shillings apeece It I give to Mercy my daughter one Bible wth a black Cover wth Bezaes notes It I give all the rest of my bookes to my sonne Samuell wch I desire my Brother Wright Will safely preserve for him. It my will is that when my daughter Mercy is fitt to goe to scole that m^rs Heeks may teach her as well as my sonne It whatsoever m^r Roger Williams is indebted to me upon my booke for phisick I freely give him Last of all whereas my wife is sick & weake I have disposed of my children to others my will is if sue recover that she have the educacon of them, & that the other gifts and legacies I have given may be pformed And if in case any of my Overseers or all of them (3) die before my children be judged by them of age of discretion then my desire is they will before such time when they dispose of their owne affaires depute some other of the Church to pform this duty of care & love towards my children, wch I allow & binde my children to obedience as before. In witnes that this is my last will & Test I have set to my hand & seale the 30th of July Anno 1633.

Samuell ffuller

Memorand that whereas the widow
Ring comitted the Oversight of her sonne
Andrew to me at her death, my will is that

m^r Prence one of my Overseers
take the charge of him & see that he be
brought up in the ffeare of the Lord
& See that he sustaine no wrong by any
                    Witnesses heerun to
                        Robt Heeks
                        John Wynslow
See his Inventory, Fol 22 (This line is in a different hand)
    A note of such debts as Sam ffuller acknowledged
    upon his death bed, at the making of the foresaid
    will
I owe to the Acco of Company in the Massachusets six or ten shillings if
ffr Johnson of Salem have not pd it   It. I owe m^r Joh Winthrop one
hogsh of Corne for lines I bought of him, but doubt whether pd or not. If
he demand it, pay it.
It. I owe him for a Sow of leade except X sh wch I have pd as appeareth
pr receipt
It. whereas Henry Wood demands an old debt due at Leyden I desire that
w^t soever he demand as due debt be pd by my overseers he dealing faithfully.
It whereas I have an herball belonging to Joh Chew of Plymouth in old
Engl. I desire when the price is known he may be pd   Also whereas there is
an Acco between Joh Jenny Manasseh Kempton & myselfe where in we are
all debtors to Joh Cheew my desire is my pt may be pd

Mention having been made of a "Fuller Fund" for the support
of the ministry of the Plymouth church, the foundation of said
fund being the proceeds derived from the sale of a plot of ground
on Leyden Street given to the church for a parsonage by Mrs.
Bridget (Lee) Fuller, widow of Dr. Samuel Fuller, and Samuel
Fuller his son, I wrote the pastor of the Congregational church in
Plymouth and received the following : "The fund you wrote about
is the "Fuller Ministerial Fund," which is used for the purpose
named in your note, but not from the source you mentioned. That
place was sold and the money used. The "fund" came from an
unborn calf. I mean that the calf was bequeathed before it came
into the world, and the proceeds of it when a cow was allowed to
accumulate, and it has grown into the thousands. This is the
history of the "Fuller Ministerial Fund."

Readers are referred to the item in Dr. Samuel's will, given above,
relative to "the first cow calfe that my Browne Cow shall have."

The Fuller Cradle.

SECOND GENERATION.

SAMUEL [2] FULLER, (*Samuel[1]*), b. ———, 1625, in Plymouth, Mass. His burial place was on the "Hill" at Plymouth, and the gravestone inscription reads: "Here lyes ye bodie of ye Rev. Samuel Fuller, who departed this life Aug. ye 17, 1695, in ye 71st year of his age. He was ye 1st minister of ye church in Middleborough."

He married Elizabeth Brewster (Records 1st Church of Middleborough, Mass.), who died in Plympton, Mass., Nov. 11, 1713. (Plympton Records.)

Samuel [2] Fuller was one of the 26 original proprietors of Middleborough. The Indians burned his home there in 1676 and he returned to Plymouth until the war with them was over. He had been educated for the ministry and preached several years at Middleborough, but was not ordained until 1694. His biographers describe him as a sober, grave, industrious, enlightened, and self-denying man.

His children were:

5.	I.	Mercy [3], b. about 1656, m. Daniel Cole.
6.	‡II.	Samuel [3], b. about 1659; m. Mercy Eaton.
7.	III	Experience [3], b. about 1661; m. April 2, 1693, James Wood and had sons Benjamin, Barnabas, Abel and Ichabod James or Jonathan
8.	‡IV.	John [3], b. 1663; m. Mercy Nelson.
9.	V.	Elizabeth [3], b. 1666; m. May 24, 1694, Samuel Eaton, b. 1665.
10.	VI.	Hannah [3], b. 1668; m Eleazer Lewis.
11	‡VII.	Isaac [3], b. 1675; m. Mary Pratt.

Settlement of Rev. Samuel Fuller's Estate.

Rev. Samuel Fuller, son of Dr. Samuel Fuller of the Mayflower, died intestate at Middleborough 17 August, 1695, and his widow Elizabeth was appointed administratrix 25 September, 1695. The record of this appointment and of the inventory taken 5 September 1695, may be found in the Plymouth County Probate Records, volume I, page 223. On page 224 is recorded the appointment of a guardian for the minor son Isaac, and on pages 246 and 247 is the agreement between the heirs.

The appointment and the administration bond are omitted here as not being of great genealogical interest.

INVENTORY.

Semtember the 5· 1695

this is a tru inventary of the Estate of mr Samuell Fuller Teacher of the church of middelbury Lately deaseased prised by us whose names are under written

his wearm cloathing woollin and linnen	09 00 00
his books	04 00 00
to bods with bedin	07 00 00
puter with table linnen	01 04 00
a still	01 00 00
the brase to kittells and a spice mortter	00 14 00
A iron pot and kittell and mortter	00 16 00
tramells tongs and pot hooks	00 08 00
chests and trays and dishes and chairs	00 15 00
tubs and pails	00 08 00
Earthen ware and glases	00 02 00
runlets and barells and a churn	00 07 00
a siften trof and a frien pan	00 04 00
a loom and taklin	01 05 00
hors taklin	00 18 00
taklin for a teem and old iron	00 12 00
a pare of oxen	05 00 00
3 cowes	04 10 00
3 heifer	03 10 00
2 Calves	00 12 00
swine	01 15 00
a hors and a mare	03 00 00
3 swarm of bees	00 08 00

atmiddelbury his dwellin hous and 20 Akers of Land and A full share of the six and twenty mens purchas only twenty five Akers and twelf Akers of Land near John haskels and a parsell of Land Cominly called the sixteen shillin purshas and A hous and Land Plimouth

more to books and a bibell	00 15 00
tow pare of scalles	00 06 00
three wheells and a pare of cards	00 10 00
A pot and a spoon	00 07 00
A gun	00 02 00
toue yarn	00 08 00
The widdows Bed not apprised	

Joseph : Vaughan

Samuell wood

Mrs Elizabeth ffuller Relict & Widdow of Saml ffuller above named made oath in Plimouth September 25th · 1695 that ye above Written is a true Inventory of ye Goods Chattels Rights & Credits of ye sd Deceased so far

as she knoweth & that if more shall come to her knowledge she will make it
known

Before William Bradford Esqr &c.

Attest Saml Sprague Register

The above written Inventory is Recorded in ye 223d page of ye first Book
of wils Recorded for the County of Plimouth.

pr Saml Sprague Register

(From Original Document.)

APPOINTMENT OF GUARDIAN.

Memorand ye 25 of Sept 1695

John Nelson of Plimouth appointed Guardian to Isaac ffuller Son of mr
Saml ffuller late of Middleborough deceased

pr William Bradford judge

(Plym. Co Prob. Rcds, I · 224)

AGREEMENT OF THE HEIRS.

This agreement made betwixt the widdow Mrs Elizabeth ffuller and all the
Children of Mr Samuel ffuller late Minister of Middleborough in ye County
of Plimouth in New England deceased Namely Samuel ffuller & Daniel Cole
and Mercy his wife James wood and Experience his wife Samuel Eaton
Elizabeth his wife Hannah ffuller and John Nelson as Guardian to Isaac
ffuller ye youngest son of sd fuller deceased and John ffuller said widdow
and all said childern have mutually and firmly Covenanted and Agreed & do
by these presents firmly Covenant and agree for themselves & every of their
heirs and assigns forever to and with each other That ye Articles herein to be
mentioned shall be and are the full & satisfying division and disposall of ye
estate of said mr ffuller deceased And that sd Widdow and all the children
above mentioned are and forever will be fully satisfied & contented with this
Settlement both of ye lands and all ye goods & chattels of sd estate as hereafter followeth.

Imprs It is agreed that Samuel ffuller ye eldest son of sd deceased Mr
ffuller Quietly possess & enjoy for his portion to him and his heirs & Assigns
for Ever that seat of land in ye Town of Plimouth aforesaid which formerly
was the possession of his said ffather and of late years Possessed by said
Samuel his son with a house Standing therupon with all uplands and
meadows & all priviledges belonging there unto Provided sd Samuel ffuller
pay or cause to be paid Annually to mrs Elizabeth ffuller Relict of his said
father ten shillings in silver money at or before the first day of each October
during ye time She remains a widow. ffurther it is agreed as aforesaid that
John ffuller ye Second son of ye said deceased have one hundred acres of
land with ye meadow lying at ye foot of said land which land said John ffuller
hath now in his possession and is Butting upon Namasket River lying in ye
lands purchased by Captain Thomas Southworth on ye North side of ye
Road from Lakenham to Namasket River with half ye meadow lying in ye
Gre at Meadow said lott of meadow is to be divided into two equall parts

and said John ffuller to take his choyce And in that purchase one share of ye undivided lands of said Purchase And if hereafter said undivided land shall be divided into lotts then said John ffuller is to have and choose his half of sd Divisions Also it is agreed as aforesaid that said Widdow Elizabeth ffuller Quietly have and possess the House and land which she now possesses in Middlebury Contayning Twenty acres more or less in ye Homestead Twelve acres more lying by ye lands of John Haskall and twenty acres of Land more or less lying at ye upei end of ye Great Meadow in said Captain Southworths purchase together with ye one half of said meadow divided and undivided belonging to sud Purchase This housing and lands mentioned the said widdow is to enjoy wholy to her own proper use and benefit untill Isaac ffuller the youngest son of sd ffuller deceased arrive at ye Age of twety one years After which said Isaac ffuller is to have the one half of said House and said Widdow to have the other half And said Isaac is then to have two thirds of said Lands and sd Widdow one third during her life and after her decease said Isaac ffuller is to have and enjoy the whole house and all said lands to him and his heirs and Assigns forever It is also further agreed as aforesaid That after all ye just debts are paid the said Widdow ffuller shall have one full third part of ye moveables of sd Estate in what specie soever it be to her own prper use and benifit for ever moreover it is agreed that if said widdow dye before her son Isaac come to ye age of one and twenty years then ye Guirdian of said Isaac hath full power and liberty to lease out said house and land for ye use and benifit of said Isaac till he Come of age to possess it   further more it is firmly Covenanted and Agreed as aforesaid that upon the decease of said Widdow the said House shall be apprised by persons (p 247) Indifferently chosen by ye children concerned and ye value of it to be divided into Six equall parts and given to Mercy Cole John ffuller Experience wood Elizabeth Laton Hannah ffuller and Isaac ffuller said Isaac ffuller Reserving his own sixth part of ye value of said House to himselfe is to pay ye Remainder of ye value of said House to his said Brother John and his said ffour sisters each of them a just proportion equally And said Isaac shall have liberty for two year before he pay said legacies to his said Brother and sisters after he comes to age if at that age of twenty one years he enter upon ye full and Intire possession of ye whole house but if it be some years after he is of age before he come fully to possess said house by ye decease of his mother then he shall be obliged to pay said legacies within a year after his taking possession of said house And if his mother dye before he sd Isaac come of age yet he shall not be obliged to pay said legacies till two years after his being of age ffurthermore it is agreed as aforesaid that for all ye lands in plimouth Township that are not before exprest in this Instrument that are part of ye estate of sd mr ffuller deceased they are hereby granted & confirmed to Mercy Cole before named to her and her heirs for ever Particularly a Grant of land by said Plimouth Town or Court to said ffuller lying at doteys meadow in said Township And for his land in ye sixteene shilling purchase and all his right of land in Assawamset Neck at or near

Middleborough aforesaid it is mutually agreed as aforesaid That said land be herby granted and confirmed to Experience Wood Elizabeth Eaton and Hannah ffuller to them their heirs and Assigns forever to be equally divided betwixt them. It is also agreed as aforesd That ye two thirds of ye moveable Estate of sd ffuller be divided into four equall parts and to be equally divided betwixt the four sisters above named Mercy Experience Elizabeth and Hannah what each of them hath already Received being to be accounted as part of their portion and accordingly ye Remainder out of these two thirds to make each of their portions alike for ye full and firm Confirmation and Establishment of all and every of said Articles the widdow and children before named have set to their hand and Seals this first day of October one thousand Six hundred Ninety and five was ye day wherein sd widdow and children made these articles of agreement.

Signed and sealed and declared to be	The E mark of
the joynt agreement of ye parties	Elizabeth ffuller (seal)
herein concerned in presence of	Samuel ffuller (seal)
William Bradford	The mark of
ye Mark of Samuel Wood	Mercy Cole (seal)
Elkanah Cushman	John ffuller (seal)
Thomas Nelson	John Nelson (seal)
	James Wood } Experience Wood } (seal)
	Samuel Eighton } The mark } (seal) Elizabeth Eaton }
	Hannah ffuller (seal)

Elizabeth ffuller Samuel ffuller Mercy Cole John ffuller John Nelson James Wood Experience Wood Samuel Eaton Elizabeth Eaton Hannah ffuller Coming all of them personally before me 27th of July 1696 did freely own and acknowledge ye Instrument above written to be their act and deed

William Bradford Justice of peace

Entered on Record Novembr 20th 1696.

pr Saml Sprague Register

(Plym. Co. Prob. Rcds., I 246,247)

THIRD GENERATION.

6. SAMUEL[3] FULLER, (*Samuel[2]*, *Samuel[1]*), b. 1659; d. Sept. 6, 1728, at Plympton, Mass., m. Jan. 7, 1685, Mercy Eaton, dau. of Samuel and Martha (Billington) Eaton and granddau. of Francis Eaton (Mayflower 1620).

Samuel[3] Fuller resided in Plympton, Mass.

His children were recorded in Plymouth, Mass., as follows:

12.	‡I.	Nathaniel[4], b. Nov. 14, 1687; m. Martha Sampson.
13.	II.	Samuel[4], b. Aug. 30, 1689; d. April 19, 1724, at Plympton.
14.	III.	William[4], b Feb. 14, 1691; d. Aug. 26, 1692.
15.	‡IV.	Seth[4], b. Aug. 30, 1692, m. 1, Sarah Wright; m. 2, Widow Deborah Cole.
16.	‡V.	Ebenezer[4], b March 24, 1695; m Joanna Gray.
17.	‡VI.	Benjamin[4], b. March 7, 1696; m. Mary (Jackson) Eddy
18.	VII.	Elizabeth[4], b March 20, 1697, m. John Eaton.
19.	‡VIII.	John[4], b. Dec. 19, 1698; m. 1, Deborah Ring; m. 2, Mrs Mercy Cushman.
20.	IX.	Jabez[4], b. June, 1701; m. 1, Deborah Soule; m. 2, Mercy Gray.
21.	X.	Mercy[4], b. Oct 3, 1702; m. Ebenezer Raymond.
22.	‡XI	James[4], b. Feb. 27, 1704, m. Judith Rickard.

8. JOHN[3] FULLER, (*Samuel[2]*, *Samuel[1]*), b. about 1668 in Plymouth or Middleboro, Mass., d. about 1710 at Middleboro; m. about 1686, Mercy Nelson.

Children, born probably in Middleboro or Halifax, Mass.:

23.	‡I.	John[4], b March 20, 1692; m 1, Hannah Thomas; m. 2, Lydia (Alden) Eddy.
24.	II.	Mercy[4], b. ———, 1693, m. 1, July 13, 1729, Jabez Wood? (H. W. Brainard MSS.)
25.	III.	Elizabeth[4], b ———, m. July 17, 1729, John Eaton of Kingston, Mass.
26.	‡IV.	Ebenezer[4], b. Nov. 1, 1697, m. Elizabeth Short.
27.	‡V.	Jabez[4], b ———, 1698; m. Priscilla Sampson.
28.	VI.	Lydia[4], b. ———, 1701; m. June 12, 1733, Francis Eaton as 2d wife and had Sylvanus[5], b. Dec. 21, 1735; John[5], b. Aug. 12, 1737, Mary[5], b. Feb. 16, 1738/9; Elijah[5], b. Nov. 7, 1740; Benjamin[5], b. March 26, 1742; and Susannah[5], b. Sept. 13, 1743.
29.	‡VII.	Samuel[4], b. ———, 1704, m. Silence Short.

30.   VIII.   Joanna[4], b. ——— ; m. Dec. 11, 1728, Thomas Doggett of Mansfield, Mass, and had *John*[5], b. 1729, *Thomas*[5], b. 1731, *Mark*[5], b. 1733; *Jabez*[5], b. March 3, 1734, *Seth*[5], b. Feb. 15, 1736, *Simeon*[5], b. Jan. 4, 1738; *Experience*[5], b May 16, 1740, and *Joanna*[5], b. March 16, 1742. (Doggett Genealogy, by S. B. Doggett.)

11.   ISAAC[3] FULLER, (*Samuel*[2], *Samuel*[1]), b. about 1675 in Plymouth, Mass.; d. 1727 in Brockton, (formerly N. Bridgewater) Mass., m. Oct. 20, 1709, Mary Pratt, married by Mr. Isaac Cushman (Plympton Records). He was a celebrated physician and resided at Halifax, Mass.

Of his children, the first two are recorded at Plympton and the others at Middleboro, Mass. :

31.   I.   Reliance[4], b. Dec. 28, 1710; m. ——— Waterman.
32.   ‡II.   Isaac[4], b. Sept. 24, 1712, m. Sarah Packard.
33.   III.   Elizabeth[4], b. July 23, 1715.
34.   ‡IV.   Samuel[4], b. Jan. 29, 1718/19; m. Elizabeth Thompson.
35.   V.   Micah[4], b. Jan. 31, 1719/20. Mr. Linus E. Fuller, of 12th Group, 8th Generation, states that his grandfather gave information to Rufus[7], his nephew, April 1, 1834, to the effect that Micah Fuller lived in Worcester, Mass., but his home was burned by Indians and he removed to Old Hadley, Mass., but was again burned out by Indians and removed to Schenectady, N. Y.; stated that Micah was wealthy; owned mills; dropped dead in a mill. Rufus[7] made a memorandum of this information which was found after his death, and a copy given to Mr. Linus E. Fuller. I have found nothing in histories of the above places relating to Micah Fuller.
36.   ‡VI.   Jabez[4], b. May 7, 1723; m. Elizabeth Hilliard.
37.   VII.   Mary[4], b. Aug. 23, 1726.

Explanation of Group Arrangement.

From this point the arrangement of the work is made similar to that found so satisfactory in the Edward Fuller volume. Sons of the third generation are made the heads of groups, and the genealogy of each group completed by itself by generations, as before, with individual numbering relative to the groups and family numbering, as before. The sons, who have had families, form heads of 14 groups arranged in order of seniority of the fathers.

Group Number	Individual Number	LINEAGE	Date of Birth
1	12	Nathaniel⁴, *Samuel³, Samuel², Samuel¹*.	Nov. 14, 1687
2	15	Seth⁴, *Samuel³, Samuel², Samuel¹*.	Aug. 30, 1692
3	16	Ebenezer⁴, *Samuel³, Samuel², Samuel¹*.	Mar. 24, 1695
4	17	Benjamin⁴, *Samuel³ Samuel² Samuel¹*.	Mar. 7, 1696 –
5	19	John⁴, *Samuel³, Samuel², Samuel¹*.	Dec. 19, 1698
6	20	Jabez⁴, *Samuel³, Samuel², Samuel¹*.	June, 1701
7	22	James⁴, *Samuel³, Samuel², Samuel¹*.	Feb. 27, 1704
8	23	John⁴, *John³, Samuel², Samuel¹*.	Mar. 20, 1692
9	26	Ebenezer⁴, *John³, Samuel², Samuel¹*.	Nov. 1, 1697
10	27	Jabez⁴, *John³, Samuel², Samuel¹*.	?
11	29	Samuel⁴, *John³, Samuel², Samuel¹*.	1704
12	32	Isaac⁴, *Isaac³, Samuel², Samuel¹*.	Sept. 24, 1712
13	34	Samuel⁴, *Isaac³, Samuel², Samuel¹*.	Jan. 29, 1718/19
14	36	Jabez⁴, *Isaac³, Samuel², Samuel¹*.	May 7, 1723

FIRST GROUP.

FOURTH GENERATION.

DESCENDANTS OF NATHANIEL⁴ FULLER.

12. NATHANIEL⁴ FULLER, (*Samuel³, Samuel², Samuel¹*), b. Nov. 14, 1687; d. April 20, 1750, in Plympton, Mass.; m. Jan. 24, 1711/12, Martha Sampson, b. Oct. 25, 1689, d. June 8, 1770.

He lived in Plympton and his children were:

1.	I.	Sarah5, b Sept 28, 1712; m. 1, Isaac Sturtevant; m. 2, Austin Bearce.
2.	II.	Ruth5, b. March 4, 1713/14; m. April 3, 1733, James Cobb Jr.
3.	III.	William 5, } twins, b. July 20, 1716; both d. 1716.
4.	IV.	Elizabeth5, }
5.	‡V.	Amos5, b. Feb. 12, 1718/19; m. 1, Abigail Harlow; m. 2, Rachel (Standish) Sampson.
6.	‡VI.	Nathaniel5, b. May 26, 1721; m. Lydia Perry.
7.	‡VII.	Barnabas5, b. Sept. 25, 1723, m. Rebecca Cushman.
8.	VIII.	Jesse5, b. Feb. 18, 1725/6; said to have d. young.
9.	IX.	Samuel5, b. Nov. 11, 1729; d. March 7, 1742/3.

FIFTH GENERATION.

5. AMOS5 FULLÉR, (*Nathaniel⁴, Samuel³, Samuel², Samuel¹*), b. Feb. 19, 1718/19, in Plympton, Mass.; d. Dec. 31, 1790; m. 1, June 11, 1744, Abigail Harlow, b. Aug. 9, 1722, d. April 15, 1755; m. 2, Oct. 25, 1759, Rachel (Standish) Sampson, who d. Oct. 13, 1809.

Children, recorded at Plympton :

10.	I.	Mary[6], b. May 24, 1745 ; d. Oct 31, 1747.
11.	II.	Martha[6], b. Dec. 15, 1746, d. Jan., 1746/7.
12.	III.	Nathaniel[6], b. Dec. 12, 1747. Nothing more found.
13.	IV.	Hannah[6], b. Oct. 1, 1749; d. March 23, 1819, at Kingston, Mass.; m 1, Dec. 3, 1767, Peleg Cook, m. 2, Samuel Drew of Kingston.
14.	V.	Sarah[6], b. April 6, 1751, m. Samuel Bradford of Plympton
15.	VI.	Abigail[6], b. June 12, 1753 ; d. Feb. 6, 1754.
16.	VII.	Amos[6], b. Oct 27, 1760; d. Nov., 1796, at Beverly, Mass.
17.	‡VIII.	Philemon[6], b. Oct. 20, 1763; m. Mercy Chipman.

6. NATHANIEL[5] FULLER, (*Nathaniel[4]*, *Samuel[3]*, *Samuel[2]*, *Samuel[1]*), b May 26, 1721, in Plympton, Mass ; d. ———— , m. June 12, 1744, Lydia Perry, who survived him, and m. May 12, 1748, Ebenezer Dunham, then of Plympton.

Children of Nathaniel and Lydia, recorded in Plympton .

| 18. | I. | William[6], b. May 15, 1744/5. Nothing further found. |
| 19. | II. | Lydia[6], b. April 22, 1746 ; d. Dec. 20, 1776. |

7. BARNABAS[5] FULLER, (*Nathaniel[4]*, *Samuel[3]*, *Samuel[3]*, *Samuel[1]*), b. Sept. 25, 1723, in Plympton, Mass., d March 24, 1814, in Hebron, Me.; m. March 16, 1747/8, Rebecca Cushman at Kingston, Mass., b. there April 9, 1730, d. April 6, 1813, dau. of Robert and Mary (Washburn) Cushman.

Barnabas Fuller is described in "Mass. Soldiers and Sailors of the Revolution" as having enlisted from Kingston in 1780; age 56 years. The U. S. Pension Records show no application for a pension.

His children, all but the last child born in Kingston, were :

20.	‡I.	Jesse[6], b. Oct 3, 1748, m Ruth Prince.
21.	‡II.	Barzillai[6], b. Jan. 17, 1751 ; m. Mary Cushman.
22.	‡III.	Robert[6], b. June 3, 1752.
23.	IV.	Martha[6], b. Jan. 11, 1754; m. Dec. 30, 1784, John[5] Fuller, (*Jabez[4], Isaac[3], Samuel[2], Samuel[1]*).
24.	V.	Azubah[6], b. June 29, 1756; m. Sept. 11, 1793, John Washburn.
25.	VI.	Joshua[6], b. Feb. 8, 1758, d. March 28, 1759.
26.	VII.	Rebecca[6], b. May 19, 1761.

27.   VIII. Ruth⁶, b. Sept. 17, 1764. The N. E. Register
              states she m Oct. 19, 1780, Ichabod, son of
              Ichabod Bradford of Kingston, while a Maine
              correspondent states she married Isaiah Wood-
              man of Minot, Me
28.   IX.   Barnabas⁶, b. June 19, 1768; d. at sea Nov. 25,
              1792.
29.   ‡X.   Isaac⁶. Date of birth not recorded. Born in
              Hebron, Maine, according to family tradition.

SIXTH GENERATION.

17. PHILEMON⁶ FULLER, (*Amos⁵, Nathaniel⁴, Samuel³, Samuel²,
Samuel¹), b. Oct 20, 1763, in Plympton, Mass., d. Dec. 6, 1838;
m. ———, 1786, Mercy Chipman, who d. Oct 23, 1847. She was
born in Kingston, Mass, June 22, 1766, dau. of Capt. Seth and
Sarah (Ripley) Chipman. A Revolutionary soldier. Lived in
Plympton

Children, recorded in Plympton :

30.   ‡I.   Charles⁷, b. April 6, 1787 ; m. ., Deborah Soule ;
              m. 2, Sarah Nye.
31.   'ᵻII. Bildad⁷, b. Nov. 23, 1789 ; m. Margaret Bonney.
32.   ‡III. Harvey⁷, b. Feb 14, 1792, m. Eliza F. Harlow.
33.   ‡IV.   Philemon⁷, b June 16, 1794; m. June 4, 1828,
              Eunice Bradford.
34.   ‡V.   Amos⁷, b Sept. 23, 1796, m. 1, Priscilla Vaughn
              Shaw, m. 2, Lucinda Sturtevant.
35.   VI.   Warren⁷, b. Oct. 5, 1799; d. July 16, 1866,
              unmarried.
36.   VII.   Sarah⁷, b. April 6, 1804, d. Aug. 2, 1894, in
              Plympton, m. Jan. 30, 1825, John Standish of
              Taunton, Mass, and had Sarah Fuller⁸, b.
              Dec. 4, 1825, Mercy Angeline⁸, b. Aug. 24, 1828;
              George Walter⁸, b. May 4, 1832, Ernest⁸, b.
              Jan. 21, 1838; and Albert Warren⁸, b. Nov. 25,
              1846.

20. JESSE⁶ FULLER, (*Barnabas⁵, Nathaniel⁴, Samuel³, Samuel²,
Samuel¹), b. Oct. 3, 1748, in Kingston, Mass ; d. Aug., 1826; m.
Jan. 11, 1778, Ruth Prince, dau. of Kimball Prince and Deborah
(Fuller) Prince.

Their children, all born in Hebron, Maine, were :

37.   ‡I.   Joshua⁷, b. Nov. 17, 1778, m. 1, Susanna Curtis ;
              m. 2, Nancy Adams.

38.   II.   Deborah[7], b. Oct. 3, 1780; m. July 9, 1801, Rev.
            Joseph Hutchinson
39   ‡III. Samuel[7], b. Aug. 27, 1782; m. Nancy Coombs.
40.   IV.   Jesse[7], b Feb. 21, 1784; d Dec. 18, 1799.
41.   ‡V.   Noah Prince[7], b. Dec. 2, 1785; m. Reliance Weed.
42.   VI.   Ruth[7], b March 2, 1788; m. Nov. 27, 1806,
            Josiah Jordan
43.   ‡VII. John[7], b. Feb. 24, 1790; m Eveline Washburn.
44.   VIII. Rebecca Cushman[7], b. Jan 8, 1792; m. Dec. 17,
            1818, Ezekiel Verrill of Minot, Me.
45.   ‡IX. Barnabas[7],   ⎫   ⎧ m. Bethia
                                 ⎬ b. June 30, 1794; ⎨   Bray.
46.   ‡X.   Kimball Prince[7], ⎭   ⎩ m. Miranda
                                                     Carmen.
47.   XI.   Martha[7], b March 18, 1797, m. March 19, 1818,
            Thomas Jackson.
48.   XII. Sarah Prince[7], b. Jan. 29, 1799; m. 1823, Levi
            Whittemore.
49.   ‡XIII. Jesse[7], b. May 14, 1801, m. ———.

21. BARZILLAI[6] FULLER, (*Barnabas*[5], *Nathaniel*[4], *Samuel*[3],
Samuel[2], *Samuel*[1]), b. Jan. 17, 1751, at Kingston, Mass.; d.
Aug. 8, 1833, at Hebron, Me., m. Feb. 20, 1786, Mary Cushman.
He was a soldier of the Revolution, who enlisted from Mass,
May 1, 1775, served 8 months; re-enlisted for one year. Enlisted
Feb, 1777, and served until Nov. 4, 1783. He applied for pension
1818 and claim was allowed. His widow was allowed a pension in
1838, at which time she was a resident of Hebron, and 87 years of
age. Her son Robert testified in the case.

Their children, recorded in Hebron, were:

50   I.   Elizabeth[7], b. July 9, 1787.
51.   ‡II. Robert[7], b. Sept. 24, 1788; m. 1, Sally Keene;
            m. 2, Almaretta Cox.

22. ROBERT[6] FULLER, (*Barnabas*[5], *Nathaniel*[4], *Samuel*[3],
Samuel[2], *Samuel*[1]), b. June 3, 1752, in Kingston, Mass.; d. ———.
He was a soldier of the Revolutionary war, enlisting from Mass., May
1, 1775, for 8 months; re-enlisted for one year. Enlisted April,
1777, and served until discharged Nov. 4, 1783. Made application
for pension April 14, 1818, and claim was allowed. Residence at
date of application, Hebron, Me. "No mention of his wife or
children, but in 1820 soldier stated that his sister, Azuba Washburn,

aged 64 years, and her granddaughter, Eunice Washburn, aged 5 years, resided with him."

29. ISAAC[6] FULLER, (*Barnabas[5], Nathaniel[4], Samuel[3], Samuel[2], Samuel[1]*), b. ————, in Hebron, Me., d. June 3, 1841, aged 70 years (Gravestone Record), in Livermore, Me.; m. ————, Sarah Houston, who d. July 23, 1854, aged 79 years (G. S. Record.)

Children, all born in Livermore, Me.:

52. I. Ruthie W.[7], b. May 11, 1800, d. Feb. 23, 1845; m. Jan. 1, 1826, Samuel Merrill; lived and d. in Livermore. Children: Lucy A.[8], b. April 2, 1827, Sarah J.[8], b. April 15, 1829; Louisa[8], b. May 18, 1831, Martha E.[8], b. Dec. 27, 1835; Ruth M[8], b Sept. 8, 1839, and Dana[8], b. March 30, 1842.

53. II. Sarah[7], b. April 11, 1802; d. Nov. 27, 1872, in Brimfield, Mass; m. Feb. 7, 1832, Abner Stebbins. Resided in Brimfield. Children: Charles Emerson[8], b. Feb. 5, 1833; Josiah[8], b. June 10, 1835; Abner Henry[8], b. April 13, 1839; and Sarah Jane[8], b. May 9, 1843.

54. ‡III. Isaiah Woodman[7], b. April 29, 1804; m. Louisa Carter Goding.

55. ‡IV. Ira[7], b. ————; m. Abigail Moore.

56. ‡V. Asa[7], b. Aug. 21, 1808, m. Hannah Stetson.

57. VI. Rebecca[7], b. ————; m. Andrew G. Day; lived and d. in Dexter, Me.

58. VII. Laura A.[7], b. March 24, 1814; d. Feb. 13, 1904, in Turner, Me.; m. Sept. 18, 1837, in Brimfield, Mass., Sewell Phillips. Resided in Livermore. Children: George Sewell[8] and Laura Ellen[8], b. Sept. 21, 1844.

SEVENTH GENERATION.

30. CHARLES[7] FULLER, (*Philemon[6], Amos[5], Nathaniel[4], Samuel[3], Samuel[2], Samuel[1]*), b. April 6, 1787, in Plympton, Mass.; d. June 19, 1862, m. 1, Deborah Soule 2d, Nov. 29, 1813; m. 2, Sept. 10, 1823, Sarah Nye, b. April 14, 1791, d. April 4, 1887.

Children, recorded in Plympton:

59. ‡I. Charles Augustus[8], b. June 30, 1816; m. Cordelia A. Douglas.

60.   ‡II   Josiah Soule[8], b. Nov. 17, 1817; m. Elizabeth Gray
               Churchill.
61.   III. Phebe Nye[8], b June 10, 1824, m Jan 18, 1846,
               Col. Godfrey Ryder and had William Henry[9], b.
               Nov 13, 1846, Charles W.[9], b. March 22, 1848;
               Winfield S[9], b. May 17, 1850; Anna H[9], b.
               March 16, 1852, Godfrey[9], b. ——— , Thomas
               Lee[9], b ——— ; Thomas Lee[9] 2d, b. ——— ;
               Frederick C.[9], b. ——— ; and Frederick C.[9] 2d, b.
               ——— .
62.   IV   Sarah Rosamond[8], b March 23, 1829; d. April 29,
               1891, m. Jan. 1, 1847, George Bonney[8] Fuller,
               (*Bildad[7], Philemon[6], Amos[5], Nathaniel[4],
               Samuel[3], Samuel[2], Samuel[1]*). Children. Juliet[9],
               b. Aug. 17, 1847; Everett S.[9], b. March 12, 1860.
63.   ‡V.   Lafayette[8], b. Feb. 16, 1834, m Eunice Ada Ellis.

31. BILDAD[7] FULLER, (*Philemon[6], Amos[5], Nathaniel[4], Samuel[3],
Samuel[2], Samuel[1]*), b. Nov. 23, 1789, in Plympton, Mass.; d.
there March 13, 1872; m. Dec. 5, 1815, Margaret Bonney, who d.
Feb 7, 1873.

Their children were

64.   ‡I.   Joseph Henry[8], b. Sept. 22, 1816, m. Eleanor F.
               Cook.
65.   II.   Darius Albert[8], b. April 7, 1819, died in early
               manhood.
66.   ‡III. George Bonney[8], b. Aug 28, 1821; m. Sarah R.[8]
               Fuller, (*Charles[7], Philemon[6], Amos[5], Nathaniel[4],
               Samuel[3], Samuel[2], Samuel[1]*).

32. HARVEY[7] FULLER, (*Philemon[6], Amos[5], Nathaniel[4], Samuel[3],
Samuel[2], Samuel[1]*), b. Feb. 14, 1792, in Plympton, Mass.; d. there
Feb 2, 1867; m. Dec. 16, 1824, Eliza F. Harlow, who d. March 7,
1878, aged 74 years.

Children, recorded at Plympton:

67.   ‡I.   Edward[8], b. Nov. 26, 1826, m. Sophia M. Phinney.
68.   ‡II. Dexter[8], b. July 12, 1831; m. Mary F. Spellman.
69.   III. George Lindley[8], b. May 14, 1834; d. Oct. 22,
               1906.
70.   IV.   Philemon[8], b. Oct. 24, 1838; d. Feb. 4, 1885.

33. PHILEMON[7] FULLER, (*Philemon[6], Amos[5], Nathaniel[4],
Samuel[3], Samuel[2], Samuel[1]*), b. June 16, 1794, in Plympton, Mass.;

d. Dec. 5, 1875, in Fairhaven, Mass.; m June 4, 1828, Eunice Bradford, b. Jan. 14, 1808, d. Dec. 22, 1882. Resided in Fairhaven.

Children, born in Fairhaven:

71.   I.   Elizabeth[8], b. Sept. 8, 1829.
72.   II.   Frederick Milton[8], b. Sept. 11, 1831.
73.   III.   Thomas Bradford[8], b. Feb., 1849; d. Oct. 15, 1886, in Fairhaven. Contributed by Mrs. Phebe Nye (Fuller) Ryder.

Philemon[7] Fuller is said to have descendants in New Bedford, Mass., but the compiler has failed to receive replies to inquiries regarding them.

34.   AMOS[7] FULLER, (*Philemon*[6], *Amos*[5], *Nathaniel*[4], *Samuel*[3], *Samuel*[2], *Samuel*[1]), b. Sept. 23, 1796, in Plympton, Mass.; d. March 3, 1875; m. 1, July 3, 1826, Priscilla Vaughn Shaw; m. 2, Aug. 4, 1836, Lucinda Sturtevant, who d Dec. 25, 1898.

Children, recorded in Plympton:

74.   I.   Amos Sumner[8], b. Feb. 10, 1827; d. March 18, 1881, m. June 8, 1850, Lucy T. Tinkham.
75.   II.   Betsey Shaw[8], b. July 8, 1829, in Coleraine, Mass.; m. Dec. 12, 1847, Charles H. Nesmith, and had Charles H.[9], Walter F.[9], and Jessie F.[9]
76.   III.   Henry[8], b. Dec 19, 1833; d. Jan. 19, 1846.
77.   ‡IV.   William[8], b. Feb. 6, 1838, m. 1, Sarah W. Ripley; m. 2, Margaret C. Thompson.
78.   V.   Lewis Warren[8], b. Feb 21, 1840. Resides in Plympton. Unmarried.
79.   VI.   Eunice[8], b. Sept. 25, 1841.
80.   VII.   Jane Helen[8], b. March 18, 1846.
81.   VIII.   Henry[8], b. June 5, 1848; m. Martha L. Foley.
82.   IX.   Albert[8], b. July 11, 1850. Resides in Plympton. Unmarried.
83.   X.   Lucinda Maria[8], b. April 4, 1852; d. March 22, 1899, m. Sept. 23, 1874, John Phinney, and had Amy B.[9], and John C.[9]

37.   JOSHUA[7] FULLER, (*Jesse*[6], *Barnabas*[5], *Nathaniel*[4], *Samuel*[3], *Samuel*[2], *Samuel*[1]), b. Nov. 17, 1778, in Hebron, Me.; d. 1856, in Castine, Me., aged 78 years; m 1, Jan. 4, 1799, Susanna Curtis; m. 2, (Int. Pub.) Nov. 26, 1808, Nancy Adams, b. Feb. 10, 1792, at Thomaston, Me.

He resided at Northport, Thomaston and Castine, was a carpenter. The "Annals of Oxford, Me.," give his name as Josiah, and his marriage to Susanna Curtis; while the History of Thomaston and the Genealogy of the Adams family of Kingston, Mass., give his name as Joshua and his marriage to Nancy Adams, with children as follows, including a "Joshua:"

84.   I.   Nancy A.^{5}, b. Dec. 18, 1809; d. 1842, m. Thomas McClellan

85.   ‡II.   Joshua^8, b. July 7, 1811; m. 1, Susan N. Robinson; m. 2, Mrs. Joanna R. Foote of Boston, Mass.; m. 3, Harriet L. Rogers.

86.   III.   Adaline P.^{8}, b. June 26, 1814; d. Nov. 12, 1840.

87.   IV   Albert^8, b. Feb. 10, 1816; m. Mary Pierson.

88.   V.   Silas M.^{8}, b Feb. 24, 1819; m. Mary A. Pitts.

89.   VI.   Thomas S^8, b. April 19, 1821; m. Elizabeth A. Lufkin.

90.   VII.   Harriet N^8, b. April 6, 1823; d. Oct. 4, 1840.

91.   VIII. Rebecca^8, b. May 7, 1825; m. Nov. 4, 1845, Charles H Averill.

92.   IX.   Ellen S.^{8}, b. July 6, 1828.

39. SAMUEL^7 FULLER, (*Jesse*^{6}, *Barnabas*^{5}, *Nathaniel*^{4}, *Samuel*^{3}, *Samuel*^{2}, *Samuel*^{1}), b. Aug. 27, 1782, in Hebron, Me.; d. Nov. 4, 1846, in Thomaston, Me.; m. July 9, 1806, Nancy H. Coombs, b. Dec. 31, 1789.

He was in trade in Lincolnville, St. George, Castine and Thomaston, Me., and later, from 1815 to 1821, deputy sheriff and subsequently postmaster. Was also first register of deeds in the Eastern District of Lincoln Co.

Their children were :

93.   I.   George Washington^8, b. May 23, 1808; d. July 1, 1808.

94.   ‡II.   Sylvester H.^{8}, b. Nov. 19, 1809, m. Amelia D. Holmes.

95.   ‡III.   Asa Coombs^8, b. March 8, 1812; m. Mary Jane Snow, m 2, Anna B. Snow.

96.   IV.   Caroline S.^{8}, b. Oct. 30, 1814; m. Oct. 10, 1834, Edwin Rose, who d. March 16, 1877. Children: Caroline E.^{9}, b. March 10, 1836; Edwin T.^{9}, b. Dec. 1, 1838; Samuel F.^{9}, b. Oct. 25, 1840; Olive F.^{9}, b. March 13, 1843; Helen D.^{9}, b. Feb. 17, 1846; Edwin S.^{9}, b. Dec. 20, 1848, and Charles A.^{9}, b. March 25, 1851.

97.   V.   Nancy^8, b. Aug. 19, 1816; d. Sept., 1860; m. March 31, 1845, Charles E. Hodgskins.

98. IV.   Sarah L.[8], b. Dec. 3, 1818; m. April 7, 1842, Capt.
            Jeremiah Murray, who d Oct. 30, 1867. They
            resided at Walnut Creek, Cal. Children: Flora
            E.[9], b. Feb. 14, 1855; Charles E.[9], b. Feb. 28,
            1856; and Sarah J.[9], b. April 7, 1862.

99. VII. Mary S.[8], b. March 18, 1821; m. Sept. 29, 1847,
            Capt. John S. Spofford, and had Samuel F.[9], b.
            July 21, 1850, Sarah M.[9], b. Nov. 29, 1853;
            Samuel F.[9], b. Aug. 20, 1855; Hannah J.[9], b.
            April 13, 1859, and Angie M[9], b. Feb. 18, 1866.

100. VIII. Isabelle Prince Bach[8], b. June 20, 1823; d. Nov.
            15, 1860, on board ship, Alice Counce, on
            passage from Melbourne to Callao; m. Sept.,
            1847, Capt. John William Singer and had Ida
            E.[9], b. July 17, 1848, and Thomas S.[9], b. July
            12, 1850

101. ‡IX. Samuel A.[8], b. July 10, 1825, m. Susan E.
            Greenlaw.

102. X.   Ruth J.[8], b. Nov. 2, 1827; d. April 19, 1850.

103. XI.   Abby[8], b. March 4, 1830; m. Oct. 3, 1852, Levi
            B. Miller, and had Lizzie H.[9], b. July 26, 1853;
            Hattie L.[9], b. May 10, 1857; and Charles M.[9], b.
            July 9, 1864.

104. XII. Jane G.[8], b. Oct. 4, 1842; d. June 6, 1874; m.
            March, 1862, Capt. William John Singer as his
            second wife.

41. Noah Prince[7] Fuller, (*Jesse*[6], *Barnabas*[5], *Nathaniel*[4], *Samuel*[3], *Samuel*[2], *Samuel*[1]), b. Dec. 2, 1785, in Hebron, Me.; d. 1858, in Lincolnville, Me., m. ———, Reliance Weed, b. Oct. 22, 1784, d. 1864. He resided in Hope, Me.

His children were:

105. ‡I.   James W.[8], b. Sept 24, 1809; m. 1, ———; m. 2,
            Margaret Wentworth, April, 1836.

106. ‡II. Jesse Prince[8], b. April 29, 1811; m. Theresa
            Walker.

107. III. Jane W.[8], b. Aug. 28, 1813; d. Sept., 1892; m.
            Jan. 5, 1834, Edward L. Eells of Camden, Me.,
            and had Delia S[9], b. Aug. 2, 1835; Ruth C.[9],
            b. April 18, 1838; Emery[9], b. July 8, 1841;
            Noah G.[9], b. June 16, 1843; Phila Ann[9], b.
            Oct. 17, 1844; Lucy E.[9], b. Sept. 28, 1846; and
            Julia G.[9], b. April 28, 1850.

108. IV.   Sally S.[8], b. Dec. 18, 1816; d. aged 3 years.

109. V.   Sally Ann[8], b. Dec. 22, 1818; m. May 2, 1835, N.

Parker of Lincolnville, Me., and had Lorna[9], Ellen[9], Annette[9], Sanford[9], Prentice[9], and Sally Ann[9].

110   ‡VI.   Hezekiah Prince[8], b. Jan. 1, 1820; m. Catherine Safford Mossman.

111.   VII.   Mary H.[8], b. Sept. 8, 1822; m. Dec. 3, 1844, Orison Bartlett.

112.   VIII.   Nancy W.[8], b. March 27, 1825; d. April, 1847; m William Athers.

43. JOHN[7] FULLER, (*Jesse[6], Barnabas[5], Nathaniel[4], Samuel[3], Samuel[2], Samuel[1]*), b. Feb. 24, 1790, in Hebron, Me., d. Aug. 13, 1856, m. June 1815, Everline Washburn, who d. Nov. 29, 1878. He was a farmer, lived in East Hebron, where both were members of the F. B. church

Their children were:

113   I.   Perley B.[8], b. May 26, 1816, d. Sept. 26, 1816.

114.   II.   Samantha P.[8], b Dec 29, 1817, d. April 1, 1898; m. Jabez Davis of Foxcroft, Me., and had Julia A[9], Samantha[9], Angelia[9] and Frank[9].

115.   III.   Jeannette W.[8], b April 11, 1820, d. June 13, 1833; m. Daniel Russell. Children: Jefferson D.[9], Sarah J.[9], Oscar[9], Everline[9] and Flora A.[9]

116.   IV.   Rebecca B[8], b. Feb. 18, 1822; d April 17, 1903; m Oct. 29, 1848, Jeremiah P. Packard, and had John H.[9], Lucillus[9], Addreanna E.[9], Frederic[9] and Frank[9]

117.   ‡V.   Josiah J.[8], b. April 13, 1823; m. 1, Margaret Foster, m 2, Mary A. Noble.

118.   VI.   Clarissa E.[8], b. Oct. 2, 1826; m. Nov. 19, 1847, William Packard, and had Sarah A.[8], Everline[9], Will H[9] and George W.[9]

119.   ‡VII.   Rufus P[8], b Nov 29, 1828; m. Lydia A. Warner.

120.   ‡VIII   Joseph D.[8], b Nov. 26, 1832, m. Mary A Chaffin.

121.   IX.   Julia A.[8], b. April 12, 1837; d. March 14, 1842.

45. BARNABAS[7] FULLER, (*Jesse[6], Barnabas[5], Nathaniel[4], Samuel[3], Samuel[2], Samuel[1]*), b. June 30, 1794, in Hebron, Me.; d. May 7, 1864, in Minot, Me.; m. April 20, 1828, Bethiah Bray, who d. Aug. 18, 1897, in Auburn, Me.

Barnabas Fuller was a Captain in the war of 1812, and his widow drew a pension. He lived and died in Minot.

Children:

122.   ‡I.   Jesse Augustus[8], b March 27, 1829; m. 1, Emma

Bean; m. 2, Josephine W. (Fuller) Wagg. Josephine W.[8] Fuller, (*Kimball P.[7], Jesse[6], Barnabas[5], Nathaniel[4], Samuel[3], Samuel[2], Samuel[1].*)

123. II. Harriet B.[8], b Dec. 25, 1831, in Minot; d. Nov. 7, 1908, in Auburn.

124. III. Barnabas[8], b Jan 21, 1833, in Hebron, Me.; m. Helen Cuningham. They reside in South Framingham, Mass.; have no children.

125. IV. George J.[8], b June 30, 1835, in Hebron; was killed in the battle of Antietam.

126. V. Bennett B.[8], b. July 4, 1837, in Minot; resides in Auburn.

127. VI. Mary Eliza[8], b. Jan. 15, 1840, in Minot; d. there May 11, 1864; unmarried.

128. ‡VII. Frank T.[8], b. Jan. 13, 1851; m. Augusta P. Keene.

46. KIMBALL PRINCE[7] FULLER, (*Jesse[6], Barnabas[5], Nathaniel[4], Samuel[3], Samuel[2], Samuel[1]*), b. June 30, 1794, in Hebron, Me.; d. Oct. 22, 1866, in Leeds, Me., m. Dec. 26, 1828, Miranda Carmen, who d. Jan. 2, 1887, at Auburn, Me.

Their children were:

129. I. William Henry[8], b. Dec. 24, 1829; d. May 18, 1863; m. Polly E Keene. No children.

130. II. Miranda[8], b. Dec. 25, 1831, in Hebron; d. April 23, 1853, in Leeds; m. George E. Williams. No children

131. III. Caroline Rose[8], b. March 20, 1835, in Hebron; d. March 26, 1855, m. June, 1854, George E. Williams. No children.

132. IV. Esther Millett[8], b. Sept. 8, 1837, in Hebron; d. Aug. 15, 1840.

133. V. Esther Millett[8], b. Jan. 27, 1840, in Leeds; m. July 20, 1860, George W. Beckler. They reside at South Leeds, Me. Children: Kimball G.[9], b. Dec. 3, 1861; Hattie Mabel[9], b. July 21, 1866 and Bert Hayes[9], b. Oct. 27, 1876.

134. VI. Kimball Verrill[8], b. May 17, 1842, in Leeds; d. July 22, 1861; unmarried.

135. VII. Josephine Whittemore[8], b. April 2, 1844, in Leeds; m. 1, Oct. 10, 1868, George W. Wagg; m. 2, 1897, Jesse Augustus[8] Fuller, (*Barnabas[7], Jesse[6], Barnabas[5], Nathaniel[4], Samuel[3], Samuel[2], Samuel[1].*)

49. JESSE[7] FULLER, (*Jesse*[6], *Barnabas*[5], *Nathaniel*[4], *Samuel*[3], *Samuel*[2], *Samuel*[1]), b. May 14, 1801, in Hebron, Me.; d. Dec. 23, 1856; m. ——.

He lived and died in Auburn, Me.

Children:

136.   ‡I.   Edward P.[8], b. —— ; m. ——.

(Compiler failed to receive information asked for.)

51. ROBERT[7] FULLER, (*Barzillai*[6], *Barnabas*[5], *Nathaniel*[4], *Samuel*[3], *Samuel*[2], *Samuel*[1]), b. Sept. 24, 1788, in Hebron, Me.; d. ——, m. 1, (Intentions entered March 16, 1818), with Sally Keene, "both of Hebron"; m. 2, ——, Almaretta Cox.

Children.

137.   I.   Ebenezer[8], b. Dec. 30, 1818; d. Feb., 1819.
138.   II.   Ansel R.[8], b. Dec. 24, 1819.
139.   III. Rebecca K.[8], b. Sept. 14, 1822.
140.   IV.   Almaretta[8], b. Feb. 5, 1833.

(No further information received.)

54. ISAIAH WOODMAN[7] FULLER, (*Isaac*[6], *Barnabas*[5], *Nathaniel*[4], *Samuel*[3], *Samuel*[2], *Samuel*[1]), b April 29, 1804, at Livermore, Me.; d. there Nov. 13, 1886, m. March 13, 1830, Louisa Carter Goding of Jay, Me., who d. Sept 10, 1872.

Their children, all born in Livermore, were:

141.   ‡I.   Elisha C.[8], b. Jan. 31, 1831, m. Antoinette A. Walker.
142.   II.   Andrew D.[8], b. March 10, 1835; d. Jan. 28, 1899; unmarried.
143.   III. Louisa C.[8] } b April 24, 1841 { d. Sept. 19, 1842.
144.   IV.   Eliza A.[8] }   { m. Jan. 1, 1882, Hiram A. Merrill. Mr. and Mrs. Merrill reside in North Livermore. They have no children.

55. IRA[7] FULLER, (*Isaac*[6], *Barnabas*[5], *Nathaniel*[4], *Samuel*[3], *Samuel*[2], *Samuel*[1]), b. ——, in Livermore, Me.; d. 1876, in Phillips, Me.; m. ——, Abigail Morse.

He lived in Livermore, Wilton and Phillips, Me.

Children:

145.   ‡I.   Henry Russell[8], b. April 27, 1841; m. 1, Sophia Parker; m. 2, Ella F. Horne.

56. ASA[7] FULLER, (*Isaac*[6], *Barnabas*[5], *Nathaniel*[4], *Samuel*[3], *Samuel*[2], *Samuel*[1]), b. Aug. 21, 1808, in Livermore, Me.; d. there May 19, 1873; m. Sept. 7, 1832, Hannah Stetson, b. Dec. 2, 1809, in Hartford, Me., d. Jan. 2, 1886, in Livermore.

Their children were all born in Livermore:

146.   I.   Angelia Arabella[8], b. March 7, 1834; d. April 29, 1886, in Livermore; m. June 24, 1858, Andrew Campbell and had Cora Hannah[9], b. Aug. 31, 1859, in Winthrop. Me, m. Oct. 14, 1878, Frank W. Cooledge of Livermore; Asa[9], b. March 2, 1862, in Winthrop, m. May 1, 1887, Anne R. Lovewell; Emma Francelia[9], b. Feb. 8, 1868, in Livermore; Myrtie Angelina[9], b. Oct. 25, 1875, m. Jan. 26, 1895, Roy Moore of Canton, Me. Mrs. Moore d. May 6, 1910.

147.   II.   Cornelia Alberta[8], b. May 6, 1836; m. Nov. 3, 1858, William H. Thompson of Hartford, Me. They reside in Livermore. Children are Cornelia Estella[9], b. Oct. 28, 1865, in Livermore, m. Jan. 14, 1893, Roswell D. Gammon of Canton, Me., and had son, Charles[10], b. in Livermore.

148.   III.   Hannah Celestia[8], b. Aug. 27, 1838, m. March 15, 1859, Lewis A. Cobb. They reside in Auburn, Me. Their only child, Frederic Augustus[9], was b. April 4, 1860, in Sumner, Me., and "passed on" before them, sad to say, April 5, 1910, only two weeks after the death of his wife. (See 5th Group, *Rebecca*[6], *Issachar*[5], *Samuel*[1], for account of union of 1st and 5th Groups by the marriage of Mr. and Mrs. Cobb.)

149.   IV.   Omar Orlistus[8], b. Jan. 17, 1842, d. March 7, 1883; m. July 7, 1866, Evelyn Conant of Canton, Me. No children.

150.   V.   Emma Francelia[8], b. Sept. 24, 1845, d. Jan. 19, 1868, in Auburn; m. Aug. 27, 1863, Rodolphus E. Hathaway of Canton, Me. No children.

151.   VI.   Aratus Asa[8], b. Jan. 29, 1847, d. Aug. 15, 1855, in Livermore.

152.   ‡VII.   Ellian Errol[8], b. Sept. 4, 1851; m. Dora M. Thompson.

153.   ‡VIII.   Aratus Carroll[8], b. Jan. 11, 1856; m. 1, Sarah C. Cummings; m. 2, Rose Hersey.

EIGHTH GENERATION.

59. CHARLES AUGUSTUS[5] FULLER, (*Charles*[7], *Philemon*[6], *Amos*[5], *Nathaniel*[4], *Samuel*[3], *Samuel*[2], *Samuel*[1]), b. June 30, 1816, in Plympton, Mass., d. Oct. 23, 1872, in Plympton, m. Sept. 20, 1848, Cordelia Douglas of Dedham, Mass., who d. April 15, 1871, in Plympton, aged 45 years.

Children :

154.   I.   Charles Warren[9], b. May 11, 1857; resides in Halifax, Mass.

60. JOSIAH SOULE[5] FULLER, (*Charles*[7], *Philemon*[6], *Amos*[5], *Nathaniel*[4], *Samuel*[3], *Samuel*[2], *Samuel*[1]), b. Nov. 17, 1817, in Plympton, Mass.; d. Jan. 27, 1874, in Faribault, Minn.; m. Dec., 1846, Elizabeth Gray Churchill of Duxbury, Mass, who d. Oct. 19, 1900, in Boston, Mass., and was buried beside her husband in Faribault.

Their children were

155.   I.   Elizabeth Parker[9], b. ———, in Provincetown, Mass., d. young.
156.   II.   Elizabeth Parker[9] 2d, b. March 5, 1857, in Provincetown.
157.   III. Effie[9],   ⎫ Twins ⎧ b. ———, in Provincetown ;
158.   IV.   Florence[9], ⎭   ⎩ d. young.
159.   V.   Orlando Wood[9], b. ———, in Provincetown ; d. young.
160.   VI.   Orlando Wood[9] 2d, b. ———, in Fairbault ; d. young.

63. LAFAYETTE[5] FULLER, (*Charles*[7], *Philemon*[6], *Amos*[5], *Nathaniel*[4], *Samuel*[3], *Samuel*[2], *Samuel*[1]), b. Feb. 16, 1834, in Plympton, Mass.; m. Aug. 12, 1862, in Middleboro, Mass., Eunice Ada Ellis.

They reside in Plympton.

Children .

161.   I.   Ida Ellis[9], b. May 31, 1863, m. Oct. 1, 1880, Darius Franklin[9] Fuller, (*Joseph H.*[8], *Bildad*[7], *Philemon*[6], *Amos*[5], *Nathaniel*[4], *Samuel*[3], *Samuel*[2], *Samuel*[1]).
162.   II.   Clara G[9], b. 1872; m. May 24, 1891, George A. Perkins, and had Robert V.[10] and Clara[10].
163.   III. A daughter, b. March 5, 1874; d. March 8, 1874.

61. JOSEPH HENRY[8] FULLER, (*Bildad*[7], *Philemon*[6], *Amos*[5], *Nathaniel*[4], *Samuel*[3], *Samuel*[2], *Samuel*[1]), b. Sept. 22, 1816, in Plympton, Mass.; d. April 16, 1900, in Brockton, Mass.; m. Dec. 9, 1841, Eleanor F. Cook, who d. March 24, 1892.

Children recorded in Plympton.

164.   I.   Mary F[9], b Nov. 11, 1843, m. Jan. 13, 1869, Josiah W. Ripley and had Herbert E.[10], who resides in Brockton

165.   II.   Darius Franklin[9], b Feb. 15, 1853, m. Oct. 1, 1880, Ida Ellis[9] Fuller, (*Lafayette*[8], *Charles*[7], *Philemon*[6], *Amos*[5], *Nathaniel*[4], *Samuel*[3], *Samuel*[2], *Samuel*[1]).

66. GEORGE BONNEY[8] FULLER, (*Bildad*[7], *Philemon*[6], *Amos*[5], *Nathaniel*[4], *Samuel*[3], *Samuel*[2], *Samuel*[1]), b. Aug. 28, 1821, in Plympton, Mass.; d. there Aug. 16, 1891, m. Jan. 1, 1847, Sarah R.[8] Fuller, (*Charles*[7], *Philemon*[6], *Amos*[5], *Nathaniel*[4], *Samuel*[3], *Samuel*[2], *Samuel*[1]).

Children recorded in Plympton:

166.   I.   Juliet Maria[9], b. Aug. 17, 1847; d. May 14, 1855.

167.   ‡II.   Everett Standish[9], b. March 12, 1860; m. Cora L. Churchill.

67. EDWARD[8] FULLER, (*Harvey*[7], *Philemon*[6], *Amos*[5], *Nathaniel*[4], *Samuel*[3], *Samuel*[2], *Samuel*[1]), b. Nov. 26, 1826, in Plympton, Mass.; m Feb. 22, 1848, Sophia M. Phinney, who d. May 29, 1888.

Children recorded in Plympton:

168.   I.   Felicia Hemans[9], b. June 12, 1848; d. Nov. 7, 1883, m. ———.

169.   II.   Edward Harvey[9], b. Sept 29, 1859, m. Aug. 13, 1884, Margaret M. Hillis. Has no children. Resides at Ladoga, Ind.

170.   III.   William W.[9], b. ———, m Mrs. Ida M. Heindall.

68. DEXTER[8] FULLER, (*Harvey*[7], *Philemon*[6], *Amos*[5], *Nathaniel*[4], *Samuel*[3], *Samuel*[2], *Samuel*[1]), b. July 12, 1831, in Plympton, Mass.; d. Aug. 20, 1906; m. Dec. 23, 1857, Mary F. Spellman.

Children :

171.   I.   Ernest Linwood[9], b. Aug. 19, 1866; d. Jan. 25, 1881.

172.   ‡II.   Frank Irving[9], b. Dec. 21, 1869; m. Mary Alice Osborne.

77. WILLIAM[S] FULLER, (*Amos*[7], *Philemon*[6], *Amos*[5], *Nathaniel*[4], *Samuel*[3], *Samuel*[2], *Samuel*[1]), b. Feb. 6, 1838, in Plympton, Mass.; m. 1, Dec. 31, 1859, Sarah W. Ripley; m. 2, Feb. 4, 1900, Margaret C. Thompson.

Children :

173.   I.   Melvin Luvelle[9], b. Sept. 1, 1861.
174.   II.   William Chester[9], b. Feb. 25, 1867.
175.   III. Laura Sherman[9], b. June 11, 1870, m. Nov. 26, 1896, Horace M. Stetson.

85. JOSHUA[S] FULLER, (*Joshua*[7], *Jesse*[6], *Barnabas*[5], *Nathaniel*[4], *Samuel*[3], *Samuel*[2]. *Samuel*[1]), b. July 7, 1811 ; d. ———; m. 1, Feb 4, 1841, Susan M. Robinson, m. 2, Dec. 5, 1855, Mrs. Joanna R. Foote of Boston, m. 3, ———, 1860, Harriet L. Rogers. He was a merchant at Thomaston, Me.

Children :

176.   I.   Ellen M.[9], b. May, 1844 ; d. Sept. 26, 1844.
177.   II.   George R.[9], b. Sept., 1846 ; d. about 1896, unmarried.
178   III. Frances R.[9], b. Oct., 1847, d. Aug. 23, 1848.
179   IV.   Susan A.[9], b. Dec., 1851 ; d. Jan. 1, 1852.
180   V.   Jessie A.[9], b. about 1856.

94. SYLVESTER H.[S] FULLER, (*Samuel*[7], *Jesse*[6], *Barnabas*[5], *Nathaniel*[4], *Samuel*[3], *Samuel*[2], *Samuel*[1]), b. Nov. 19, 1809, in Castine, Me., d. Jan. 10, 1885, in Rockland, Me.; m. April 8, 1837, Amelia Doyle Holmes.

He was a hotel keeper at Owls Head, Me., and was also in business several years in California.

Children, born at Owls Head :

181.   I.   Mary Amelia[9], b. April 13, 1838; d. June 12, 1880; m. 1, May 31, 1856, Capt. John Lancaster Crocker and had one child, Jennie L.[10]; m. 2, in Boston, Herbert G. Emerson and had Margaret[10] and George M.[10]
182.   II.   Charles H.[9], b. Sept. 25, 1839; d. June 6, 1872, in San Francisco ; unmarried.
183.   III. Frances Berry[9], b. Jan. 31, 1843 ; m. 1, Sept. 17, 1860, Judson M. Kalloch and had son, Kendall Kalloch; m. 2, Selleck Raphael. Resides N. Y. C.
184.   IV.   Martha[9], b. Jan. 30, 1846; d. June 22, 1885 ; m.

June 7, 1872, Joshua O. Snell of New Bedford, Mass., and had Fanny[10], b. May 29, 1876; Carrie A.[10], b. Feb. 4, 1877, Amy V.[10] and Charles R.[10]

185.   V. Caroline Rose[9], b Dec. 25, 1850, d. April 24, 1895; m. Jan., 1869, William H. Dutcher of Boston and had William A., b. March 15, 1872.
Holmes Genealogy. Gamble Genealogy.

95. Asa Coombs[8] Fuller, (*Samuel[7]*, *Jesse[6]*, *Barnabas[5]*, *Nathaniel[4]*, *Samuel[3]*, *Samuel[2]*, *Samuel[1]*), b. March 18, 1812; d. Dec. 16, 1874, in Lawrence, Mass; m. 1, July 5, 1846, Mary J. Snow, b. Sept. 9, 1823, d. Aug. 1, 1857, m. 2, Anna B. Snow, b. April 21, 1840, d. June 17, 1898.

He was a trader and a deputy collector of internal revenue in Thomaston, Me., removed to Derry, N. H., and thence to Lawrence.

Children, all born in Thomaston except Asa E., b. in Derry, N. H.:

186. ‡I. Frederick Gillmore[9], b. June 7, 1849; m. Caroline J. Evans.

187. ‡II. William Frank[9], b. July 22, 1851; m. Elizabeth B. Cameron.

188. III. Nancy High[9], b. April 17, 1853; d. April 30, 1856.

189. IV. Julia Adelia[9], b Jan. 26, 1855; m. John R. Dean and had Clarence W.[10], b. Oct. 6, 1882, Isabel[10], b. Jan. 13, 1885, Ruth[10], b. Jan. 18, 1887 and Walter E.[10], b. Jan. 25, 1893. Reside in Lawrence, Mass.

190. V. Lizzie Josephine[9], b. June 29, 1857; m. Dec. 1, 1877, Otto Kress and had Edward F.[10], b. Feb. 4, 1877 and Eva B.[10], b. June 5, 1883.

191. ‡VI. Sylvester Heuse[9], b. Jan. 21, 1860; m. H. Pomeroy.

192. VII. Mark Ingraham[9], b. Feb. 14, 1862; m. Lizzie Runnels; resides at Lawrence.

193. VIII. Nancy High[9] 2d, b. April 19, 1864; d. July 6, 1898, m. Fred H. Libby and had Frederick[10], b. April 27, 1895, and Anna Maybelle[10], b. July 6, 1898.

194. IX. Anna Belle[9], b. April 20, 1866; m. Sept. 27, 1899, Thomas Hay and had Jessie[10], b. July 16, 1901, and James[10], b. April 18, 1906; reside in Lawrence.

195.   ‡X. Asa Edmund[9], b Jan. 13, 1873, m. Linnie M.
               Nicholson.

   101. SAMUEL A.[8] FULLER, (*Samuel[7], Jesse[6], Barnabas[5],
Nathaniel[4], Samuel[3], Samuel[2], Samuel[1]*), b. July 10, 1825, in
Boston, Mass, m. May 17, 1855, Susan E. Greenlaw.
   He was a portrait painter and landscape artist; was chaplain of
the First Maine Cavalry; entered the ministry of the Methodist
Episcopal church; preached in Newport, Bremen, Dresden, Sears-
mont, Oldtown, Winterport and Searsport, Me.; Leicester, N.
Brookfield, Millbury and Topsfield, Mass.
   Children :
196.   ‡I.   William John[9], b Feb. 26, 1856; m. Ada
               Spaulding
197.   II.   Katie Isabella[9], b. May 28, 1857, in Bremen, Me.;
               m. Charles A Huntington and had Edgar A.[10], b.
               Aug 22, 1885, at Nashua, N. H, Helen A[10], b.
               April 7, 1888; Anna May[10], b. June 12, 1893,
               and Isabella F.[10], b March 30, 1895.
198.   III. Samuel A.[9], b. Feb. 22, 1859, m. Isabella S. Dean.

   105. JAMES W.[8] FULLER, (*Noah P.[7], Jesse[6], Barnabas[5],
Nathaniel[4], Samuel[3], Samuel[2], Samuel[1]*), b. Sept 24, 1809; d.
Dec. 1, 1892, in Searsmont, Me.; m 1, ———; m. 2, Margaret
Wentworth of Searsmont.   He owned farms; burnt lime and
operated mills.
   Children by first wife.   All children born in Searsport, Me. :
199.   I.   A daughter[9], b. ———.
   By second wife :
200.   II.   Mary Jane[9], b. ———; m. and had 5 children.
               Parents both dead.
201.   ‡III. James[9], b. ———, m. Sarah Spence.
202.   IV.   Alden[9], b. ———; removed to California; d.
               unmarried.
203.   V.   Andrew[9], b. ———; removed to the West; d.
               there unmarried.
204.   VI.   Abby[9], b. ———, d. in childhood.
205.   VII. Lovicia[9], b. ———.
206.   VIII. Obed[9], b. ———; m. ———; res. Searsmont. No
               children.
207.   IX   Frank[9], b. ———; resides at Searsmont.
208.   X.   Edward[9], b. ———; removed to the West.

209.   XI.   Noah⁹, b. ——, killed in mill machinery in
               childhood.
210.   XII.   Julia⁹, b. ——; m. ——; resides in Mass.
211.   XIII.   Rosanna⁹, b. ——; m. ——; resides Belfast,
               Me No children.
212.   XIV.   John⁹, b ——; lives in Maine; unmarried.
213   XV.   Elizabeth⁹, b. (the youngest); m. —— Burrage;
               res. W. Camden, Me.; two children.

It is said there were 19 in all, and that the others died in
childhood.

106. JESSE PRINCE⁸ FULLER, (*Noah P.⁷, Jesse⁶, Barnabas⁵,
Nathaniel⁴, Samuel³, Samuel², Samuel¹*), b. April 29, 1811; d.
——, 1839; m April, 1835, Theresa Walker of Appleton, Me.
   Children:
214.   Lorna⁹, b——; d. young.

110. HEZEKIAH PRINCE⁸ FULLER, (*Noah P.⁷, Jesse⁶, Barnabas⁵,
Nathaniel⁴, Samuel³, Samuel², Samuel¹*), b. Jan. 1, 1820, in Hope,
Me.; d. Oct. 16, 1903, in Searsmont, Me.; m. March 4, 1847,
Catherine Safford Mossman, b. Feb. 18, 1827, in Thomaston, Me.,
d. July 29, 1881, in Searsmont.
   Their children, all born in Hope, Me., were:
215.   I.   Lucy Safford⁹, b. Jan. 22, 1848; m. Nov. 11, 1871,
               Leonard W. Luce and had Nellie A.¹⁰, b. June 2,
               1874, in Searsmont; Charles E.¹⁰, b. May 8,
               1876, in Hope, and Clifford L.¹⁰, b. Nov. 14, 1884,
               in Searsmont, d. there March 26, 1895.
216.   II.   Sarah Hale⁹, b. May 12, 1850; m. Aug. 8, 1870,
               H. A. Thorndike of Augusta, Me., and has one
               son, b Nov. 2, 1873, in Augusta.
217. ‡III.   George Washington⁹, b. Aug. 7, 1853; m. Mary
               Ellen Pease.
218.   IV.   Charles Henry⁹, b. Nov. 4, 1855.*
219.   V.   Orison Bartlett⁹, b. Sept. 2, 1857.*

117. JOSIAH J.⁸ FULLER, (*John⁷, Jesse⁶, Barnabas⁵, Nathaniel⁴,
Samuel³, Samuel², Samuel¹*), b. April 3, 1823, in Hebron, Me., d.
Aug. 18, 1909; m. 1, 1848, Margaret A. Foster of Buckfield, Me.,
who d. 1854; m. 2, March, 1855, Mary A. Noble of Auburn, Me.

---

*No reply received to letters of inquiry.

For a number of years he had a general merchandise store at East Hebron. Contractor on Portland and Buckfield, R. R. in 1862.

Children by first wife.

220.   I.   Clifton J.9, b. ———.
221.   II. Sylvester9, b. ———.

By second wife .

222.   III. Jesse E 9, b. ———; m. Dec. 10, 1889, Emily Louisa Howard   No children.*
223.   IV.   Cora M.9, b. ———.
224.   V.   Clara9, b. ———.
225.   VI.   Nettie F.9, ———.
226.   VII. Lura M 9, b. ———.
227.   VIII. Alta A.9, b. ———.
228   IX.   Frank J.9, b. ———.

(The compiler has failed to receive replies from children to whom he was referred for information)

119. RUFUS P.8 FULLER, (*John 7, Jesse 6, Barnabas 5, Nathaniel 4, Samuel 3, Samuel 2, Samuel 1*), b Nov. 29, 1828, in Hebron, Me ; d. May 15, 1908 ; m. ———, Lydia A. Warner of Sumner, Me.

Children :

229.   I. A son b. ———— .

120. JOSEPH DANA 8 FULLER, (*John 7, Jesse 6, Barnabas 5, Nathaniel 4, Samuel 3, Samuel 2, Samuel 1*), b. Nov. 26, 1832, in Hebron, Me., d. Feb. 14, 1902 ; m. ———, Mary Augusta Chaffin.

Children .

230.   ‡I.   Charles Rodney9, b. Dec. 31, 1853 ; m. Ada Foster.
231.   II.   Mary Jane9, b May 9, 1856, at Portland, Me. ; m. Oct 12, 1865, in Boston, Mass., William J. Mayo of Portland, and had Walter Huntington10, b. Feb. 24, 1876, in Portland ; Arthur Jewett10, b. March 5, 1878, in Portland ; Ida May10, b. June 9, 1880, in Boston and Bessie Reynolds10, b. June 5, 1883, in Boston.
232.   III.   Agnes Angelia9, b. Jan. 25, 1858, at East Hebron, Me. ; m. Jan. 25, 1882, in Boston, Robert F. Piper of Boston. Their children are Ethel May10, b. Sept. 18, 1884 and Edith Waldron10, b. April 25, 1888.
233.   IV.   Ida Ellen9, b. March 22, 1860, at E. Hebron ; m. Sept. 23, 1890, at Medfield, Mass., Daniel

———————
*Bellows Family Genealogy.

Thomas of Walpole, Mass. They have had
Frank Waldron[10], b. Oct 3, 1892, d. Oct. 4,
1892; Grace Chaffin[10], b. March 10, 1894, d.
March 20, 1894; Carl Webster[10], b. April 21,
1896; Eva Gladys[10], b. Nov. 25, 1897, Bessie
Church[10], b. Sept. 3, 1899 and Earl Gordon[10],
b. 1903, at Walpole.

234. ‡V. Frederick D[9], b. Nov. 22, 1862; m. Helen C.
Clark.

235. VI. Carrie Clark[9], b. Feb 22, 1868, in Portland, Me.;
m March 19, 1890, in Medfield, Mass., Edward
C. Snyder of Boston, Mass., and has Charles
Edward[10], b. Dec. 25, 1891, in Medfield;
Waldron Lewis[10], b. Jan. 11, 1893, Lester
William[10], b Sept. 9, 1894, and Grace Reed[10], b.
Oct. 13, 1895, the last three b in Boston.

236. ‡VII. Louis Edward[9], b. Feb. 23, 1871; m. Mabel E.
Allen.

237. VIII. Emma B.[9], b. Dec. 31, 1872, in Boston; m. Nov. 9,
1893, in Medfield, Robert Busby Newcomb.

238. IX. Julia Smith[9], b. Jan. 20, 1875, in Boston; m.
June 26, 1895, in Boston, Frank N. Spear of
Walpole, Mass., and has George Dana[10], b.
Nov. 18, 1895; Marjorie Fuller[10], b. May 5,
1899 and Henry Dyke Newcomb[10], b. Jan. 27,
1906; all born in Walpole.

122. JESSE AUGUSTUS[8] FULLER, (*Barnabas[7], Jesse[6], Barnabas[5],
Nathaniel[4], Samuel[3], Samuel[2], Samuel[1]*), b. March 27, 1829, in
Hebron, Me.; d Jan. 2, 1900, m. 1, Feb. 24, 1868, in Boston,
Emma Bean; m. 2, ———, 1897, Josephine W.[8] (Fuller) Wagg,
(*Kimball P.[7], Jesse[6], Barnabas[5], Nathaniel[4], Samuel[3], Samuel[2],
Samuel[1]*).

Children by first wife:

239. I. ———.
240. II. ———.
241. III. ———.

(I have failed to obtain further data in regard to this family.)

128. FRANK T.[8] FULLER, (*Barnabas[7], Jesse[6], Barnabas[5],
Nathaniel[4], Samuel[3], Samuel[2], Samuel[1]*), b. Jan. 13, 1851, in
Minot, Me.; m. Oct. 20, 1873, Augusta P. Keene.

He removed to Boston in 1878, where he is now in business;
resides in Dorchester, Mass.

Children·

242.   I.   Alice Mae[9], b Sept. 29, 1882, in Boston; m. April
                    5, 1905, Charles W. Homeyer, and has son, Frank
                    Fuller[10], b. Dec. 30, 1907.
243.   II. Carrie Belle[9], b. Feb. 18, 1885.

136. EDWARD P.[8] FULLER, (*Jesse[7]*, *Jesse[6]*, *Barnabas[5]*,
Nathaniel[4], *Samuel[3]*, *Samuel[2]*, *Samuel[1]*), b. ———; d. ———;
m. ———.

He resided in Auburn, Me.

The following names of the children have been mentioned,
presumably not in order of birth:

244.   I.   Charles[9], b. ———, removed to Minnesota.
245.   II. Dora[9], b. ———; m. ——— Humbert and removed
                    to Arizona.
246.   III. Mary[9], b. ———, removed to Arizona.
247.   IV. Edward[9], b. ———.

141. ELISHA C.[8] FULLER, (*Isaiah W.[7]*, *Isaac[6]*, *Barnabas[5]*,
Nathaniel[4], *Samuel[3]*, *Samuel[2]*, *Samuel[1]*), b. Jan. 31, 1831, in
Livermore, Me., d. June 21, 1909, in Bath, Me.; m. Aug. 16, 1857,
Antoinette A. Walker, who d. Mar. 12, 1898.

He resided at North Livermore.

Children:

248.   I.   Jessie L.[9], b. July 10, 1862, in Framingham, Mass.;
                    m. 1, Oct. 18, 1882, Charles S. Loring, who d.
                    March 31, 1887; m. 2, Nov. 24, 1906, Frank W.
                    Merritt, M. D. They reside in Jay, Me. Her
                    children are Bertha May[10] Loring, b. Oct. 31,
                    1883, of Mt. Holyoke College, 1904/5, Pratt
                    Institute, 1906, now in Commercial Art work in
                    New York City; Charles Sewall[10] Loring, b. June
                    22, 1887, entered Univ. of Me., 1907.
249.   II. Annette M.[9], b. April 28, 1864, in Livermore.
250.   III. N. Bonaparte[9], b. June 5, 1868, in Livermore; m.
                    Oct. 7, 1907, Evelyn L. Wyman.
251.   ‡IV. Victor S.[9], b. April 9, 1870, in Livermore; m. 1,
                    Lula A. Pomeroy, m. 2, Bertha A. Sinnette.

145. HENRY RUSSELL[8] FULLER, (*Ira[7]*, *Isaac[6]*, *Barnabas[5]*,
Nathaniel[4], *Samuel[3]*, *Samuel[2]*, *Samuel[1]*), b. April 27, 1841, in
Livermore, Me.; d. Dec. 6, 1907, in Temple, Me.; m. 1, in N. Y.
City, Sophia Parker of Jay, Me.; m. 2, July 3, 1889, Ella F. Horne

of Temple, Me. He was a harness maker; a violinist, and in his later years a guide for sportsmen in the Maine woods.

Children, by first wife ·

252. ‡I. Charles Henry[9], b. March 11, 1865; m. Helen L. Foster.
253. II. Josephine Lee[9], b. Oct. 7, 1866, in N. Y. City; m. Aug. 31, 1889, Frederick L. Johnson, and has a son, Benjamin W.[10], b. Jan 30, 1890.
254. III. Leonie May[9], b. Nov. 3, 1868, in Phillips, Me.; resides in Lynn, Mass.
255. IV. Georgia Lillian[9], b. May 7, 1862, in Phillips; m. June 23, 1905, George W. Walsh.
256. ‡V. Frederick Russell[9], b. Aug. 17, 1879; m. Grace N. Barry.

By second wife:

257. VI. A child that died in infancy.

152. ELLIAN ERROL[8] FULLER, (*Asa*[7], *Isaac*[6], *Barnabas*[5], *Nathaniel*[4], *Samuel*[3], *Samuel*[2], *Samuel*[1],) b. Sept. 4, 1851, in Livermore, Me., m. May 10, 1876, Dora M. Thompson of Hartford, Me.:

Their children are:

258. I. Orlistus Conant[9], b. April 16, 1881, in Livermore.
259. II. Cornelia Mahala[9], b. April 30, 1891, in Livermore.

153. ARATUS CARROLL[8] FULLER, (*Asa*[7], *Isaac*[6], *Barnabas*[5], *Nathaniel*[4], *Samuel*[3], *Samuel*[2], *Samuel*[1]), b. June 1, 1856, in Livermore, Me.; m. 1, Dec. 25, 1878, Sarah C. Cummings of Livermore, who d. Feb. 2, 1886; m. 2, June 28, 1890, Rose Hersey of Auburn, Me.

Children:

260. I. Addie Reed[9], b. March 21, 1880; m. Nov. 6, 1899, Leon L. Morton of Canton, Me. They reside in Hemet, Cal.
261. II. Celestia Emma[9], b March 2, 1882; m. April 28, 1904, Ernest R. Wills of Auburn, Me., and had Rose Alberta[10], b. June 27, 1906. They reside in Hemet, Cal.
262. III. Errol Omar[9], b. June 22, 1884; d. Oct. 27, 1886.
263. IV. Carroll Millett[9], b. May 31, 1886.
264. V. Edward Hersey[9], b. July 3, 1891. Class of 1912 Bates College. Director of the College Band and Orchestra; Secretary Auburn and Lewiston Musicians' Union (1910).

NINTH GENERATION.

170. Everett Standish[9] Fuller, (*George B.*[8], *Bildad*[7], *Philemon*[6], *Amos*[5], *Nathaniel*[4], *Samuel*[3], *Samuel*[2], *Samuel*[1]), b. March 12, 1860, in Plympton, Mass.; m. Cora L. Churchill, who d. Sept., 1908.

He resides in Middleboro, Mass.

Children :

265.   I.   Nellie L.[10], b. Aug. 18, 1884; d. July 20, 1897, in Plympton.

175. Frank Irving[9] Fuller, (*Dexter*[8], *Harvey*[7], *Philemon*[6], *Amos*[5], *Nathaniel*[4], *Samuel*[3], *Samuel*[2], *Samuel*[1]), b. Dec. 21, 1869; m. 1888, Mary Alice Osborne.

Children, recorded in Plympton, Mass.:

266.   I.   Lillian Frances[10], b. 1888, m. Feb. 25, 1905, Freeman N. Stevens.
267.   II.   Earnest Walter[10], b. Sept. 20, 1893
268.   III.   Frederick Martin[10], b. July 13, 1897.
269.   IV.   Ruby Osborne[10], b July 13, 1900.
270.   V.   Pearl[10], b. Dec. 20, 1901.

186. Frederick Gillmore[9] Fuller, (*Asa C.*[8], *Samuel*[7], *Jesse*[6], *Barnabas*[5], *Nathaniel*[4], *Samuel*[3], *Samuel*[2], *Samuel*[1]), b June 7, 1849, m. July 21, 1872, Caroline J. Evans.

He is a farmer residing in Berlin, N. H.

Children .

271.   ‡I.   Albert C.[10], b. July 26, 1873; m. Mary A. Calkins·
272.   II.   Harry R.[10], b. Jan. 13, 1876; d. March 28, 1881.
273.   III.   Edith L.[10], b. Aug. 20, 1877; m. Dec. 17, 1900, Alfred C. Whitherbee. They reside in Berlin, N. H., and children are: Alfred C.[11], b. March 20, 1902, Caroline F.[11], b. Sept. 2, 1903 and Beryle Sylvia[11], b. April 7, 1908.

187. William Frank[9] Fuller, (*Asa C.*[8], *Samuel*[7], *Jesse*[6], *Barnabas*[5], *Nathaniel*[4], *Samuel*[3], *Samuel*[2], *Samuel*[1]), b. July 22, 1851, in Thomaston, Me.; d. May 10, 1909, in Brentwood, N. H.; m. 1, Elizabeth B. Cameron, who d. ———— ; m. 2, Dec. 21, 1889, Theresa L. Cartlidge, who resides in Lawrence, Mass.

Children :

274.   I.   Ethel[10], b. Aug. 16, 1895, in West Andover, Mass.

191. SYLVESTER HUESE[9] FULLER. (*Asa C.[8], Samuel[7], Jesse[6], Barnabas[5], Nathaniel[4], Samuel[3], Samuel[2], Samuel[1]*), b. Jan. 21, 1860, in Thomaston, Me.; m. —— H. Pomeroy?
Resides in Dorchester, Mass.
Children:

275.　　　I. Clara[10], b. ——. Resides in Boston, Mass.

195. ASA EDMUND[9] FULLER, (*Asa C.[8], Samuel[7], Jesse[6], Barnabas[5], Nathaniel[4], Samuel[3], Samuel[2], Samuel[1]*), b. Jan. 13, 1873, in Derry, N. H.; m. Linnie M. Nicholson.
Resides in Lawrence, Mass.
Children, born in Lawrence:

276.　　　I. Ernest W.[10], b. Sept. 9, 1904.
277.　　　II. Charles E.[10], b. Oct. 14, 1907.

196. WILLIAM JOHN[9] FULLER, (*Samuel A.[8], Samuel[7], Jesse[6], Barnabas[5], Nathaniel[4], Samuel[3], Samuel[2], Samuel[1]*), b. Feb. 26, 1856, at Newport, Me.; m. Ada Spaulding of Somerville, Mass.
Resides in Derry, N. H.
Children, all born in Derry, N. H..

278.　　　I. Samuel A.[10], b. Nov. 26, 1891.
279.　　　II. William J.[10], b. Sept. 25, 1893.
280　　　III. James S.[10], b. Sept. 23, 1895.

201. JAMES[9] FULLER, (*James W.[8], Noah P.[7], Jesse[6], Barnabas[5], Nathaniel[4], Samuel[3], Samuel[2], Samuel[1]*), b. ——, in Searsmont, Me., m. Sarah Spence.
Resides in Searsmont.
Children:

281.　　　I. A daughter, b. ——.
282.　　　II. A daughter, b. ——.
283.　　　III. A daughter, b. ——.

217. GEORGE WASHINGTON[9] FULLER, (*Hezekiah P.[8], Noah P.[7], Jesse[6], Barnabas[5], Nathaniel[4], Samuel[3], Samuel[2], Samuel[1]*), b. Aug. 7, 1853, in Hope, Me.; m. May 1, 1880, Mary Ellen Pease.
They reside in North Searsmont, Me.
Their children are:

284.　　　‡I. Clarence Hezekiah[10], b. Aug. 14, 1881; m. Alma Mae O'Hara.

285.   II.   Arthur Samuel [10], b. Aug. 21, 1884.
286.   III.   Albert Brown [10], b. May 29, 1888.
287.   IV.   Everett George [10], b. Jan. 19, 1896.

230. CHARLES RODNEY[9] FULLER, (*Joseph D.*[8], *John*[7], *Jesse*[6], *Barnabas*[5], *Nathaniel*[4], *Samuel*[3], *Samuel*[3], *Samuel*[1]), b. Dec. 31, 1853, at East Hebron, Me., m. July 10, 1889, Ada Foster of Boston, Mass. They have no children. Mr. Fuller is a Boston grocer, director in "The National Association of Retail Grocers of the United States," and President of the Boston Retail Grocers Association.

The compiler is indebted to him for much information concerning the descendants of John[7] Fuller (*Samuel*[1]).

234. FREDERICK DANA[9] FULLER, (*Joseph D.*[8], *John*[7], *Jesse*[6], *Barnabas*[5], *Nathaniel*[4], *Samuel*[3], *Samuel*[2], *Samuel*[1]), b. Nov. 22, 1862, in East Hebron, Me., m. March 14, 1889, Helen C. Clark of Portland, Me.

Mr. Fuller is a lawyer in Boston, residing in Newton, Mass.

Children, all born at Topeka, Kan.:

288.   I.   Dana Clark [10], b March 2, 1890; d. March 4, 1890.
289.   II.   Warren Clark [10], b. April 16, 1892.
290.   III.   Elizabeth Clark [10], b. May 23, 1894.

236. LOUIS EDWARD[9] FULLER, (*Joseph D*[8], *John*[7], *Jesse*[6], *Barnabas*[5], *Nathaniel*[4], *Samuel*[3], *Samuel*[2], *Samuel*[1]), b. Feb. 22, 1871, at Portland, Me.; d. June 10, 1907, at Walpole, Mass.; m. Sept. 9, 1893, in Newton, Mass., Mabel E. Allen.

Their children are:

291.   I.   Mildred Allen [10], b. June 2, 1894, in Waltham, Mass.
292.   II.   Helen Chaffin [10], b. Nov. 17, 1895, in Waltham.
293.   III.   Florence Leda [10], b. Jan. 23, 1897, in Somerville, Mass.

251. VICTOR S.[9] FULLER, (*Elisha C.*[8], *Isaiah W.*[7], *Isaac*[6], *Barnabas*[5], *Nathaniel*[4], *Samuel*[3], *Samuel*[2], *Samuel*[1]), b. April 9, 1870, in Livermore, Me.; m 1, Jan. 12, 1888, Lula A. Pomeroy, who d. Aug. 31, 1899, m. 2, May 12, 1903, Bertha A. Sinnette.

Resides in Bath, Me.

Children, all born in Livermore, Me.:

294.   I.   Vivia Maude[10], b. Nov. 16, 1888, m. Sept. 2, 1907, Walter F. Norton and has Carrie Ardell[11], b. Feb. 16, 1909. They reside in Bath, Me.
295.   II.   Paul Jones[10], b. Dec. 14, 1889.
296.   III.   Guy Soult[10], b. June 12, 1891.
297.   IV.   Everett Ney[10], b. March 7, 1893.
298.   V.   Lannes M.[10], b Oct. 31, 1894.
299.   VI.   Harry L.[10], b. Aug. 18, 1897.
300.   VII.   Carl Woodman[10], b. April 8, 1899.

252. CHARLES HENRY[9] FULLER, (*Henry R.*[8], *Ira*[7], *Isaac*[6], *Barnabas*[5], *Nathaniel*[4], *Samuel*[3], *Samuel*[2], *Samuel*[1]), b. March 1, 1865, in Brooklyn, N. Y., m. Aug. 16, 1888, Helen L. Foster.

They reside in Lynn, Mass.

Their children are:

301.   I.   Walter Russell[10], b Dec. 11, 1899.
302.   II.   Harry Earle[10], b. Dec. 8, 1904.

256. FREDERICK RUSSELL[9] FULLER, (*Henry R.*[8], *Ira*[7], *Isaac*[6], *Barnabas*[5], *Nathaniel*[4], *Samuel*[3], *Samuel*[2], *Samuel*[1]), b. Aug. 17, 1879, in Phillips, Me.; m. July 3, 1902, Grace N. Barry.

They reside in Lynn, Mass.

Children:

303.   I.   Dorothy N.[10], b. ———.

TENTH GENERATION.

271. ALBERT COLE[10] FULLFR, (*Frederick G.*[9], *Asa C.*[8], *Samuel*[7], *Jesse*[6], *Barnabas*[5], *Nathaniel*[4], *Samuel*[3], *Samuel*[2], *Samuel*[1]), b. July 26, 1873; m. April 12, 1898, in South Framingham, Mass., Mary A. Calkins.

They reside in Fitchburg, Mass.

Children:

304.   I.   Thelma Grace[11], b. March 18, 1899, in South Framingham.
305.   II.   Harry Raymond[11], b. Jan. 6, 1901, in Fitchburg.
306.   III.   Merle Evans[11], b. Aug. 11, 1909, in Fitchburg.

280. CLARENCE HEZEKIAH [10] FULLER, (*George W.[9], Hezekiah P.[8], Noah P.[7], Jesse[6], Barnabas[5], Nathaniel[4], Samuel[3], Samuel[2], Samuel[1]*), b. Aug. 14, 1881, in Searsmont, Me.; m. June 8, 1901, Alma Mae O'Hara.

They reside in Searsmont.

Their children, all born in Searsmont, are:

307.   I.   Wilbur Clarence[11], b. March 29, 1902.
308.   II. Lytle Ella[11], b. Nov. 26, 1904.

SECOND GROUP.

FOURTH GENERATION.

SETH⁴ FULLER, AND SOME OF HIS DESCENDANTS.

15. SETH⁴ FULLER, (*Samuel³, Samuel², Samuel¹*), b. Aug. 30, 1692 (Plymouth Records) ; date and place of death not found ; m. 1, May 12, 1720, Sarah Wright (Plympton Records), who d. June 7, 1726, at Plympton, and Plympton Records also state that Seth Fuller m. March 8, 1727, Deborah Cole, widow of Samuel Cole.

Children, recorded at Plympton

1.   ‡ I.   Archippus⁵, b. May 17, 1721 ; m. 1, Mary Pratt ;
                   m. 2, Maria (Rider) Churchill.
2.   II.   Sarah⁵, b. Jan. 27, 1728.

FIFTH GENERATION.

1. ARCHIPPUS⁵ FULLER, (*Seth⁴, Samuel³, Samuel², Samuel¹*), b. May 17, 1721, in Plympton, Mass.; d. 1811, in Hartford, Vt., aged 91 years; m. 1, Aug. 23, 1748, Mary Pratt (Plympton Records) ; m. 2, Sept. 26, 1753, Maria (Rider) Churchill, "and removed to Woodstock, Vt." (Churchill Family Genealogy.)

May 5, 1782, Archippus Fuller and "Meriah," his wife, were received into full communion in the Woodstock Congregational church.

Children :

3.   ‡ I.   Seth⁶, b. ——— ; m. Olive Dutton.
4.   ‡ II.   Samuel⁶, b. 1764 ; m. Sarah Freeman.

And perhaps others.

SIXTH GENERATION.

3. SETH[6] FULLER, (*Archippus[5]*, *Seth[4]*, *Samuel[3]*, *Samuel[2]*, *Samuel[1]*), b. ——— ; d ———, 1837, m. about 1780, Olive Dutton, b. Aug. 17, 1761, d. Aug. 16, 1828, dau of Samuel Dutton, who removed from Woodbury, Ct., to Woodstock, Vt., in 1778, and remained there until 1796. (Tucker's Hist. of Hartford, Vt.) Seth Fuller was a fifer in the Revolutionary war. He and his father each bought a 100-acre lot in the western part of Woodstock in 1784, and sold property in 1792, and the last deed mentions Seth as of Hartford, Vt.

Children :

5.	I.	Lois[7], bapt. June 1, 1783 (Cong. church records, Woodstock) ; m Stephen Parker. "Of their children three daughters lived and two married."
6.	‡II.	Oliver[7], b. March 13, 1785 ; m. Sarah Thorn.
7.	III.	Adelaide[7], b. ——— ; d. young.
8.	IV.	Abner[7], bapt. May 12, 1787 ; d. Nov. 12, 1868, aged 81 years, 3 m. (Hartford, Vt, Rec.) ; m. 1, Jan. 26, 1814, Olive Savage ; m. 2, Mary Savage. No children. He was a deacon in the Cong. church.
9.	V.	Amelia[7], b. ——— ; d. young.
10.	VI.	Susan[7], b. ——— ; d. young.
11.	VII.	Deborah[7], b. Jan. 8, 1792, bapt. Feb. 19, 1792 ; d Jan. 4, 1858, m. Dec 23, 1813, Solomon Hazen, b. Aug. 22, 1788, d. Oct. 29, 1834 ; had three sons, Carleton[8], Edward[8] and Norman[8].
12.	VIII.	Sarah[7], b. ———, bapt. March 16, 1794 ; d. ——— ; m. July 4, 1815, Hastings Savage, b. Nov. 20, 1789.
13.	IX.	Abigail[7] (Nabby), b. ——— ; bapt. May 15, 1795 ; d. June, 1862, aged 66 ; m. Joseph Crandall, who d Aug. 28, 1856. They lived in Hartford, Vt., and had six children, four of whom lived to maturity.
14.	X.	Mary[7], b. ——— ; m. Jacob Black of Stowe, Vt.
15.	XI.	John[7], b. 1799 ; d. Sept. 14, 1861, aged 72 yrs., 1 m., 1d. (Hartford, Vt., Rec.) ; m. 1, ——— Dewey of Ct. (See Dewey Gen.), m. 2, Feb. 22, 1849, Caroline Savage, who d. Feb. 3, 1879. He had children by first wife that d. in infancy ; none by second wife. John Fuller was a deacon in the W. Hartford, Vt., Congregational church.

4. SAMUEL[6] FULLER, (*Archippus*[5], *Seth*[4], *Samuel*[3], *Samuel*[2], *Samuel*[1]), b. about 1764, perhaps in Woodstock, Vt.; d. April 17, 1849, aged 85, in Stowe, Vt., m. Sarah Freeman, who d. Sept. 13, 1851, aged 75 years. Samuel Fuller removed to Stowe, Vt., in 1807, probably from Woodstock, since it was there his son Joseph was born. Probably he was the Samuel Fuller of Woodstock, mentioned in Dana's Hist. of Woodstock, as owning an interest in a saw-mill in the northwest part of the town.

Children:

16.   ‡I.   Joseph[7], b. about 1797, in Woodstock; m. Mercy Hodgman
17.   ‡II.   Archippus[7], b. Nov. 19, 1798; m. Esther Sartle.
18.   ‡III. Bethuel Washburn[7], b. Sept. 4, 1800; m. 1, Abigail Head; m. 2, Dolly (Head) Barrows.
19.   ‡IV.   Madison[7], b. ———; m. Althea Parcher.
20.   ‡V.   Samuel Freeman[7], b. May 6, 1803; m. Elizabeth Kingsley.
21.   VI.   Myron[7], b. ———; m. and removed to N. Y. state.
22.   ‡VII. George[7], b. ———; m. ———.
23.   VIII. Hawley[7], b. ———, d. in early manhood; was a lawyer.
24.   IX.   Charles[7], b. ———, d. about 1848, aged 40; unmarried.
25.   X.   Maria[7], b. ———; d. about 1841, in Stowe, Vt.; m. Josiah Keith.

SEVENTH GENERATION.

6. OLIVER[7] FULLER, (*Seth*[6], *Archippus*[5], *Seth*[4], *Samuel*[3], *Samuel*[2], *Samuel*[1]), b. March 13, 1785, in Woodstock, Vt.; d. Nov. 15, 1855, in Stowe, Vt.; m. Sept. 10, 1807, Sarah Town, b. Aug. 31, 1787, in Sharon, Vt.

Children:

26.   I.   Elvira[8], b. June 9, 1808, in Stowe, Vt.; d. ———; m. Charles Brigham of Morristown; had one child.
27.   ‡II.   Seth[8], b. Feb. 8, 1811; m. Pamelia Bingham.
28.   III.   Lucy[8], b. Oct. 21, 1812, in Stowe, Vt.; never married.
29.   ‡IV.   Salem[8], b. July 11, 1814, in Stowe, Vt.; m. Mehitable Cheney.

16. JOSEPH[7] FULLER, (*Samuel[6], Archippus[5], Seth[4], Samuel[3], Samuel[2], Samuel[1]*), b. March 13, 1797, in Woodstock, Vt.; d. Nov. 6, 1881, in Stowe, Vt., m. 1824, Mercy Hodgman, b. March 26, 1797, in Hartland, Vt, d. Jan. 31, 1885.

Children :

30.	‡I.	Philo Francis[8], b. Sept. 25, 1825; m. Candace Richardson.
31.	II.	Caroline Cordelia[8], b. May 18, 1829; d. April 17, 1888; m. David Brown of Stowe, Vt., and had Hollis M.[9], b. Aug. 7, 1851 and Hattie M.[9], b. Oct. 26, 1856.
32.	‡III.	Samuel Thomas[8], b. Feb 16, 1831, m. Elizabeth Town
33.	IV.	Vodica Maria[8], b May 1, 1833, d Dec. 6, 1893, in Framingham, Mass., m May 11, 1852, Joseph J. Boynton, and had Alice Bingham[9], b. Oct 30, 1855, Ada Delano[9], b. March 31, 1860; Joseph Stannard[9], b May 12, 1863, Elsie Maria[9], b Aug 9, 1871, who m. Sept. 15, 1892, Clarence Edward Dunavan of the National Shawmut Bank of Boston.
34.	V.	Mary Churchill[8], b. May 4, 1835; m. 1, July 19, 1863, Otis G. Hatch; m. 2, J. A. Smith of Orleans, Vt. Children (Hatch) : Seward[9], b. Jan. 16, 1866; Ola M.[9], b. Dec. 25, 1867 and Jessie M.[9], b. Dec 2, 1869.
35.	VI.	Joseph Henry[8], b. Aug. 7, 1837; d. March, 1838.
36.	VII.	Sarah Eunice[8], b May 28, 1840; m. 1, Feb. 9, 1866, W. H. H. Poor, who d. April, 1870; m. 2, Oct. 14, 1877, Henry Clough of Troy, Vt. Children : Mary Eunice Poor, b. Feb. 5, 1867; Howard Harrison Poor, b. May 27, 1868 and Ernest Albert Clough, b. Sept. 23, 1878.
37.	VIII.	Claribel Alantha[8], b. Nov. 13, 1845; m. 1, ——— Gould, m 2, George Hall of Springfield, Vt.

17. ARCHIPPUS[7] FULLER, (*Samuel[6], Archippus[5], Seth[4], Samuel[3], Samuel[2], Samuel[1]*), b. Nov. 19, 1798, in Hartland, Vt., d. Oct. 28, 1888, in Tarkio, Mo., m. June 5, 1823, in Stowe, Vt., Esther Sartle, b. Aug. 9, 1806, in Stowe, d. June 22, 1862, in Independence, Ia.

He removed to Ashburnham, Mass., about 1853 and about 1856 to Des Moines, Ia., with wife and four youngest children.

Their children were ·

38.	I.	Julius Vilroy[8], b. June 25, 1824; d. May, 1849.

39.   II.   Henry^S, b. -——, 1826 ; d. in infancy.
40.   III.   Louisa Jane^S ⎫ twins, b. July 4, 1827 ⎰ d in infancy.
41.   IV.   Eliza Ann^S ⎭   ⎱ d. Mar., 1896,
            in Des Moines, Ia.; m. 1, ——— Pierce, who d.
            ——— ; m. 2, ——— Rice. She had a dau,
            Eda Pierce, who m. but d. without issue.
42.   ‡V.   Charles Carroll^S, b. May 21, 1829; m. Stella
            Anstess Hosley.
43.   VI.   Elvira Jane^S, b April 13, 1831 ; d. about 1864, in
            Iowa, m. ——— Sparling and had Elfreda^9, b.
            1858; Susan^9, b. about 1860 and Oscar^9, b.
            1865.
44.   ‡VII.   George Hawley^S, b. Aug. 14, 1841 ; m. 1, Adelaide
            Boome ; m. 2, ———.
45.   ‡VIII.   Oscar Martin^S, b. Sept 5, 1844, m. ———.
46.   IX.   Susan Maria^S, b. April 18, 1846; d. March, 1904,
            in Iowa; was a fine scholar; taught school
            several years; m. ——— Harwood; had three
            children ; children and parents dead.

18.   BETHUEL WASHBURN^7 FULLER, (*Samuel^6, Archippus^5, Seth^4,
Samuel^3, Samuel^2, Samuel^1*), b. Sept. 4, 1800, in Woodstock, Vt.;
d. July 19, 1867, in Montgomery, Vt.; m. 1, Abigail Head of
Montgomery, who d ———, m. 2, her sister, Mrs. Dolly (Head)
Barrows. He was a physician in Montgomery for many years.
    Children, b. in Montgomery :

47.   I   William^S, b. Oct. 8, 1832 ; d. in the army ; enlisted
            and raised a company, of which he was Captain,
            in the Civil war.
48.   ‡II.   George H.^{S}, b. March 31, 1835 ; m. Jane
            Wightman.
49.   III.   Hattie^S, b. March 17, 1837 ; m. 1855, George L.
            Clapp of Montgomery, Vt., and had William J.^{9},
            b. Nov. 28, 1857 and Charlotte^9, b. April 3, 1866.
50.   IV.   Abigail^S, b. Sept. 8, 1839 ; m. Warren Rawson and
            had Charles Fuller^9 and Isabel^9.
51.   V.   Cornelia^S, b. March 11, 1842.
52.   VI.   Nancy^S, b. April 29, 1844 ; m. James E. Smith of
            Montgomery, and had 10 children, of whom six
            are now (1910) living, Hattie^9, Sadie^9, James^9,
            Henry^9, Ethel^9 and Hazel^9.

19.   MADISON^7 FULLER, (*Samuel^6, Archippus^5, Seth^4, Samuel^3,
Samuel^2, Samuel^1*), b. ——— ; d. ——— ; m. ———, Althea
Parcher.

He was a mason. The family removed to Minneapolis, Minn., where his descendants live.

Children :

53.	I.	Ellen[8], b. ———.
54.	II.	Delia[8], b ———.
55.	III.	Myra[8], b. ———.
56.	IV.	A son, b. ———; d. in childhood.

20. SAMUEL FREEMAN[7] FULLER, (*Samuel[6], Archippus[5], Seth[4], Samuel[3], Samuel[2], Samuel[1]*), b. May 6, 1803, in Woodstock, Vt.; d. Oct. 19, 1866, in Montgomery, Vt.; m. Sept. 19, 1841, Elizabeth Kingsley of Montgomery, who d. April 18, 1881.

He was a farmer and a shoemaker.

Children :

57.	I.	Maria Elizabeth[8], b. April 15, 1843, d. Jan. 31, 1873.
58.	‡II.	Bethuel Hawley[8], b. Jan. 9, 1846; m. Caroline J. Noyes.
59.	‡III.	Jonathan Kingsley[8], b. May 13, 1848; m. Gertrude F. Smith.

22. GEORGE[7] FULLER, (*Samuel[3], Archippus[5], Seth[4], Samuel[2], Samuel[1]*), b. ———, d. ———; m. ———, Jane ———.

Lived in Milton, Vt., many years, and then removed to Minnesota. He was a musician.

Children :

60.	I.	George[8], b. ———.
61.	II.	Jed[8], b. ———.
62.	III.	Don[8], b. ———.

EIGHTH GENERATION.

27. SETH[8] FULLER, (*Oliver[7], Seth[6], Archippus[5], Seth[4], Samuel[3], Samuel[2], Samuel[1]*), b. Feb. 8, 1811, in Hartford, Vt.; d. ———; m. Dec., 1837, Pamelia Bingham.

Children :

| 63. | I. | Harriet[9], b. Sept. 19, 1838; d. Sept., 1860; unmarried. |
| 64. | II. | Ellen L.[9], b. Feb. 13, 1845; m. March 28, 1865, Joseph S. Wheeler and had Stedman C.[10], b. March 1, 1867 and Lillian H.[10], b. Jan. 23, 1872, d. Nov. 21, 1874. They reside in Waterbury, Vt. |

65.   III.   Mary⁹, b. Feb. 26, 1847; d. April 14, 1865; unmarried.

66.   IV.   Emma C.⁹, b. Sept. 7, 1852; m. Oct., 1870, George Sawyer of Stowe, Vt.

29. SALEM⁸ FULLER, (*Oliver⁷, Seth⁶, Archippus⁵, Seth⁴, Samuel³, Samuel², Samuel¹*), b. July 11, 1814, in Stowe, Vt.; d. —— ; m. ——, Mehitable Cheney.

Children:

67.   I.   Berton⁹, b. ——; d. ——; m. and had one son.

68.   II.   A dau.⁹, b. ——; d. ——; m. and had one dau.

30. PHILO FRANCIS⁸ FULLER (*Joseph⁷, Samuel⁶, Archippus⁵, Seth⁴, Samuel³, Samuel², Samuel¹*), b. Sept. 25, 1825, in Stowe, Vt.; d. Dec. 10, 1905; m. Sept., 1854, Candace Richardson, Stowe, Vt.

Children.

69.   I.   Frank⁹, b. —— Resides in Hadley, Mass.

70.   II.   Mary⁹, b.——; m. —— Wood. Resides in Chester, Vt.

71.   III.   Irving⁹, b. —— ; d. ——.

72.   IV.   Elsworth⁹, b. ——. Resides in Michigan.

73.   V.   A son, } twins, { b. ——; d. ——.
74.   VI.   A dau., }

32. SAMUEL THOMAS⁸ FULLER, (*Joseph⁷, Samuel⁶, Archippus⁵, Seth⁴, Samuel³, Samuel², Samuel¹*), b. Feb. 16, 1831, in Stowe, Vt.; d. there April 26, 1905; m. March 30, 1862, Elizabeth Town, now (1910) living in Stowe.

Children, born in Stowe:

75.   I.   Sarah E.⁹, b. May 15, 1866; d. July 19, 1902; m. Jan. 8, 1889, Andrew J. Magoon.

76.   ‡II.   Herbert G.⁹, b. May 18, 1869; m. Clara Louise Jacobs.

42. CHARLES CARROLL⁸ FULLER, (*Archippus⁷, Samuel⁶, Archippus⁵, Seth⁴, Samuel³, Samuel², Samuel¹*), b. May 21, 1829, in Stowe, Vt.; m. April 22, 1851, in Gardner, Mass., Stella Anstess Hosley, b. June 25, 1834, in Jamaica, Vt.; d. Dec. 30, 1891, in Riverside, R. I.

He resides in Pittsfield, Mass.

Children born to them were:

77.   I.   Eda Emogene[9], b. Dec. 14, 1851, in Gardner, m.
              Irving Ballou and resides in Swansey, N. H.
              They have three children, Unabella[10], Bernice[10]
              and Carrie E[10]

78   II. Calista E[9], b. Dec. 9, 1853, d. March 12, 1867.

79.   III. Lizzie Augusta[9], b. Jan. 31, 1856; d. Sept. 8, 1878.

80.   IV. Carrie Elzada Maria[9], b. July 2, 1858, in
              Ashburnham, Mass.; m. Aug. 22, 1877, Albert
              C. Coleman. They reside in Gardner and have
              three children, all b. there: Ethel[10], b. May 17,
              1880, a teacher in Springfield, Mass.; Blanche
              U.[10], b Sept 8, 1885, a teacher in Chicopee,
              Mass., and Leon N.[10], b. Jan. 4, 1887, resides in
              Gardner.

81.   V.   Nellie Eliza Lovinia[10], b. Nov. 8, 1860, in
              Ashburnham; m. June, 1885, Frank H.
              Goodspeed, and has dau, Helen F[10], b. May 12,
              1886 They reside in Gardner.

82.   ‡VI Julius Vilroy[9], b Jan. 14, 1864; m. Carrie L.
              Coleman.

83   VII. Samuel Elwin[9], b. Aug. 11, 1866; d. Sept. 10,
              1867.

84.   VIII. Mary Louise[9], b. Oct. 23, 1868; m. Dec. 24, 1887,
              Chester H. Learned and had Mildred A.[10], b.
              July 17, 1891, in Gardner.

85   IX   Albertie[9], b. Jan. 24, 1871, d. in infancy.

86.   X.   Francis Merriam[9], b. Jan. 25, 1874, in Gardner;
              m. Feb. 22, 1910, Carrie L. (Coleman) Fuller.

44. GEORGE HAWLEY[8] FULLER, (*Archippus*[7], *Samuel*[6],
Archippus[5], *Seth*[4], *Samuel*[3], *Samuel*[2], *Samuel*[1]), b. Aug. 14, 1841,
probably in Stowe, Vt; d. March 26, 1906, in Tarkio, Mo.; m.
about 1873, Adelaide Boone, who d. about 1898, m. 2, ———.

Dr. George H. Fuller was a soldier of the Civil war, and after its
close completed his education as a physician and began the practice
of his profession in Iowa. He was greatly beloved by all, and was
called the poor man's friend.

Children:

87.   I.   Albert[9], b. Sept. 28, 1905.

45. OSCAR MARTIN[8] FULLER, (*Archippus*[7], *Samuel*[6], *Archippus*[5],
Seth[4], *Samuel*[3], *Samuel*[2], *Samuel*[1]), b. Sept. 5, 1844, probably in
Stowe, Vt., m. about 1873, ———.

Oscar M. Fuller removed with his father from Mass. to Iowa in 1856. He was a soldier of the Civil war; came out of it broken in health and has been a sufferer ever since; is a resident of Seattle, Wash.

88.   I.   A son, b. ———— , d. about 1906.

89.   II.   George[8], b. about 1871 ; resides in Seattle; is in railway mail service.

46. George H.[8] Fuller, (*Bethuel W.[7], Samuel[6], Archippus[5], Seth[4], Samuel[3], Samuel[2], Samuel[1]*), b. March 31, 1835, in Montgomery, Vt.; served nine months in the Civil war; d. May, 1909 ; m. Jane Weightman of Richland, Vt.

Children :

90.   I.   William[9], b. ————.

91.   II.   Beecher[9], b. ————.

92.   III.   George[9], b. ————.

58. Bethuel Hawley[8] Fuller, (*Samuel F.[7], Samuel[6], Archippus[5], Seth[4], Samuel[3], Samuel[2], Samuel[1]*), b. Jan. 9, 1846, in Montgomery, Vt. , m. Nov. 22, 1877, Caroline J. Noyes, b. Nov. 7, 1851.

They reside in Montgomery.

Their children are .

93.   I.   Clayton J.[9], b. July 30, 1882.

94.   II.   Elizabeth K[9], b Jan. 5, 1888.

59. Jonathan Kingsley[8] Fuller, (*Samuel F.[7], Samuel[6], Archippus[5], Seth[4], Samuel[3], Samuel[2], Samuel[1]*), b. May 13, 1848, in Montgomery, Vt , m. Sept. 16, 1875, Gertrude F. Smith, b. Feb. 12, 1856, in Richford, Vt.

Mr. Fuller studied law and later took a theological course, and entered the ministry in 1874. He was pastor at Bakersfield, Vt., Congregational church, 1876–1889, then at Bakers' Landing, later at the Old South church at Windsor, Vt., and at present is chaplain of the Vermont State Prison.

Their children were :

95.   I.   John Harold[9], b. June 27, 1876, in Richford; m. 1, July 7, 1904, Caroline Houghton of Lyndonville, Vt , who d. Nov. 16, 1907 ; m. 2, Sept. 1, 1909, Olicta Longworthy of Brandon, Vt. No children.

96.   II.   Hawley Leigh[9], b. July 28, 1878, at Bakersfield,
                      Vt.; d. May 9, 1895.
97.   III.   Raymond G.[9], b. March 26, 1886, at Bakersfield.
98.   IV.   Robert Samuel[9], b. Feb. 28, 1893.

NINTH GENERATION.

76. HERBERT G.[9] FULLER, (*Samuel T.[8], Joseph[7], Samuel[6], Archippus[5], Seth[4], Samuel[3], Samuel[2], Samuel[1]*), b. May 18, 1869, in Stowe, Vt.; m. Sept 25, 1895, Clara Louise Jacobs, b. Sept. 12, 1874.

Mr. Fuller is a farmer in Stowe.

Children:

99.   I.   Elizabeth J.[10], b. Jan. 27, 1897.
100.   II.   Ada Louise[10], b. Feb. 28, 1898.
101.   III.   Roger Grant[10], b Oct. 2, 1899, d. April 2, 1901.
102.   IV.   Clara Beatrice[10], b. Oct. 26, 1900.
103.   V.   Reba Dorothy[10] } twins { b. Oct. 12, 1902.
104.   VI.   Rollo Downer[10] }
105.   VII.   Theodore H.[10], b. May 26, 1904.
106.   VIII. Hilda Carlotta[10], b. Nov. 2, 1907.

77. JULIUS VILROY[9] FULLER, (*Charles C.[8], Archippus[7], Samuel[6], Archippus[5], Seth[4], Samuel[3], Samuel[2], Samuel[1]*), b. Jan. 14, 1864, in Ashburnham, Mass.; d. Aug. 25, 1907, in Pittsfield, Mass.; m. May, 1889, Carrie L. Coleman, in Pittsfield.

Children:

107.   I.   Lulu[10], b. Dec. 16, 1890, in Pittsfield.

THIRD GROUP.

FOURTH GENERATION.

EBENEZER⁴ FULLER, (*Samuel³*) AND SOME OF HIS DESCENDANTS.

16. EBENEZER⁴ FULLER, (*Samuel³, Samuel², Samuel¹*), b. March 24, 1695, in Plymouth, Mass.; d. May 2, 1759, in Kingston, Mass.; m. Int. Pub. March 17, 1721, with Joanna Gray.

Plymouth Probate Records, Vol. 2, p. 192: Will of Ebenezer Fuller of Kingston, dated 1755, mentions wife Joanna, sons Josiah and Ebenezer, and daughters Rebecca, Lois and Eunice.

Children, recorded in Plymouth:

1.	‡I.	Josiah⁵, b. May 15, 1722; m. Lydia Cushman.
2.	II.	Samuel⁵, b. Oct. 14, 1723, d. April 22, 1724.
3.	III.	Rebecca⁵, b. April 23, 1725; m. Aug. 31, 1783, Elijah Alden.

Recorded at Kingston (Rebecca as above), and:

4.	IV.	Hannah⁵, b. June 8, 1727; d. Aug. 20, 1736.
5.	V.	Mercy⁵, b. Aug. 29, 1730, d. Jan. 8, 1733/4.
6.	VI.	Lois⁵, b. Nov. 16, 1733; d. Feb. 25, 1790; m. May 2, 1764, Nicholas Davis.
7.	VII.	Eunice⁵, b. May 5, 1736; m. 1760, Ebenezer (or Jeduthan) Robbins.
8.	‡VIII.	Ebenezer⁵, b. Feb. 16, 1737/8; m. Int. 1, Lois Rider; 2, Hannah Rider.

FIFTH GENERATION.

1. JOSIAH⁵ FULLER, (*Ebenezer⁴, Samuel³, Samuel², Samuel¹*), b. May 15, 1722, in Plymouth, Mass.; d. Sept. 3, 1805, in Kingston,

Mass.; m Jan. 21, 1746, Lydia Cushman, b. Sept. 29, 1726, d. April 3, 1784.

He was a blacksmith, and lived in Kingston, Dartmouth and Duxbury.

Children, the first two as recorded at Kingston; the others as given in H. W. Brainard's MSS, which says b. in Kingston:

9.	I.	Hannah[6], b. Nov. 15, 1747, d. Nov. 27, 1747.
10.	‡II.	Josiah[6], b. Oct. 31, 1748; m. Elizabeth Holmes.
11.	‡III.	Zephaniah[6], b. 1750, m. Mary Loring.
12.	IV.	Thankful[6], b. 1751; m. Oct. 24, 1771, Sylvanus Everson.
13.	V.	Malachi[6], b. 1753.
14.	VI.	Lemuel[6], b. 1755.
15.	VII.	Lavia[6], b. 1757.
16.	VIII.	Lydia[6], b. Aug. 21, 1759; d. July 17, 1842, m. 1, May 15, 1780, Elisha Cushman; m. 2, Perez Bradford of Kingston. She had a son, Thomas[7], b May 15, 1781, at Kingston.
17.	IX.	Joanna[6], b 1761; d. young.
18.	X.	Joanna[6] 2d, b. 1763; m. ——— *Sampson* (H. W. B MSS), m. Aug. 14, 1799, Jeremiah *Sumner* (Kingston and Taunton Records).
19.	XI.	James[6], b. 1768
20.	XII.	Eleazer[6], b ———.

8. EBENEZER[5] FULLER, (*Ebenezer[4]*, *Samuel[3]*, *Samuel[2]*, *Samuel[1]*), b. Feb. 16, 1737/8 (Kingston Records), d. ——— , m. Int. Pub. Nov. 6, 1756, with Lois Rider (Plymouth Record); m. Dec. 1, 1756 (Middleboro Record), m. Int. Pub. Aug. 15, 1761, with Hannah Rider (Plymouth Records); m. Oct. 21, 1761 (Bailey, Mass, Records).

Children, born to " Ebenezer Fuller and Lowis his wife " :

21.	I.	Ebenezer[6], b. Feb 17, 1758. (Plymouth Record.)

Plymouth, Mass, Deeds, Vol 56, p. 245, dated July 11, 1772: Ebenezer Fuller of Kingston, mariner, to Josiah Fuller of Kingston, yeoman, three rights or shares in 30 acres of woodland, being 3-6 parts of the whole, given by John Gray of Kingston, deceased, to his daughter Joanna Fuller; also: that part of the homestead lands and buildings belonging to the estate of my honored father Ebenezer Fuller, late of Kingston, deceased, which he gave me in his last will.

No further record found of this family.

SIXTH GENERATION.

10. JOSIAH[6] FULLER, (*Josiah*[5], *Ebenezer*[4], *Samuel*[3], *Samuel*[2], *Samuel*[1]), b. Oct. 31, 1748, at Kingston, Mass.; d. ——; m. Nov. 12, 1772, Elizabeth Holmes, who d. Aug. 10, 1829.

Children, recorded in Kingston:

22.   I.   John Holmes[7], b. Oct. 28, 1774; d. March 12, 1860.
23.   II.   Content[7], b. Nov. 27, 1777; d. May 19, 1784.
24.   III.   Lemuel[7], b June 25, 1781.
25. ‡IV.   Josiah[7], b. Dec. 11, 1783; m. Lucy Bradford.
26. ‡V.   Ephraim Holmes[7], b. Aug. 6, 1786; m. Lydia Johnson.

11. ZEPHANIAH[6] FULLER, (*Josiah*[5], *Ebenezer*[4], *Samuel*[3], *Samuel*[2], *Samuel*[1]), b. 1750, at Kingston, Mass.; d. ——; m. Dec. 11, 1781, Mary Loring.

Children, recorded in Kingston:

27.   I.   Sarah[7], b. Sept. 3, 1782; m. 1, —— Carey; m. 2, —— Shipley.
28.   II.   Zephaniah[7], b. Jan. 13, 1784, d. Oct. 3. 1806.
29. ‡III.   George[7], b. Aug. 1, 1785; m. 1, Sarah Kuhn; m. 2, Susannah Gill.
30. ‡IV.   Ebenezer[7], b. Aug. 6, 1788; m. Harriet Blanchard.
31.   V.   Loring[7], b Nov. 19, 1789.
32.   VI.   Perez[7], b. Jan. 11, 1797; m. Elizabeth Adams.

SEVENTH GENERATION.

25. JOSIAH[7] FULLER, (*Josiah*[6], *Josiah*[5], *Ebenezer*[4], *Samuel*[3], *Samuel*[2], *Samuel*[1]), b. 1783, at Kingston, Mass.; d. Aug. 14, 1868; m. Nov. 29, 1807, Lucy Bradford of Plymouth, who d. Jan., 1870.

Children, born at Kingston:

33.   I.   Josiah[8], b. Sept. 16, 1808.
34. ‡II.   Charles Warren[8], b. April 29, 1810; m. Maria Bisbee.
35.   III.   Elizabeth Holmes[8], b. Jan. 12, 1812; m. June 3, 1832, Thomas Howe of Boston.

26. EPHRAIM HOLMES[7] FULLER, (*Josiah*[6], *Josiah*[5], *Ebenezer*[4], *Samuel*[3], *Samuel*[2], *Samuel*[1]), b. Aug. 6, 1786, in Kingston, Mass.; d. there Aug. 29, 1872; m. 1812, Lydia Johnson, who d. Sept. 29, 1880, aged 91 y. 8 m.

Children, recorded at Kingston :

36.   I. Lydia[8], b. Oct. 1, 1812 ; m. Oct. 23, 1831, Leavitt
           T. Robbins of Plymouth, Mass.
37.   II. Lemuel[8], b. July 22, 1814 ; d. at sea July 8, 1837.
38.   III. Deborah C.[8], b. March 12, 1816 ; m. Int. Pub.
           April 23, 1827, with Elbridge G. Winsor.
           Children, all born in Kingston, were . Mary
           Helen[9], b. April 19, 1841, d. July 20, 1845 ;
           Eugenia[9], b. March 6, 1847, m. Sept. 25, 1872,
           Francis H. Webb, and Clara[9], b. Aug. 30, 1853,
           d. Sept. 16, 1872.
39.   IV. Content, b. Feb. 12, 1818 ; d. Oct. 18, 1840.

29. GEORGE[7] FULLER, (*Zephaniah[6], Josiah[5], Ebenezer[4], Samuel[3], Samuel[2], Samuel[1]*), b. Aug. 1, 1785 ; d. —— ; m. 1, Sarah Kuhn of Duxbury, Mass., Nov. 29, 1812 ; m. 2, March 26, 1835, Susannah B. Gill.

Children :

40.   I. Sarah Kuhn[8], b. Sept. 14, 1813 ; m. John L.
           Hunnewell.
41.   II. George James[8], b. Nov. 19, 1815 ; d. Dec. 25,
           1841, at St. Croix ; unmarried.
42.   ‡III. John Kuhn[8], b. April 30, 1817 ; m. Harriet West.
           (F. A. Fuller MSS.)

30. EBENEZER[7] FULLER, (*Zephaniah[6], Josiah[5], Ebenezer[4], Samuel[3], Samuel[2], Samuel[1]*), b. Aug., 1788, in Kingston, Mass. ; d. —— ; m. April 11, 1816, Harriet Blanchard. .

Children :

43.   I. Edward E.[8], b. ——, 1821 ; d. ——, 1833.
44.   II. James M.[8], b. June 20, 1824 ; m. Dec. 18, 1851,
           Jane A. Spelman.
45.   III. Caroline W.[8], b. March 31, 1828.
46.   IV. George W.[8], b. May 20, 1831 ; m. Elizabeth
           Pinckney, Sept. 2, 18 ?
47.   V. Martha C.[8], b. June 7, 1833 ; m. William F. Miller,
           June 7, 1854. (F. A. Fuller MSS.)

EIGHTH GENERATION.

34. CHARLES WARREN[8] FULLER, (*Josiah[7], Josiah[6], Josiah[5], Ebenezer[4], Samuel[3], Samuel[2], Samuel[1]*), b. April 29, 1810, at Kingston, Mass.; d. Jan. 27, 1840, at Mt. Clemens, Mich.; m. Oct. 16, 1831, Maria Bisbee.

Children:

48.   I.   Lucy Bradford[9], b. Feb. 17, 1832.
49.   II. Abby Standish[9], b. Jan. 28, 1834.
50.   III. Elizabeth Howe[9], b. June 9, 1838, at Mt. Clemens, Mich.

42. JOHN KUHN[8] FULLER, (*George*[7], *Zephaniah*[6], *Josiah*[5], *Ebenezer*[4], *Samuel*[3], *Samuel*[2], *Samuel*[1]), b. April 30, 1817; m. Nov. 16, 1840, Hannah West.

Children:

51.   I.   Harriet L.[9], b. May 17, 1842; d. 1844.
52.   II. John F.[9], b. Jan. 9, 1844, d. 1850.
53.   III. Mary E.[9], b. Oct. 16, 1845; d. 1850.
54.   IV. Anna W.[9], b. Nov. 30, 1848; m. Edward Lawrence.
55.   V. John E.[9], b. Feb. 25, 1851; d. 1871.
56. ‡VI. Henry A.[9], b. Sept. 22, 1853; m. Jessie Clark.
              (F. A. Fuller MSS.)

NINTH GENERATION.

56. HENRY A.[9] FULLER, (*John K.*[8], *George*[7], *Zephaniah*[6], *Josiah*[5], *Zephaniah*[4], *Samuel*[3], *Samuel*[2], *Samuel*[1]), b. Sept. 22, 1853; m. Jessie Clark.

Children:

57.   I. John Henry[10], b. ———.
58.   II. Lawrence[10], b. ———. (F. A. Fuller MSS.)

FOURTH GROUP.

FOURTH GENERATION.

BENJAMIN⁴ FULLER, AND SOME OF HIS DESCENDANTS.

17. BENJAMIN⁴ FULLER, (*Samuel³, Samuel², Samuel¹*), b. March 7, 1696 (Plymouth Records), d. ———, m. Mary Jackson? (Eddy, dau. of Obidiah Eddy?)   (H. W. Brainard's MSS)
Children, recorded at Plympton :

1.	I.	Jeptha⁵, b July 26, 1720.
2.	II.	Hazadiah⁵, b. March 3, 1721/2; "m. May 22, 1740, James Sturtevant." (H. W. B. MSS.)
3.	‡III.	Samuel⁵, b. May 14, 1724.

3. SAMUEL⁵ FULLER. (*Benjamin⁴, Samuel³, Samuel², Samuel¹*), b. May 14, 1724, at Plympton, Mass. , d. ———, m. Oct. 27, 1747, Anna Tinkham of Kingston, Mass.   (Plympton Records.)
Children, recorded in Plympton :

4.	I.	Mary⁶, b Nov. 23, 1748.
5.	II.	Rube⁶, b. Jan. 20, 1751.
6.	III.	Benjamin⁶, b. Dec. 20, 1752.
7.	IV.	Sylvannus⁶, b. March 16, 1755.
8.	V.	Anna⁶, b. May 14, 1757.

(I have found nothing more in regard to this group.)

FIFTH GROUP.

FOURTH GENERATION.

JOHN⁴ FULLER, (*Samuel³*) AND SOME OF HIS DESCENDANTS.

19. JOHN⁴ FULLER, (*Samuel³, Samuel², Samuel¹*), b. Dec. 19, 1698, at Plympton, Mass.; "d. Sept. 25, 1778 in 80th year" (Gravestone at Kingston, Mass.), m. 1, Feb. 7, 1722/3, Deborah Ring, b. 1699, d. Nov. 8, 1763 (Gravestone, Kingston); m. 2, May 2, 1764, Mrs. Mercy Cushman, who d. May 3, 1796, ae. 94 y. (Gravestone record at Kingston.)

John Fuller was a physician, and a deacon in the Kingston church.

Children, recorded at Kingston:

1.	I.	Eleazer⁵, b. Nov. 3, 1723; d. Aug. 20, 1736.
2.	‡II.	Issachar⁵, b. July 8, 1725, m. 1, Elizabeth Doten; m. 2, Lucy Tinkham.
3.	III.	John⁵, b. Sept. 16, 1727; d. July 30, 1742.
4.	IV.	Deborah⁵, b. Dec. 14, 1729; d. March 4, 1826; m Nov. 2, 1749, Kimball Prince and had: Christopher⁶, b. July 11, 1751, Kimball⁶, b. July 20, 1753; Sarah⁶, b. Jan. 15, 1756, Ruth⁶, b. May 7, 1758; Deborah⁶, b. July 13, 1760; Noah⁶, b. Jan. 18, 1763, Job⁶, b. March 22, 1765, John⁶, b. Feb. 23, 1768, and Hezekiah⁶, b. Feb. 7, 1771.
5.	V.	Susannah⁵, b. Nov. 18, 1731; m. April 5, 1753, Jacob Dingley.
6.	VI.	Noah⁵, b. May 31, 1734; d. Aug. 6, 1736.
7.	‡VII.	Ezra⁵, b. April 23, 1736; m. Elizabeth Weston.
8.	‡VIII.	Consider⁵, b. July 7, 1738; m. Lydia Bryant.

9.   ‡IX.   Eleazer[5], b. April 27, 1740; m. Elizabeth Holmes.
10.   X.   Hannah[5], b. April 30, 1743; m. Benjamin Bisbee.

FIFTH GENERATION.

2.   ISSACHAR[5] FULLER, (*John*[4], *Samuel*[3], *Samuel*[2], *Samuel*[1]), -
b. July 8, 1725, in Kingston, Mass ; d. Oct. 31, 1822, in Carver,
Mass.; m. 1, Jan. 19, 1747 (Plympton Records), Elizabeth Doten;
m. 2, Dec. 26, 1785, Lucy Tinkham, who d. April 30, 1847, aged 95.
  Children, recorded at Kingston

11.   I.   Lydia[6], b. May 1, 1749; m. Nov. 16, 1769, John
                Lucas.
12.   ‡II.   Isaac[6], b Feb 8, 1751 ; m. Lydia Ellis.
13.   ‡III.   John[6], b. March 18, 1753; m. Betty Smith.
14.   IV.   Deborah[6], b. Feb 18, 1756; m. Consider Clark of
                Plymouth, Mass.   (Hayford Genealogy)
15.   ‡V.   Noah[6], b. March 26, 1758; m. Sarah Smith.
16.   VI.   Sylvia[6], b. April 13, 1760; m. Nov. 4, 1779,
                Sylvannus Stephens.
17.   ‡VII.   Issachar[6], b March 22, 1762 ; m. Rebecca Tillson.
18.   VIII.   Elizabeth[6], b. Feb. 10, 1764 ; m. Nathaniel Harlow
                of Plympton
  Children, recorded in Carver, Mass. :

19.   ‡IX.   Edward[6], b. Aug. 25, 1768 , m. Hannah West.
20.   X.   Rebecca[6], b. June 27, 1772 ; d. Dec. 27, 1843 ; m.
                Feb. 27, 1791 (Carver Record), Timothy Cobb
                and removed to Maine. They had two sons,
                Stephen[7] and Ezra[7], and several daughters.
                Stephen[7] was b. May 26, 1794, in Sumner, Me.;
                he married and his son, Lewis A.[8] Cobb of
                Auburn, Me., married March 15, 1859, Hannah
                Celestia[8] Fuller, (*Asa*[7], *Isaac*[6], *Barnabas*[5],
                Nathaniel[4], *Samuel*[3], *Samuel*[2], *Samuel*[1]), thus
                uniting the first and fifth groups. Their only
                child, Frederic Augustus[9] Cobb, b. April 4, 1860,
                in Sumner, Me., d. April 5, 1910, in Haverhill,
                Mass.

21.   XI.   Abigail[6], b. July 18, 1774; d. Sept. 11, 1824, at
                Canton, Me.; m. Aug. 13, 1797, Gustavus
                Hayford, b. Jan. 7, 1773, at Pembroke, Mass.
                Their children were : Sophronia[7], b. June 4, 1801 ;
                Abigail[7], b. Sept. 25, 1803 ; Alvira[7], b. Nov. 27,
                1805 ; Gustavus[7], b. July 2, 1808; Alvarado[7], b.
                Nov. 25, 1811; Elizabeth D.[7], b. June 8, 1815,
                and Stillman[7], b. Sept. 29, 1818.

22.   XII.   Lucy[6], b. Nov. 4, 1786, m. 1, Dec. 14, 1806,
            Nathaniel Shaw of Carver, Mass.; m. 2,
            Ebenezer Cobb of Carver.
23.   XIII. Deborah[6], b. March 3, 1788; m. Sept. 8, 1808,
            Ezra Shaw (Carver Records) of Rochester, Mass.
24.   ‡XIV. Ebenezer[6], b. Oct. 26, 1789; m. Mary Atwood.
25.   XV.   Hannah[6], b Sept. 5, 1792; m. Luther Shurtleff.
26.   XVI. Priscilla[6], b. Feb. 16, 1794; m. George Barrows
            and removed to Vermont.

7.   Ezra[5] Fuller, (*John[4], Samuel[3], Samuel[2], Samuel[1]*), b.
April 23, 1736, at Kingston, Mass.; d. May 24, 1771 (Gravestone at
Kingston); m. Elizabeth Weston.
   Children, recorded at Kingston:
27.   I.   Samuel[6], b. Nov. 14, 1759.
28.   II.   Susannah[6], b. May 30, 1761; d. March 30, 1862,
            in Duxbury, Mass, aged 100 ys. 10 mos.; m.
            1779, Thomas Hunt of Duxbury.
29.   III. Molly[6], b. May 31, 1763.
30.   ‡IV   Consider[6], b. Sept. 19, 1765, m. 1, Sarah Tilden;
            m. 2, Hannah Eaton.
31.   ‡V.   James[6], b. Feb. 2, 1768; m. Mary Perkins.

8.   Consider[5] Fuller, (*John[4], Samuel[3], Samuel[2], Samuel[1]*), b.
July 7, 1738, in Kingston, Mass.; d. ——— ; m. Feb. 25, 1759,
Lydia Bryant of Plympton, Mass.
   Children, recorded in Halifax, Mass.:
32.   I.   Luna[6], b. Feb. 17, 1760.
33.   II.   Eliphalet[6], b. Oct. 23, 1761. An Eliphalet Fuller,
            aged 16 years, enlisted at Kingston in 1777.
   H. W. Brainard's MSS. gives also ·
34.   ‡III. Consider[6], b. May 31, 1780, m. Elizabeth
            Cummings.

9.   Eleazer[5] Fuller, (*John[4], Samuel[3], Samuel[2], Samuel[1]*),
b. April 27, 1704, in Kingston, Mass., date and place of death not
found, m. Jan. 6, 1763, Margaret Holmes.
   Children on Kingston Records
35.   I.   Abigail[6], b. March 29, 1764.
36.   II.   Daniel[6], b. Aug. 29, 1765.
37.   III. Jenny[6], b. Aug. 18, 1769.
38.   IV.   Sally[6], b. July 9, 1771, m. Barnabas, b. Nov. 20,
            1769, "son of Noah Thompson" (H. W.
            Brainard), m. Nov. 27, 1792 (Halifax Records).

SIXTH GENERATION.

12. ISAAC[6] FULLER, (*Issachar[5], John[4], Samuel[3], Samuel[2], Samuel[1]*), b. Feb. 8, 1751, in Kingston, Mass., d. April 27, 1833, in Livermore, Me.; m. Nov. 20, 1777, Lydia Ellis (Middleboro, Mass., Records), who d. May 28, 1836, aged 83 years.

As a soldier in the war of the Revolution Isaac Fuller enlisted April 30, 1777, serving eight months in Capt. John Bridgham's Co.; again enlisted as Sergeant in Capt. Samuel Bradford's Co. for one year. He was at the battle of Bunker Hill. Some years after the war he removed to Hebron, Me.; thence to Hartford, Me., and finally to Livermore.

His first four children were born at Plympton, Mass., and are named and recorded as follows "Children of Isaac Fuller by Lydia, his wife. Her maiden name was Lydia Ellis, daughter of John Ellis":

39.   I.   "Sarah, b. Nov. 7, 1778"; d. Feb., 1859, at Livermore, Me ; unmarried.

40.   ‡II.   "Isaac, b Jan. 14, 1781"; m. Sally Ames.

41.   III.   "Lydia, b. Jan. 19, 1783"; d. March 22, 1856, at Fort Fairfield, Me., m. in 1800, Freeman Ellis of Hartford, Me, who d. Jan. 13, 1866, at Ft. Fairfield, aged 86 y 2 m. 13 d. Their children were: Phebe[8], b. Feb. 6, 1801; Freeman[8], b. July 24, 1802, Lydia[8], b. June 1, 1804; Isaac Fuller[8], b. Oct. 5, 1806, Benjamin[8], b Aug 3, 1808; Gideon Bradford[8], b. July 22, 1811; Mercy Hayford[8], b. Feb. 14, 1813; Alyndia Fuller[8], b. July 21, 1815; Frederick[8], b. April 12, 1817, Sarah[8], b. June 24, 1819; Joanna[8], b. Sept. 17, 1821; Caleb Holt[8], b. April 26, 1824, and Christina Hayford[8], b. April 30, 1826.

42.   ‡IV.   "Samuel, b. Dec. 3, 1784"; m. Lydia Leavitt.

43.   V.   Deborah[7], b. 1787; d. March 30, 1851, at Hartford, Me.; m. in 1807, Lemuel Stevens of Hartford, who d. July 16, 1844, aged 62 years. Their children were: Ellura[8], b. May 21, 1808; Issachar[8], b. Oct. 8, 1810; Melintha[8], b. July 15, 1812; Phylinda[8], b. Aug. 18, 1814; Deborah[8], b. Sept. 14, 1817, Phebe[8], b. Nov. 28, 1820, and Edward[8], b. July, 1822.

44.   ‡VI.   Ezra[7], b. Sept., 1789; m. Sally Soule.

45.   VII.   Ada[7], b. Sept. 30, 1792; d. Feb. 10, 1864, at

Livermore, Me.; m. Joseph Tobin of Hartford,
Me., b. March 10, 1790, d. Oct. 21, 1868.
Children · Matthew[8], b. June 15, 1814, Joseph[8],
b. March 19, 1816, Ezra F.[8], b. Feb. 15, 1818;
Jane Angeline[8], b. Feb 21, 1820; Albion K.[8], b.
April 29, 1822; Ada F.[8], b. Feb. 15, 1824;
John[8], b. March 13, 1826, Lydia[8], b. Dec. 29,
1827, Albina M.[8], b. Feb. 15, 1830; Marcellus[8],
b. March 29, 1832, and Augustus[8], b. Nov. 25,
1835

46.   VIII.   Linda[7], b. Nov. 2, 1795; d. Oct. 17, 1862, at
Livermore, Me.; m. in 1817, Hezekiah Griffith
of Livermore, Me., who d. July 23, 1878, aged
86 y. 4 m. 10 d. They had Jane[8], b. July 5,
1818, Rufus Newman[8], b. Sept. 18, 1820;
Sabra Ann[8], b. Oct. 26, 1822; Lyndia Maria[8],
b. July 24, 1826, Charles Roscoe[8], b. March 9,
1829, Lorinda Adelia[8], b. July 6, 1831;
Stephen[8], b. Nov. 19, 1833, and Flora[8], b. April
21, 1835.

13. JOHN[6] FULLER, (*Issachar[5]*, *John[4]*, *Samuel[3]*, *Samuel[2]*,
Samuel[1]), b. March 18, 1753, in Kingston, Mass., d. April 15,
1809, at Middleboro, Mass.; m. July 29, 1779, at Plympton, Mass.,
Betty Smith, who d. Sept. 3, 1832, aged 75 years.

Children, recorded at Middleboro:

47.	I.	Elizabeth[7], b. Sept 28, 1781.
48.	II.	Sophia[7], b. Jan. 27, 1784; m. 1818, John Warren.
49.	III.	Betsey[7], b. Nov. 28, 1786; d. Feb. 16, 1814.
50.	‡IV.	John Smith[7], b. Nov. 19, 1789.
51.	V.	Sylvia[7], b. July 10, 1792; d. April 18, 1866.
52.	‡VI.	Consider[7], b. Feb. 20, 1795; m. 1, Mercy Thomas; m. 2, Mary H. Southworth.
53.	VII.	Allen[7], b. April 23, 1798, d. about 1862; m. a Southern lady; no issue; was a clergyman and author.
54.	VIII.	Lauretta Ann[7], b. July 29, 1809; m. Oct. 1, 1829, Alanson Darling.*

15. NOAH[6] FULLER, (*Issachar[5]*, *John[4]*, *Samuel[3]*, *Samuel[2]*,
Samuel[1]), b. March 26, 1758, in Kingston, Mass.; d. Nov. 9, 1843,
in Lempster, N. H.; m. May 31, 1787, Sarah Smith, who d. April
28, 1813.

---

* C. M. Thatcher.

They lived in Middleboro, Mass., until 1802, and then removed to Lempster, Mrs. Fuller riding on horseback most of the way. Noah Fuller was a Revolutionary soldier; after marriage a farmer until later a severe illness left him a cripple, able to walk only with his hands resting on his knees, but he arranged wheels and an axle on which he could hang a basket and rest his hands, and so get about his place doing some light work.

Children, the first five b. in Middleboro, the others in Lempster:

55.   I.   Bethia[7], b. May 19, 1788; d. June 29, 1826; unmarried.

56.   II.   Susanna[7], b. July 13, 1791, d. April 7, 1866; unmarried.

57.   III. Sarah[7], b. Dec. 20, 1793; d. Aug. 3, 1835; unmarried.

58.   IV.   Sabina[7], b Feb. 5, 1798; d. July 11, 1876; m. Dec. 28, 1817, George Way and had Sarah[8], b. Nov., 1818, Caroline[8], Herman[8], Henry S.[8], Gilbert[8], and Celia M.[8], b. Sept. 4, 1838, all born in Lempster, N. H.

59.   V.   Rebecca[7], b. April 17, 1800; d. May 11, 1881; unmarried.

60.   VI.   Asenath[7], b Dec. 14, 1802; d. Nov. 27, 1812.

61.   ‡VII.   Sylvannus[7], b. Aug. 23, 1806; m. Sarah M. Taylor.

62.   VIII. Sylvia[7], b. Nov. 22, 1809; d. Dec. 5, 1840; m. Freeman Clark and had a daughter, Sylvia F.[8] Clark, b. Nov. 26, 1840, in Hubbardston, Mass., m. March 1, 1867, John W. Knox of Southfield, Mass., and had Harry A.[9] Knox, b. Jan. 19, 1875, at Westfield, Mass, who m. June 4, 1904, Mildred Janet[11] Fuller (*Merrick L.*[10], *Lathrop L.*[9], *Lyman*[8], *Ezekiel*[7], *Joshua*[6], *Young*[5], *Matthew*[4], *Samuel*[3], *Samuel*[2], *Edward*[1]), thus uniting the Edward and Dr. Samuel Fuller lines. They reside in Springfield, Mass.

63.   ‡IX.   Benoni[7], b. April 23, 1813; m. Dorothy Wadsworth.

17. ISSACHAR[6] FULLER, (*Issachar*[5], *John*[4], *Samuel*[3], *Samuel*[2], *Samuel*[1]), b. March 22, 1762, at Kingston, Mass. He is said to have been lost at sea in a ship that sailed from Boston in 1794 and was never heard from. He m. Dec. 11, 1788, Rebecca Tillson of Carver, Mass.

Their children were:

64.   ‡I.   Tillson[7], b. Sept. 5, 1789; m. Edith Eloisa Craven.

65. II. Phebe[7], b. ———— , d. before 1842 ; m. ————
Thomas, probably Josiah C Thomas, Int. Pub.
Nov. 3, 1812 , m. Nov. 22, 1812, in Pembroke,
Mass., and had sons, Josiah[8] and Isaac[8].

66 ‡III. Issachar[7], b. Aug. 19, 1794 , m. Matilda C. Nichols.

19. EDWARD[6] FULLER, (*Issachar[5], John[4], Samuel[3], Samuel[2],
Samuel[1]*), b. Aug. 25, 1768, in Carver, Mass.; d. April 17, 1854, in
Montrose, Pa.; m. Dec. 24, 1795, Hannah West, b. in Bozrah, Ct,
the sixth child of Capt. Elias and Mary (Lathrop) West.

Capt. Elias West was son of Nathan West of Bozrah, and served
as Lieutenant in the Revolutionary war   Mary Lathrop was from
Norwich, Ct. Elias West, brother of Hannah, m. Mary Armstrong
and lived in Montrose. Hannah (West) Fuller d. Dec. 14, 1861, in
Scranton, Pa., and was buried at Montrose, Dec. 17, 1861. Edward
Fuller came to Montrose in 1806 and settled on a farm near the
village , appointed Sheriff in 1812, he removed to the village.

Their children were :

67. ‡I. Charles[7], b March 1, 1797 , m. Maria Scovill.
68. II. Mary[7], b. Feb. 20, 1799 ; d. Aug 28, 1820.
69. III. Edward W.[7], b Oct. 10, 1800, in Norwich, Ct.; d.
Feb. 22, 1891 (probably in Cohoes, N. Y.) ;
unmarried.
70. ‡IV. George[7], b. Nov. 7, 1802 ; m. Mary Barnard.
71. V. Elizabeth Harlow[7], b. Jan. 1, 1805 ; d. June 13,
1871 ; m. Nov. 24, 1829, Ebenezer Kingsbury,
b. June 18, 1804, d. April 15, 1844. Their
children were   Henry Augustus[8], b. Dec. 10,
1830 ; Edward Payson[8], b. April 12, 1832, d.
July 31, 1833, Edward Payson[8], b. Aug. 19,
1834, Mary Elizabeth[8], b. June 6, 1836, d. May
3, 1884 ; Emeline Chapman[8], b. July 1, 1838, d.
Jan. 19, 1860, and Caroline Neal[8], b. May 19,
1843, who m. Jan. 24, 1865, Frederick L.
Hitchcock, and their dau , Elizabeth Fuller[9]
Hitchcock, b. May 19, 1873, m. Sept. 15, 1903,
George B. Dimmick and has Caroline Eleanor[10]
Dimmick, b. Aug. 28, 1904, and George B.[10]
Dimmick, b. March 1, 1906. They reside in
Scranton. (See also the Kingsbury Family
Genealogy.)
72. ‡VI. Henry D.[7], b. March 29, 1807 ; m. Catherine
Byce.

73.   ‡VII. Francis⁷, b. May 14, 1809 ; m. Polly Ann Vaughn.
74.   ‡VIII. Isaac⁷, b. Feb. 2, 1812 ; m. Abigail A Sutton.
75.   IX.   Deborah West⁷, b. Feb 13, 1814; d. June 20,
             1880; m. June 6, 1830, Dr. John Newman
             Sumner, b Dec 17, 1807, d. Oct. 26, 1850.
             Their children were · Mary⁸, b. Nov. 2, 1833, d.
             young, Elizabeth⁸, b. Nov. 2, 1833, d. about
             1854, John Newman⁸, b. May, 1835, d. Jan. 10,
             1851, and Alfred Wright⁸, b. Feb. 4, 1839.

24. EBENEZER⁶ FULLER, (*Issachar* ⁵, *John* ⁴, *Samuel*³, *Samuel*²,
*Samuel*¹), b. Oct 26, 1789, in Carver, Mass., d. Sept. 9, 1865, in
Carver; m. July 12, 1810, Mary Atwood, who d. Feb. 23, 1870. He
lived and died at the old homestead

Their children, all born in Carver, were :
76.   I.   Mary Atwood⁷, b. Oct. 10, 1811 ; m. Dec. 2, 1832,
             Levi Cobb and had : Levi⁸, Joseph⁸, Lysander⁸,
             Ezra⁸, Mary⁸, Irena⁸, and Hannah⁸.
77.   ‡II.   Ebenezer⁷, b. April 5, 1813, m. Jane H. Packard.
78.   ‡III. Ezra⁷, b. Sept. 13, 1814, m. Elizabeth A. Buffington.
79.   ‡IV.   Joseph⁷, b. Feb. 16, 1817, m. Matilda Luce.
80.   ‡V.   Stillman⁷, b. July 9, 1820; m. ——.
81.   VI.   John⁷, b July 26, 1822.
82.   VII.   Sarah⁷, b. Feb. 9, 1826, residing in Watertown
             1878 ; unmarried.

30. CONSIDER⁶ FULLER, (*Ezra* ⁵, *John* ⁴, *Samuel*³, *Samuel*²,
*Samuel*¹), b. Sept. 19, 1765, at Kingston, Mass.; d April 20, 1829,
in Kingston; m. 1, April 9, 1789, Sarah Tilden of Pembroke, who
d. Sept. 19, 1805, m. 2, July 13, 1806, Hannah Eaton of Plympton,
who d. Aug. 1, 1830.
Children :
83.   ‡I.   Ezra⁷, b. Jan. 19, 1791 ; m. Eliza Cobb.
84.   II.   Elizabeth⁷, b. Nov. 30, 1792, d. Dec. 4, 1836, m.
             Nov. 25, 1814, Linus Drake. Lived at Easton,
             Mass.
85.   III.   Joanna Tilden⁷, b. Dec. 26, 1794, d. April, 1861;
             m. 1815, Ichabod Bassett of Taunton, Mass.
86.   IV.   Sarah⁷, b. Feb. 23, 1799, m. Nov. 20, 1823, Elijah
             Bird of Stoughton, Mass.
87.   ‡V.   John⁷, b. Jan. 12, 1801, m. 1, Nov., 1820, Caroline
             Bisbee ; m. 2, 1858, Elizabeth Bartlett.
88.   VI.   Caleb Tilden⁷, b. Oct. 26, 1802 ; d. Oct. 24, 1806.
89.   VII.   Nathan Thompson⁷, b. June 12, 1807 ; m. Nov. 30,
             1828, Cornelia A. Cook, no children.

90. ‡VIII. Smith[7], b. Sept. 5, 1809, m. Eliza Churchill.
91. IX. Daniel W[7], b. Jan. 5, 1812; d June 7, 1894.
92. ‡X. Samuel[7], b. June 29, 1814, m. Maria Churchill.
93. XI. Hannah[7], b. May 29, 1819; m. Aug. 29, 1841, Hiram Field of Taunton, Mass.
94 ‡XII. Waldo Ames[7], b. Feb. 20, 1821; m. Sarah A. Stetson.

31. JAMES[6] FULLER, (*Ezra[5], John[4], Samuel[3], Samuel[2], Samuel[1]*), b. Feb. 2, 1769, in Kingston, Mass.; d. Dec. 29, 1830, in Salem, Mass.; m Dec. 15, 1796, Mary Perkins.

Their children were:

95. I. Ezra[7], b. May 20, 1798, d. Nov. 17, 1824; unmarried.
96 ‡II. James[7], b. May 14, 1802; m. Elizabeth Norton.
97. III. Mary[7], b. April 17, 1804; m. Theodore Bartlett of W. Newbury, Mass
98. IV. Lucy Sturtevant[7], b. March 18, 1810; d. Aug. 17, 1830.
99. ‡V. Edward[7], b. Nov 24, 1813, m. Eliza A. Little. (F. A. Fuller's MSS.)

34. CONSIDER[6] FULLER, (*Consider[5], John[4], Samuel[3], Samuel[2], Samuel[1]*), b. May 31, 1780?, d. ——, m. about 1825? Elizabeth Cummings.

The History of Woodstock, Me, states Consider Fuller moved into Woodstock in 1801, enlisted as a private in 1814, and mentions children of Consider as follows

100. I. Christiana[7], b. ——; m. Charles B. Brooks.
101. II. Chloe[7], b. ——, m Rufus Farrar, b. Dec. 18, 1808.

SEVENTH GENERATION.

40. ISAAC[7] FULLER, (*Isaac[6], Issachar[5], John[4], Samuel[3], Samuel[2], Samuel[1]*), b. Jan. 13, 1781, d. Sept 13, 1856, in Hartford, Me., m. 1805, Sally Ames of Groton, Mass., b. April 6, 1785, d. Nov. 15, 1851, in Hartford, Me.

They came to Livermore, Me., where their first child was born; later they removed to Hartford, settling on the intervale at the head of Bear Pond, where they died. Capt. Fuller served in the war of 1812–1815. He was a man of sterling character and much respected.

Their children were :

102.   I.   Adeline B.8, b. Feb. 24, 1806, in Livermore, Me., d.
                 Aug. 16, 1888, m. June 30, 1832, Ezekiel Fogg,
                 b. Feb. 21, 1807, d Sept 13, 1888   They lived
                 in Woodstock, Me, for many years. Their
                 children were · Emily A.9, b Dec. 25, 1832;
                 Ezekiel F.9, b. Feb 7, 1834, Adeline C.9, b. Feb.
                 7, 1834; Adeliza M.9, b. Sept. 29, 1835,
                 Elbridge9, b April 26, 1839; Ephraim9, b. Sept.
                 5, 1840; Elliott L.9, b. Jan. 13, 1842, killed at
                 Gettysburg, July 3, 1863, Amanda M.9, b. June
                 5, 1844, Isaac F.9, b. Oct. 28, 1845, and Elzira
                 M.9, b. April, 1848.
103.   ‡II.   Edward8, b. June 13, 1807, m. Celia B. Stevens.
104.   ‡III.   Ezekiel8, b April 22, 1809, m. 1, Asenath Ames;
                 m 2, Maria Farrar.
105.   IV. Ephraim8, b Jan. 24, 1811; d. Oct. 3, 1838.
106.   ‡V.   Eland8, b. Dec. 25, 1812; m Elzira Hood
107.   ‡VI.   Elbridge G.8, b. Jan. 29, 1815, m. Sarah J.
                 Mitchell.
108.   ‡VII.   Essec8, b. April 26, 1817; m. Maria Vose.
109.   ‡VIII.   Elonzo8, b. March 25, 1819, m. Aurelia Foye.
110.   IX.   Adeliza8, b. July 15, 1821, d. Aug. 9, 1907; m.
                 Elisha Reynolds, b. Dec. 2, 1816, d. Feb. 21,
                 1903. They lived in Hartford, Me., a few years,
                 then removed to N Bridgewater, Mass. (now
                 Brockton), and later to Fort Fairfield, Me.
                 Children: Everett E.9, b. Aug. 3, 1847; Ellen
                 M.9, b June 17, 1849, Herbert R.9, b. Nov. 10,
                 1850; Frank A.9, b. Jan 15, 1855, and Mary V.9,
                 b. Sept., 1856
111.   X.   Arethusa8, b Sept. 24, 1824; d. Jan. 27, 1827.
112.   ‡XI.   Emery L.8, b. Feb. 14, 1826; m. Eunice Records.
113.   XII. Edwin E.8, b. Sept 8, 1827, d. March 4, 1890, in
                 Turner, Me.; m. April 12, 1859, Lydia J.
                 Records, b. May 12, 1831. He was in California
                 several years in the "early fifties", then lived
                 a while in Massachusetts, then removed to Peru,
                 Me., and thence to Turner. He served as a
                 soldier in the Civil war in the 23d Maine Regt.
                 They had no children.

After Ephraim died it was nearly 50 years before there was a
death among the ten remaining children in this family.

42. SAMUEL7 FULLER, (*Isaac*6, *Issachar*5, *John*4, *Samuel*3,
*Samuel*4, *Samuel*1), b. Dec. 3, 1784, at Plymouth, Mass.; d. Sept.

Edward Hersey Fuller.

Everett L. Philoon.

16, 1855, at Livermore, Me.; m. Int entered June 3, 1809, with Lydia Leavitt, b. Sept. 5, 1784, at Rochester, Mass., d. June 1, 1885, at Livermore, aged 100 y. 8 m. 27 d.

Their children were .

114.   I. Lydia^S, b. April 23, 1810; d. Dec. 31, 1857; unmarried.
115.   II. Lois L.^{S}, b. Jan. 25, 1812; d. Nov., 1907; m. Lorin Bryant, who d. April, 1883; no issue.
116. ‡III. Samuel^S, b. April 26, 1814, m. Louise Carver.
117.   IV. Nancy D^S, b. Sept 7, 1816, at Livermore, Me.; d. June 18, 1894, at Auburn, Me.; m. March 8, 1840, James Philoon, b. July 15, 1809, in Abington, Mass, d. March 22, 1886, at Auburn, Me She had three children (1) Dr. Charles E. of Auburn, Me., who m. and had George M^{10}, b. Feb. 3, 1874, Byron S.^{10}, b. March 28, 1876, and Loverna E.^{10}, b. 1878, d. 1880; (2) Loverna E.9, b. ———, d. ———; (3) Everett L.9 of Auburn, b. Oct. 30, 1848, in Livermore, m Oct 5, 1875, Mary A. Lara, children: Daniel L.^{10}, b. Aug. 28, 1877, in Livermore, James T.^{10}, b April 23, 1879, d. Feb. 15, 1880, Wallace C.^{10}, b. Oct. 13, 1883, West Point graduate 1909, James E.^{10}, b. May 1, 1887.
118.   V. Elizabeth^S, b. Nov. 1, 1818; d. Sept. 25, 1863; unmarried.
119.   VI. John^S, b. March 12, 1820, d. Nov. 23, 1882; m. Nov. 4, 1849, Ruth Upham; no issue.
120. ‡VII. Philander B.^{S}, b. Aug. 31, 1823; m. Lucinda Beals.
121.   VIII. Lysander^S, b. July 2, 1827; d. Dec. 16, 1860; m. Mary G. Humphrey; no issue.

44. Ezra7 Fuller, (*Isaac^6, Issachar^5, John^4, Samuel^3, Samuel^2, Samuel^1*), b. Sept., 1789; d. March 3, 1864, in Hartford, Me.; m. Sally Soule.

They resided in Hartford.

Their children were ·

122.   I. Elvira^S, b. Oct. 6, 1822, d. Sept. 1, 1885; m. Nov. 5, 1851, Horace Ames and had: Fisher9, b. Feb. 25, 1855, George C9, b. Nov. 17, 1857; Elizabeth B.9, b. Sept. 6, 1859. Elvira lived and died in Bridgewater, Mass.
123.   II. Abigail^S, b. Nov. 2, 1824, d Aug. 26, 1901, in Chicago, Ill.; m. 1846, John D. Sawin and had: Ella Arline9, b. July 8, 1848; Prescott Dana9,

		b. Oct. 7, 1853; Ella Arline 9, m. July 8, 1867, Charles A. Loomis of Chicago and has five children. (See Loomis Family Genealogy.)
124.	III.	Amanda 8, b. 1826; d. Dec. 21, 1907; m. John C. Dearborn, who d Feb. 5, 1908. They had Mabel F.9, b. June 5, 1858, d. Oct. 25, 1881.
125.	IV	Oscar 8, b 1827, d. 1901 ; unmarried.
126.	V.	Marcellus 8, b. 1833, d. 1854, in Cambridge, Mass.; unmarried.
127.	‡VI.	George Henry 8, b. March 26, 1839; m. Harriet Parsons.

50. JOHN SMITH 7 FULLER, (*John*6, *Issachar*5, *John*4, *Samuel*3, *Samuel*2, *Samuel*1), b Nov. 19, 1789, at Middleboro, Mass.; d. July 3, 1865, in Dover, N. H.; m. Oct. 9, 1821, Ann Guppy Hanson, b. Dec. 18, 1792, in Wells, Me., d. Feb. 18, 1871, in Dover, N. H. He was a soldier in the war of 1812.

Children, the first three b. in Boston, the others in Barrington, N. H..

128.	‡I.	John H.8, b. Sept. 19, 1822; m. ———.
129.	‡II	Edward Newton 8, b Dec. 6, 1824, m Augusta Elizabeth Morrison.
130.	‡III.	Frank 8, b. Sept. 25, 1827; m. Annie W. Thompson.
131.	IV.	Elizabeth W 8, b. Aug. 22, 1834; d. March 18, 1871 ; unmarried.
132.	V.	George W.8, b. Oct 28, 1838; d. June 12, 1864; unmarried.

52. CONSIDER 7 FULLER, (*John*6, *Issachar*5, *John*4, *Samuel*3, *Samuel*2, *Samuel*1), b. Feb. 20, 1795, in Middleboro, Mass., d. there Feb. 16, 1875, m. 1, March 25, 1818, in Halifax, Mass., Mercy Thompson, m 2, March 16, 1869, Mary H. Southworth

Children :

133.	I.	Betsey 8, b. June 29, 1818.
134.	II.	Sarah Smith 8, b. March 7, 1821 ; d. Dec. 20, 1898 ; m. Dec. 18, 1842, Nathan 8 Fuller Jr. (*Nathan* 7, *Chipman*6, *Ebenezer*5, *Ebenezer*4, *John*3, *Samuel*2, *Samuel*1), of Halifax and had: Emily French 9, b. Dec. 21, 1843, a dau., b. March 8, 1846, and Edmund Herbert 9, b. June 13, 1849.
135.	‡III.	Charles Thompson 8, b. Aug. 30, 1823; m. Mary C. Benson.
136.	IV.	Nancy Caroline 8, b. Jan. 5, 1826; d. Jan. 11, 1903;

m. Int. Pub. May 17, 1846, with Benjamin
Freeman
137.   V.   Mary J.[S], b. June 19, 1828.*
138.   VI.   Maria A.[S], } b. 1832.*
139.   VII.   Mercy A.[S], }
140.   VIII. Olive Francis[S], b. May 5, 1835; d. May 27, 1857.

61. SYLVANUS[7] FULLER, (*Noah[6], Issachar[5], John[4], Samuel[3], Samuel[2], Samuel[1]*), b. Aug. 23, 1806, in Lempster, N. H.; d. there Oct. 29, 1891; m. March 17, 1835, Sarah M. Taylor of Lempster, who d. Oct. 11, 1889.

He was a farmer and lived and died at the homestead where his father lived.

Their children, all b. in Lempster, were ·

141.   ‡I.   Homer T.[S], b Nov. 15, 1838; m. Amerette Jones.
142.   ‡II. Horace C.[S], b. Jan. 3, 1841; m. Emily E. Boutelle.
143.   III. Sarah M.[S], b. Dec 7, 1842, living in Leominster, Mass., 1910.
144.   IV. John W.[S], b. May 16, 1848, d. Oct. 2, 1866.
145.   ‡V. Irving H.[S], b. Aug. 2, 1852, m. 1, Celia M. Piedmont; m. 2, Emma L. Packard.

63. BENONI[7] FULLER, (*Noah[6], Issachar[5], John[4], Samuel[3], Samuel[2], Samuel[1]*), b. April 23, 1813, in Lempster, N. H.; d. Jan. 19, 1892, in Peterboro, N. H., m. March 23, 1849, Dorothy Wadsworth of Henniker, N. H., b. Aug. 7, 1813, d. Jan. 20, 1892.

He worked as tanner for many years in Lempster, then removed to Peterboro and engaged in farming about 1870.

Their children were b. in Lempster:

146.   I. Harriet Louisa[S], b. Jan. 12, 1850; d. Sept., 1864.
147.   ‡II. George Herbert[S], b. Aug. 29, 1852; m. Clara L. Kent.

64. TILLSON[7] FULLER, (*Issachar[6], Issachar[5], John[4], Samuel[3], Samuel[2], Samuel[1]*), b. Sept. 5, 1789, in Middleboro, Mass.; d. July 1, 1844, in Brownsville, Pa.; m. Feb. 2, 1812, Edith Eloisa Craven, who d. May 6, 1872, in Brownsville.

Tillson Fuller followed a seafaring life a while; was a member of the Boston Militia in war of 1812; then settled in Mifflin, Pa., and after marriage removed to Millertown, Pa., finally settling in Browns-

---

*Newton Fuller gives these according to Brainard's MSS , the others are from Middleboro Records

ville, where he was a highly respected citizen and a deacon of the First Baptist church.

Their children were:

148.   I.   James Craven[8], b Jan. 20, 1820, in Mifflin; d. Sept 3, 1854, near Uniontown, Pa.
149.   ‡II.   Josiah Tillson[8], b. Nov. 22, 1822; m. Irene Parker.
150.   III.   Thomas Edwin[8], b June 20, 1825; d. March 8, 1826, in Brownsville.
151.   IV.   Phebe Anna[8], b. Feb. 13, 1827; d. July 6, 1848, in Bridgeport, Pa.
152.   V.   Orrin Augustus[8], b. Jan 4, 1830; d March 18, 1838, in Bridgeport, Pa.
153.   VI.   Rebecca Tillson[8], b. Feb. 10, 1833; d. ——, at Madison, Ohio, m. Jan. 4, 1859, Henry W. Patton, who d. Aug. 25, 1864, in Andersonville, Ga., Prison. They had two daughters living in 1910.
154   VII.   Martha Maria[8], b. Oct. 12, 1835; resides (1910) at Brownsville; unmarried.
155   ‡VIII.   Orrin Augustus[8] 2d, b. Aug. 1, 1838; m. Sophia Fuller.
156.   IX.   Sarah Matilda[8], b. June 6, 1841; resides (1910) at Brownsville; unmarried.
                      Also one other child that died on the day of its birth.

66.   ISSACHAR[7] FULLER, (*Issachar[6], Issachar[5], John[4], Samuel[3], Samuel[2], Samuel[1]*), b. Aug. 19, 1794, in Middleboro, Mass.; d. Feb. 11, 1866, at Hingham, Mass.; m. Jan. 27, 1822, Matilda C. Nichols, who d. Sept. 3, 1887, aged 84, at Hingham.

By trade he was a cooper; was for many years postmaster; was also messenger to the General Court, and deacon of the Baptist church at Hingham.

Children.

157.   I.   Thomas Baldwin[8], b. July 24, 1825, at Cohassett, Mass   Dead.
158.   II.   Eliza Nichols[8], b. May 28, 1829, at Cohassett; m. Dec. 5, 1848, James G. Graves of Weymouth, Mass., and had Carrie M.[9] and Abbott F.[?]
159.   ‡III.   Tillson[8], b. Dec. 25, 1831; m. Lydia Stowell Switzer.
159½.   IV.   Joshua Thayer[8], b. May 25, 1833, at Hingham; m. at Melrose, Mass., Aug. 13, 1854, Sarah Pike, who d. Dec. 15, 1908. He d. March 27, 1906,

Isaac Fuller.

Mrs. Abigail (Sutton) Fuller.

1899, in Scranton, Pa.; m. May 16, 1842, Polly Ann Vaughn, b. Aug. 9, 1814, d. Feb. 4, 1897.

Children ·

185.   ‡I.   Albert^S, b. Aug. 13, 1843; m. 1, Anna Mary
              Phelps; m. 2, Clara ———; m. 3, Anne Scott.
186.   II.   Anna Eliza^S, b. June 15, 1849.
187.   III. Ella Gertrude^S, b. April 26, 1857.

74. ISAAC^7 FULLER, (*Edward^6, Issachar^5, John^4, Samuel^3, Samuel^2, Samuel^1*), b. Feb. 2, 1812, in Montrose, Pa.; d. Oct. 14, 1898, in Poughkeepsie, N. Y., and was buried at Seneca Falls, N. Y.; m. Jan. 3, 1833, Abigail A. Sutton, b. Nov. 17, 1814, d. Jan. 24, 1899.

"Isaac Fuller learned the printer's trade, and at 18 was editing "The Independent," at Montrose, Pa., and later "The Wayne County Herald." He removed to Seneca Falls in 1837, and founded the "Seneca County Courier." He was active in political affairs and a leader in the county, was postmaster 1841–1845; county clerk 1853, postmaster again 1861–1869; then proof reader in the government printing office for 24 years until his resignation in 1893.

"Mr. Fuller was a man of peculiarly pure life. He was honest, energetic, upright, courteous and affable. He never used tobacco or liquors in any form. His temperament was extremely buoyant. He always saw the bright side of affairs, and was singularly sensitive to the humorous. His hearty laugh and genial greeting are remembered by all who knew him, yet was he a vigorous fighter, sturdy, resolute and resourceful, as his opponents in the old days were well aware." (Seneca County Courier, Oct. 20, 1898.)

Children born to them were :

188.   I.   Charles Francis^S, b. July 8, 1834; d. July 24, 1834.
189.   II.   George Williston^S, b. Aug. 16, 1835; d. Sept. 4,
              1835.
190.   III. Edward West^S, b. March 2, 1837; d. Sept., 1838.
191.   IV.   Henry Clay^S, b. July 25, 1839; d. June 25, 1907.
192.   V.   James Sutton^S, b. Nov. 9, 1841; d. Jan. 1, 1901.
193.   VI.   Ella Augusta^S, b. Feb. 23, 1844; m. June 19, 1867,
              Archibald Winnie, b. Feb. 1, 1846, and had:
              Clara^9, b. Jan. 6, 1869, d. Aug. 16, 1869; Jennie
              Louise^9, b. Dec. 9, 1872, and John^9, b. Sept. 6,
              1875.

194.   VII.   Clara Catlin[8], b. Aug. 7, 1846, m. July 2, 1868, Alexander Livingston Fryer, b. May 8, 1839, and had · (1) Ella Augusta[9], b. March 23, 1870; (2) Mary Margaretta[9], b. Jan. 13, 1872, in Albany, N. Y., m. June 12, 1895, Lieut. Spencer Shepard Wood, U. S. N., children: Margaretta[10] Wood, b. Aug. 28, 1899, in Flushing, L. I., and Anne Elizabeth[10] Wood, b. Sept. 29, 1906, in Washington, D. C., (3) Alexander Livingston[9] Fryer, b. June 18, 1880; (4) Edith Livingston[9] Fryer, b. July 14, 1883.

195.   ‡VIII. George[8], b. April 24, 1850; m. Mary Jamison.

77. EBENEZER[7] FULLER, (*Ebenezer[6], Issachar[5], John[4], Samuel[3], Samuel[2], Samuel[1]*), b. April 5, 1813, in Carver, Mass.; d. there Feb. 1, 1884, m. 1, Int Pub. May 13. 1838, with Jane H. Packard, who d Jan. 26, 1843, in her 21st year; m. 2, Sept. 14, 1846, Hannah F. Wilbur, b. in Norton, Mass., who d. April 1, 1881.

Children :

196.   I.   Sarah Frances[8], b. Aug 25, 1839; m. Wm. Irvine; resided in Chatsworth, Ill.

197.   II.   Andrew Austin[8], b. Sept. 12, 1842; d. in the Civil war.

198.   III.   Ebenezer Barton[8], b. March 17, 1850, d. April 6, 1885.

78. EZRA[7] FULLER, (*Ebenezer[6], Issachar[5], John[4], Samuel[3], Samuel[2], Samuel[1]*), b. Sept. 13, 1814, in Carver, Mass.; d. there Jan. 25, 1857, m. Elizabeth A. Buffington.

Children :

199   ‡I.   Noel B.[8], b. Oct. 15, 1841; m 1, Mary L. Wilbur; m. 2, Anjenette J. Manchester.

200   II.   Ezra M. B.[8], b. 1847; d. Aug 22, 1847.

201.   III.   Edwin C.[8], b. Dec. 21, 1855, d. Dec. 28, 1855.

79. JOSEPH[7] FULLER, (*Ebenezer[6], Issachar[5], John[4], Samuel[3], Samuel[2], Samuel[1]*), b. Feb. 16, 1817, in Carver, Mass.; d. ——; m. Matilda Luce.

Edward[6] Fuller of Montrose, Pa., wrote in a letter to relatives in Lempster, N. H., dated in 1848, that "Joseph and Stillman Fuller are living in this county. Joseph has bought a farm about 2½ miles from this village (Montrose)." This is probably the Joseph above,

Mrs. Clara C. (Fuller) Fryer.

Miss Ella Augusta Fryer.

as he had a brother Stillman. Ebenezer[7], brother of Joseph, wrote in 1879 to a relative in N. H., that "Joseph went to New York, then got married, his wife's name was Matilda Luce and his children's names were :

202.   I. "Sumner," b. ———.
203.   II. "Lucius," b. ———.
204.   III. "Charles," b. ———.
205.   IV. "Emma," b. ———.

(I have obtained no further information about this family)

80. STILLMAN[7] FULLER, (*Ebenezer[6], Issachar[5], John[4], Samuel[3], Samuel[2], Samuel[1]*), b. July 9, 1820, in Carver, Mass.; d. before 1879, in North Carolina ; m. 1, ——— ; m. 2, ———.

Letters of Ebenezer Fuller in 1879 stated that his brother Stillman had had two wives ; had one son by first wife ; that he was a Freewill Baptist minister, that Stillman and his second wife in time of the war went to North Carolina and had 500 colored people under their care, teaching them, that Stillman died there.

Children .

206.   I. A son, b. ———.

83. EZRA[7] FULLER, (*Consider[6], Ezra[5], John[4], Samuel[3], Samuel[2], Samuel[1]*), b. Jan. 19, 1791, at Kingston, Mass.; d. ——— ; m. Oct. 8, 1818, to Eliza Cobb of Carver, Mass, by Rev. Elijah Dexter. (Plympton, Mass, Records.)

Children :

207.   I. Sarah Tilden[8], b. May 19, 1822 (Davis' Plymouth) ; d. Sept. 17, 1822.
208.   II. Eliza Barker[8], b. May 26, 1823 ; m. Nov. 8, 1848, Daniel P. Sherman of North Bridgewater, Mass.
209. ‡III. Ezra Tilden[8], b. May 5, 1825 ; m. Mary J. Dunbar, Aug. 23, 1849
210.   IV. Betsey[8], b. April 3, 1827 ; d. June 14, 1881 ; m. April 4, 1848, Andrew J. Forbes of Bridgewater, Mass., and had : Melvin Jackson[9], b. Dec. 31, 1848 ; Sarah Emily[9], b. Nov. 21, 1851 ; Clara Augusta[9], b. May 25, 1854, and Angeline Allen[9], b. Sept. 23, 1861 ; all born in Bridgewater.
211.   V. Angelina Wood[8], b. April 15, 1831 ; d. Sept. 23, 1869 ; m. Henry Allen of East Bridgewater.
212.   VI. Sarah[8], b. May 11, 1832 ; d. Nov. 29, 1896 ; m. Sept. 7, 1853, Robert Clark of North Bridgewater and had : Frederick Clinton[9], b. Aug. 17,

1860, and Herbert Warren[9], b. July 12, 1870, in Plymouth, Mass.

213   ‡VII.   Isadas[8], b. March 4, 1834 ; m. Mary A. Mendell.
214.   VIII.   Truman Holmes[8], b. Nov. 29, 1839, m. Dec. 24, 1868, Mary Eliza Bartlett. Resides in Kingston, Mass. No children.
215.   IX.   Mary Frances[8], b. July 30, 1841.

87.   JOHN[7] FULLER, (*Consider*[6], *Ezra*[5], *John*[4], *Samuel*[3], *Samuel*[2], *Samuel*[1]), b. Jan. 12, 1801, at Kingston, Mass.; d. ———, m. 1, Nov. 1, 1829, Caroline Bisbee of Kingston, who d. Dec. 1, 1856; m. 2, Jan. 6, 1859, Elizabeth (Hyler), widow of Henry Bartlett of Kingston. She d. July 6, 1899, aged 87 y. 8 m. 7 d.

Children :

216.   ‡I.   John Andre[8], b. Aug. 1, 1830, m. Minerva Horsford.
217.   II.   Caroline Elizabeth[8], b. June 17, 1833; m. 1, April 2, 1853, Thomas H Bartlett of Kingston; m. 2, George M. Skinner of North Bridgewater.
218.   III.   Emily Jane[8], b. Jan. 14, 1841, d. Nov., 1858.

90.   SMITH[7] FULLER, (*Consider*[6], *Ezra*[5], *John*[4], *Samuel*[3], *Samuel*[2], *Samuel*[1]), b. Sept. 5, 1809, in Kingston, Mass.; d. Sept. 17, 1894 ; m. Int. Pub Jan. 2, 1830, with Eliza Churchill.

He lived on the old homestead at Kingston.

Children born to them were .

219.   ‡I.   Ansel[8], b 1831, m Salome Maria Bent.
220.   II.   Louisa[8], b. June 17, 1832; m. March 19, 1848, John Vaille.
221.   III.   Hannah[8], b. May 14, 1834 ; d. Aug. 26, 1852.
222.   IV.   Joanna[8], b. Oct. 14, 1836.
223.   ‡V.   Nathan Thomas[8], b. Dec. 8, 1841 ; m. Martha A.   C.   Woodward.   (Churchill   Genealogy. Kingston   Records.)   (Chas.   M.   Thatcher Middleboro Genealogies.)

92.   SAMUEL[7] FULLER, (*Consider*[6], *Ezra*[5], *John*[4], *Samuel*[3], *Samuel*[2], *Samuel*[1]), b. June 29, 1814, in Kingston, Mass.; d. Jan. 20, 1892; m. April 7, 1836, Maria Churchill of Plympton.

They resided in Kingston.

Children born to them were :

224.   I.   Maria Thomas[8], b. April 6, 1837; m. Nov. 26, 1854, Andrew Demerrit.   (Carver Records.)

225. II. Lois Frances[8], b. Aug 30, 1842 ; m. Oct. 20, 1861,
      Daniel Bisbee of Kingston.
226. III. Waldo Ames[8], b. Nov. 16, 1851 ; d. Oct. 17, 1852.
      (Churchill Genealogy.)
227. IV. A dau., b. July 12, 1854.

94. WALDO AMES[7] FULLER, (*Consider*[6], *Ezra*[5], *John*[4], *Samuel*[3], *Samuel*[2], *Samuel*[1]), b. Feb. 20, 1821, in Kingston, Mass.; d. March 22, 1872 ; m. Aug. 29, 1852, Sarah Amanda Stetson of Kingston, who d. March 17, 1871.

Children :

228. I. Charles Waldo[8], b. 1854.
229. II. Anne A.[8], b. 1859. (F. A. Fuller MSS.)

96. JAMES[7] FULLER, (*James*[6], *Ezra*[5], *John*[4], *Samuel*[3], *Samuel*[2], *Samuel*[1]), b. May 14, 1802 ; d. —— ; m. Jan. 2, 1828, Elizabeth Martin.

Resided at Georgetown, Mass.

Children :

230. I. John S.[8], b. Oct. 3, 1828.
231. II. James E.[8], b. May 30, 1830
232. ‡III. Josiah W.[8], b. Oct. 13, 1832 ; m. Harriet Boynton.
233. IV. Hannah W.[8], b. May 2, 1834. (F. A. Fuller MSS.)

99. EDWARD[7] FULLER, (*James*[6], *Ezra*[5], *John*[4], *Samuel*[3], *Samuel*[2], *Samuel*[1]), b. Nov. 10, 1813, at Salem, Mass.; d. there Oct. 3, 1888 ; m. April 23, 1840, Eliza A. Little of West Newbury, Mass., who d. Oct. 30, 1896.

Resided in South Danvers, Mass.

Children :

234. ‡I. Edward Little[8], b. April 11, 1841 ; m. Mary C.
      Doane.
235. II. Robert Melvin[8], b. June 3, 1843 ; d. Sept. 22, 1852.
236. III. Alfred Augustus[8], b. Aug. 21, 1847 ; m. July 20,
      1891, Mary Florence Mayhew.
237. IV. Louis Sturtevant[8], b. Sept. 13, 1852 , d. Oct. 21,
      1863.

EIGHTH GENERATION.

103. EDWARD[8] FULLER, (*Isaac*[7], *Isaac*[6], *Issachar*[5], *John*[4], *Samuel*[3], *Samuel*[2], *Samuel*[1]), b. June 13, 1807 ; d. March 16, 1890 ;

m. Jan. 20, 1833, Celia B. Stevens, b. May 26, 1812; d. Sept. 21, 1866.

They lived for a time in Hartford, Me., and then removed to North Turner, Me.

The children of this union were:

238   I. Elbridge Gerry[9], b. May 18, 1834, d. Dec. 4, 1837.

239   ‡II. Isaac Arnaldo[9], b. Feb. 12, 1837; m. Sarah E. Smith.

240.   III. Octavus Wright[9], b Jan. 17, 1839, d Sept. 15, 1840.

241.   ‡IV. Octavus Wright[9] 2d, b. Jan. 24, 1841; m. Omelia Jones.

242.   V. Celia Emeline[9], b. March 22, 1843; d. June 14, 1843.

243.   VI. Celia Genevra[9], b. Nov 26, 1844; m. Dec. 8, 1863, Charles A Dresser, b Jan. 19, 1843, reside at Turner, Me. Children: Edward Lucius[10], b April 8, 1865, Inez Celia[10], b. Feb. 28, 1867, and Bert Arthur[10], b. May 2, 1875.

244.   VII. William Edward[9], b. March 11, 1848, m. 1878, in Detroit, Mich., Mary Downey, b March 5, 1850. He has lived in several Western cities and is at present (1910) residing in Mishawaka, Ind. They have no children.

245.   VIII. Sarah Adel[9], b. March 26, 1850; d. Aug. 11, 1850.

104. EZEKIEL[8] FULLER, (*Isaac[7], Isaac[6], Issachar[5], John[4], Samuel[3], Samuel[2], Samuel[1]*), b. April 22, 1809; d Nov. 23, 1896, in Hartford, Me.; m. 1, Asenath Ames, who d. Feb. 7, 1840, aged 23 years; m. 2, June 27, 1840, Maria Farrar, b. April 21, 1814, d. June 27, 1890.

He lived in Hartford, Turner, Livermore and Buckfield. By an accident in middle life he lost an eye, and much impaired his health.

His children were, by his first wife:

246.   ‡I. Henry W.[9], b. June 1, 1838; m. Huldah Glover.

By second wife .

247.   II. Zipporah[9], b. Sept. 4, 1841; d. June 4, 1876; m. 1868, James Conwell, who d. April 12, 1877. Their children were: Adelbert L.[10], b. March 9, 1869; Bertie A.[10], b. March 9, 1869, and James M.[10], b. Oct. 4, 1876.

Essec Fuller.

His children were :

267. I. Edwin A.⁹, b. ———— ; d. Jan. 18, 1857, aged five years.
268. II. Essec⁹, b. ———— ; d. Jan. 14, 1857, aged three years.
269. III. Elonzo⁹, b. ———— ; d. March 3, 1862, aged six years.
270. IV. Edith⁹, b. ———— ; d. March 7, 1862, aged four years.
271. V. May Forest⁹, b. ———— ; d. Aug. 22, 1891 ; m. Jan. 15, 1862, Charles T. Hobbs of Turner, Me., and had · Edith M.¹⁰, b. June 1, 1883, and Lillian F.¹⁰, b. Sept. 10, 1886.

112. EMERY L.⁸ FULLER, (*Isaac⁷, Isaac⁶, Issachar⁵, John⁴, Samuel³, Samuel², Samuel¹*), b. Feb. 14, 1826, d. April 9, 1908, near North Turner, Me.; m. June 5, 1851, Eunice Records of Turner, Me., b. Oct. 27, 1833.

They lived in Hartford, Me.; removed to Peru, Me.; thence to Turner, Me , and finally to North Turner.

Their children were :

272. I. William B.⁹, b. Sept. 1, 1853.
273   ‡II. Calvin R⁹, b Oct. 20, 1856.
274. ‡III. Charles E.⁹, b. May 20, 1858 ; m. Emma Trevett.

116. SAMUEL⁸ FULLER, (*Samuel⁷, Isaac⁶, Issachar⁵, John⁴, Samuel³, Samuel², Samuel¹*), b. April 26, 1814, probably at Livermore, Me.; d. Aug. 14, 1906 ; m. May 26, 1843, Louisa Carver.

Children :

275. I. Louisa⁹, b. Feb. 26, 1844 ; d. April 17, 1861.

120. PHILANDER BRYANT⁸ FULLER, (*Samuel⁷, Isaac⁶, Issachar⁵, John⁴, Samuel³, Samuel², Samuel¹*), b. Aug. 31, 1823 ; d. Aug. 31, 1898, in Livermore, Me.; m. Jan. 1, 1871, Lucinda W. Beals.

Children :

276. I. Louisa C.⁹, b. Jan. 23, 1872 , m. Dec. 25, 1897, Frank C. Morrison of West Farmington, Me., and have three children . Leonard F.¹⁰, b. Oct. 21, 1898 ; Esther L.¹⁰, b. April 23, 1901, and F. Clinton ¹⁰, b. May 9, 1907.
277. II. Ethel L.⁹, b. Dec. 23, 1874.

Edward Newton Fuller.

Frank Fuller.

Homer Taylor Fuller.

Yours most cordially

Homer T. Fuller

Their children, born in Leominster, are:

293.   I.   Walter B.[9], b. July 30, 1872; m June 16, 1903, M. Florence Dow of Arlington, Mass. He is a graduate of Worcester Technical Institute, and a draftsman for the Pennsylvania Steel Co.; residing in Harrisburg, Pa.

294.   II.   Arthur T.[9], b. Feb. 13, 1876; graduate Worcester "Tech.;" is a draftsman, residing in Holyoke, Mass.

145.   IRVING H.[8] FULLER, (*Sylvanus[7], Noah[6], Issachar[5], John[4], Samuel[3], Samuel[2], Samuel[1]*), b. Aug. 2, 1852, in Lempster, N. H.; m. 1, Oct. 6, 1875, Celia M. Piedmont at Lempster; m. 2, Nov. 21, 1898, Mrs. Emma L. Packard of Fitchburg, Mass.

He resided in Lempster until after the death of his father in 1891, when he removed to Fitchburg.

His children were born in Fitchburg:

295.   I   Elsie M.[9], b. Aug. 23, 1876; m. June, 1900, Charles T. Staniels of Fitchburg, where they reside.

296   II.   Howard B.[9], b. June 13, 1878, m. Sept. 15, 1903, Etta Florence Bowen of Leominster, Mass., where they reside.

147.   GEORGE HERBERT[8] FULLER, (*Benoni[7], Noah[6], Issachar[5], John[4], Samuel[3], Samuel[2], Samuel[1]*), b. Aug 29, 1852, at Lempster, N. H., d. March 28, 1908, at Roxbury, Mass; m. Sept. 25, 1877, Clara L. Kent of Lawrence, Mass., who d Jan. 8, 1882.

He was a bookkeeper; resided in Boston, Mass, after his wife's decease.

They had one child:

297.   I.   George Wadsworth[9], b. April 24, 1879, at Lawrence, Mass.; m. Sept. 18, 1909, Marion Lawrence Hill, b. Aug. 14, 1880, at Roxbury. He is in business in Boston; resides at Roxbury.

149.   JOSIAH TILLSON[8] FULLER, (*Tillson[7], Issachar[6], Issachar[5], John[4], Samuel[3], Samuel[2], Samuel[1]*), b. Nov. 22, 1822; d. Nov. 22, 1863, in Louisville, Ky.; m. Irene Parker.

Children:

298.   I.   May Belle[9], b. Oct., 1856; d. ———, in Chicago, Ill., m. June, 1852, Frederick Mueller of Louisville and had Frederick Ferdinand [10].

155. ORRIN AUGUSTUS[8] FULLER, (*Tillson*[7], *Issachar*[6], *Issachar*[5], *John*[4], *Samuel*[3], *Samuel*[2], *Samuel*[1]), b. Aug. 11, 1838, in Browns-ville, Pa ; d. July 2, 1904, in Philadelphia, Pa.; m. Jan. 28, 1874, Sophia Fuller, b. Jan. 16, 1853, in Petersburg, Pa., dau. of James, son of Jacob Fuller

Mrs. Fuller resides (1910) in Philadelphia.

Their children were ·

299.	‡I.	Harry Tillson[9], b. Jan. 3, 1875; m. Margaret Young Galbraith.
300.	II.	James Robert[9], b. Sept. 15, 1876; d. Nov. 17, 1881, in Philadelphia.
301.	III.	Herbert Leslie[9], b. Feb. 9, 1880.
302.	IV.	Edith May[9], b. Sept. 23, 1884, m. Sept. 23, 1909, Frederick Rudolph Raeuchle, b. Oct. 12, 1878, in Pottsville, Pa.; residing in Mahanoy City, Pa.
303.	V.	Randall Mershon[9], b. June 30, 1886; d. April 4, 1887.
304.	VI.	Anna Louise [9], b. Dec. 5, 1890.

159. TILLSON[8] FULLER, (*Issachar*[7], *Issachar*[6], *Issachar*[5], *John*[4], *Samuel*[3], *Samuel*[2], *Samuel*[1]), b. Dec. 25, 1831, at Pembroke, Mass., d. April 10, 1908, in Charleston, Me.; m. Feb. 1, 1862, Lydia Stowell Sweetser, who d Nov. 13, 1872.

Children, all born in Hingham, Mass. ·

305.	I.	Nancy Jane[9], b. Jan. 6, 1865; m Aug 27, 1897, George Franklin Hardy and had: George Gresham[10], b. Sept. 14, 1898; Jack[10], b. April 14, 1901, and Phillip[10], b Sept. 20, 1903.
306.	II.	Harriet Adaline[9], b. July 12, 1867; m. Oct. 12, 1892, Rev. Nathan Hunt. Children. Merle[10], b. May 24, 1894; Esther Elizabeth[10], b. March 13, 1900, and Katherine[10], b. March 13, 1900. They reside in Charleston, Me.
307.	III.	Marion Lovett[9], b. Nov. 13, 1868; m. July 25, 1899, Louis Peterson Maynard. Children: Percival Hardy[10], b. May 16, 1900, and Tillson Fuller[10], b. Sept. 29, 1902.
308.	IV.	Lydia Florence[9], b. April 17, 1870; d. Nov. 13, 1872.

160. JOHN NICHOLS[8] FULLER, (*Issachar*[7], *Issachar*[6], *Issachar*[5], *John*[4], *Samuel*[3], *Samuel*[2], *Samuel*[1]), b. June 26, 1837, at Hingham, Mass., m. Sarah E. Thayer.

Children :

309.   I. Arthur Gregg[9], b. ———— ; d. Aug. 21, 1861, aged 3 months.

161. CHARLES MASON[8] FULLER, (*Issachar*[7], *Issachar*[6], *Issachar*[5], *John*[4], *Samuel*[3], *Samuel*[2], *Samuel*[1]), b Feb. 17, 1844, at Hingham, Mass.; m. Mary W. Clapp of Boston, Mass.

Capt. Fuller, formerly of the U. S. Navy, resides in Dorchester, Mass., with offices in State street, Boston. He is a dealer in investment securities and a public lecturer on various popular and interesting subjects.

Children :

310.   I. Alice De Carteret[9], b. ————.

162. JAMES SCOVILL[8] FULLER, (*Charles*[7], *Edward*[6], *Issachar*[5], *John*[4], *Samuel*[3], *Samuel*[2], *Samuel*[1]), b. Sept. 24, 1819, in Wyoming, Pa ; d. Jan. 2, 1877, in Scranton, Pa.; m. 1, Feb. 26, 1846, Martha Sharp, who d. May 2, 1847, m. 2, 1857, Mercy Barnum Porter.

Children :

311.   I Martha Maria[9], b. Jan. 10, 1847 ; m. May 1, 1873, Dr. William Elting Johnson, b. Oct. 17, 1837.

165. EDWARD CHARLES[8] FULLER, (*Charles*[7], *Edward*[6], *Issachar*[5], *John*[4], *Samuel*[3], *Samuel*[2], *Samuel*[1]), b. Jan. 8, 1826, in Wyoming, Pa., d. in Scranton, Pa. , m. Jan. 2, 1849, Helen Ruthven.

Edward C. Fuller came to Scranton while it was yet a village and was one of its most prominent and influential citizens. He was a druggist.

Their children were :

312.   ‡I. Charles Ruthven[9], b. Oct. 2, 1849; m. 1, Fanny Maria Penman ; m. 2, Catherine Rayner Scranton.

313.   ‡II. Edward Laton[9], b. Oct. 10, 1851 ; m. Helen Maria Silkman.

314.   ‡III. James Alexander[9], b. May 9, 1855; m. Eva Margaret Davis.

315.   ‡IV. Harry Grafton[9], b. -———— ; m. Ida Estelle Frink.

316.   V. Marion[9], b. ————.

317.   VI. Helen Ruthven[9], b. ————.

169. JOHN DORRANCE[8] FULLER, (*Charles[7], Edward[6], Issachar[5], John[4], Samuel[3], Samuel[2], Samuel[1]*), b Nov. 6, 1834, in Wyoming, Pa.; d. Oct. 29, 1898, in Elmhurst, Pa., m Feb. 10, 1863, Emma Chase Lathrop, b. Sept. 9, 1843, d. Nov. 1, 1879.

Was in fire insurance business and lived in Scranton, Pa.

Children :

318.	I.	Frank[9], b. Dec 2, 1863, d. Jan. 8, 1864.
319.	II.	Nellie[9], b Oct. 29, 1865, m. Nov. 17, 1887, Charles Richardson Smith, b. July 11, 1847, d. June 28, 1909. To Mr. Smith is due the credit for the collection of most of the genealogical data relating to the descendants of Edward[6] Fuller of Montrose, Pa The children of Mr. and Mrs. Smith are. Kenneth[10], b. Sept. 12, 1888, Mildred[10], b. May 4, 1890; Ruth Fuller[10], b Nov. 1, 1891, Phillip Lathrop[10], b. Feb. 23, 1895, and Allan Breed[10], b. Aug. 7, 1896; all of Scranton, Pa.
320.	III.	Hattie Geer[9], b. Aug. 27, 1868, d. July 20, 1869.
321	IV.	Emma Lathrop[9], b Sept 24, 1870
322.	V.	Lucy Leonard[9], b. Oct. 30, 1872.
323.	‡VI.	John Dorrance[9], b Feb. 6, 1875; m Ruth Davis.
324.	VII.	Mary Lathrop[9], b. Jan. 10, 1877 (name changed by law of N. Y. state to Mary Lathrop Johnson); m. May 16, 1905, William Boyd Stamford, and had Martha Fuller[10], b. May 26, 1907.

173. WILLIAM HENRY[8] FULLER, (*George[7], Edward[6], Issachar[5], John[4], Samuel[3], Samuel[2], Samuel[1]*), b. Aug. 10, 1829; d. Sept. 18, 1898, in Scranton, Pa., m. Oct 6, 1857, Mary Wheeler, b. Aug. 7, 1832, d. Oct. 23, 1903.

He lived in Scranton, and for years was ticket agent for the D. L. & W. R. R. Co.

Children :

325.	I	William Marshall[9], b. March 2, 1862.
326.	II.	Eliza Wheeler[9], b. May 6, 1864, m. Feb. 22, 1886, Charles Bartlett Macquivey, b. Jan. 19, 1859, and had Earl Wadleigh[10], b. Sept. 14, 1886.

175. ISAAC FRANCIS[8] FULLER, (*George[7], Edward[6], Issachar[5], John[4], Samuel[3], Samuel[2], Samuel[1]*), b. March 10, 1832; m. Nov. 19, 1856, Hettie Carling, b. Oct. 1, 1833.

Lives in Scranton, Pa.

Children :

327.   I. Mary Florence9, b. Feb. 20, 1860; m. May 7, 1884, Charles Edward Wade, b. Oct. 11, 1859, and had : Clara Buckley10, b. Feb. 20, 1885, and Charles Edward 10, b. April 2, 1887.

328.   II. Anne Meixsell9, b. Oct. 12, 1866; m. Sept. 16, 1886, Winfield Fremont Ward and had : Fremont Fuller10, b. Nov. 18, 1887 ; Florence Elizabeth10, b. Aug. 22, 1892, and Donald Carling10, b. Oct. 5, 1897.

329.   III. Samuel Barnard9, b. Feb. 3, 1872 ; d. July 21, 1872.

330.   ‡IV. Francis Carling9, b. Oct. 12, 1875; m. Bertha Lorine Powell.

177. GEORGE AUGUSTUS 8 FULLER, (*George*7, *Edward*6, *Issachar*5, *John*4, *Samuel*3, *Samuel*2, *Samuel*1), b. Sept. 9, 1835 ; d. Jan. 20, 1908, in Glenburn, Pa.; m. Oct. 5, 1859, Elizabeth Whitfield Scranton, b. March 17, 1838, d. Jan. 22, 1894.

He resided in Scranton and Glenburn, Pa.

Children :

331.   I. George Whitfield Scranton9, b. Nov. 24, 1860 ; d. April 5, 1909.

332.   II. Jane Scranton9, b. Nov. 24, 1863 ; m. June 2, 1886, Arthur Hovey Storrs and had : Janet 10, b. July 24, 1887 , William R. 10, b. July 24, 1889, d. Jan. 13, 1890, and Elizabeth Scranton10, b. April 6, 1891.

333.   III. Frederick9, b. Sept. 24, 1866 ; d. April 10, 1869.

334.   IV. William Augustus9, b. March 20, 1870.

335.   V. Lawrence Barnard9, b. April 19, 1875 ; m. June 20, 1908, Elizabeth S. LaTourette.

178. FREDERICK 8 FULLER, (*George*7, *Edward*6, *Issachar*5, *John*4, *Samuel*3, *Samuel*2, *Samuel*1), b. May 13, 1837 ; m. June 6, 1866, Laura Pardee Gay, b. Feb. 3, 1843.

He is a member of the Board of Aldermen, Scranton, Pa.

Children :

336.   I. Frederick Pardee9, b. May 18, 1871.

337.   ‡II. Theodore Sedgwick9, b. Nov. 23, 1872 ; m. Margaret Stevens Cissel.

183. HENRY V.8 FULLER, (*Henry*7, *Edward*6, *Issachar*5, *John*4, *Samuel*3, *Samuel*2, *Samuel*1), b. March 25, 1860; m. May, 1872,

Children :

338.   I.   A daughter, b. May 18, 1875; m. Joseph Fuller
                 Slater.
339.   ‡II.   Edward K.[9], b. Oct. 21, 1877; m. ———.

185.   Albert[S] **Fuller,** (*Francis*[7], *Edward*[6], *Issachar*[5], *John*[4], *Samuel*[3], *Samuel*[2], *Samuel*[1]), b. Aug. 13, 1843; m. 1, Anna Mary Phelps; m. 2, Clara ———; m. 3, Anna Scott.
Resides in New York City.   Employed in the navy yard.
Children :

340.   I.   Alice Louise[9], b. Nov. 24, 1866, m. Harry Tisdale
                 and had : Laura Louise [10] and Ethel Maria [10].
341.   II.   Francis William[9], b. Feb. 18, 1869; m. ———.
342.   III.   Cyrus Edward[9], b. ———; m. ———.

195.   George[S] **Fuller,** (*Isaac*[7], *Edward*[6], *Issachar*[5], *John*[4], *Samuel*[3], *Samuel*[2], *Samuel*[1]), b. April 24, 1850, m. June 11, 1879, Mary Jamison.
He resides at Cohoes, N. Y.
Children :

343.   I.   Stuart Jamison[9], b. May 4, 1880.
344.   II.   Isaac Sutton[9], b. Feb. 25, 1886.

199.   Noel B.[S] **Fuller,** (*Ezra*[7], *Ebenezer*[6], *Issachar*[5], *John*[4], *Samuel*[3], *Samuel*[2], *Samuel*[1]), b. Oct. 15, 1841, in Somerset, Mass.; d. Feb. 25, 1901, in Taunton, Mass.; m. 1, April 12, 1860, Mary L. Wilbur, b. in Winthrop, Me.; m 2, Nov. 24, 1883, Angenette J. Manchester, who resides (1909) in Taunton, Mass.
Children

345.   I.   Ella E.[9], b. 1860; d. March 12, 1861, in Taunton.
346.   II.   Elizabeth S[9], b. Nov. 8, 1886, in Taunton.   (Car-
                 ver, Middleboro and Taunton Records.)

209.   Ezra Tilden[S] **Fuller,** (*Ezra*[7], *Consider*[6], *Ezra*[5], *John*[4], *Samuel*[3], *Samuel*[2], *Samuel*[1]), b. May 5, 1825; m. Aug. 23, 1849, Mary J. Dunbar of East Bridgewater, Mass.
They resided in East Bridgewater.
Their children were :

347.   I.   Ezra Edgar[9], b. Dec. 28, 1857; d. Dec. 10, 1864.
348.   II.   Percy Dunbar[9], b. July 31, 1864.

Mrs. Mary Eliza (Fuller) Alexander.

John Knowles Alexander.

349.   III.   Carlotta Estelle[9], b Sept. 30, 1867; m. Sept. 25, 1889, Charles Raymond Ransden.

213. Isadas[8] Fuller, (*Ezra*[7], *Consider*[6], *Ezra*[5], *John*[4], *Samuel*[3], *Samuel*[2], *Samuel*[1]), b. March 4, 1834, in Kingston, Mass.; m. July 25, 1859, Mary Allen Mendell.

They reside at East Bridgewater, Mass.

Children:

350.   I.   Mary Eliza[9], b. May 3, 1860, in Campello, Mass.; m. June 2, 1892, John Knowles Alexander and had: John Herbert[10], b. Oct. 30, 1893; Grace Fuller[10], b. July 3, 1896; Andrew Jackson Bradford[10], b. Feb. 8, 1898, and Beatrice May[10], b. Aug. 1, 1901; reside at East Bridgewater.

351.   ‡II.   Frederick E.[9], b. Sept. 10, 1862; m. Mary Stanton Keith.

352.   III.   Moses Mendell[9], twins; b. Dec. 7, 1865, at East Bridgewater; d. Jan. 13, 1866.

353.   IV.   Maria Washburn[9], m. Aug. 1, 1895, William T. Leonard and had Albert Mendell[10], b. July 23, 1905. They reside at Elmwood, in East Bridgewater.

216. John Andre[8] Fuller, (*John*[7], *Consider*[6], *Ezra*[5], *John*[4], *Samuel*[3], *Samuel*[2], *Samuel*[1]), b. Aug. 1, 1830, in Kingston, Mass.; m. in California, Minerva A. Horsford of Norwich, N. Y.

They resided in Kingston.

Children:

354.   I.   John Andre[9], b. Nov. 27, 1855.
355.   II.   Benjamin C.[9], b. Feb. 8, 1858; d. Dec. 27, 1858.
356.   III.   Emily Jane[9], b. Dec. 15, 1859.
357.   IV.   Caroline Bisbee[9], b. Jan. 24, 1863.

219. Ansel[8] Fuller, (*Smith*[7], *Consider*[6], *Ezra*[5], *John*[4], *Samuel*[3], *Samuel*[2], *Samuel*[1]), b. 1831, at Kingston, Mass.; m. May 18, 1863, Salome Maria Bent.

Children:

358.   I.   Herman W.[9], b. Sept. 5, 1867, at Carver; m. Dec. 29, 1896, Addie Wardell.
359.   ‡II.   Otis Granville[9], b. 1869; m. Lottie M. Wentworth.
360.   ‡III.   Adelbert W.[9], b. 1871; m. Alice Doolan.
361.   IV.   A son, b. March 9, 1872; d. July 11, 1872. (Charles M. Thatcher, and Carver Records.)

223. NATHAN THOMAS[5] FULLER, (*Smith*[7], *Consider*[6], *Ezra*[5], *John*[4], *Samuel*[3], *Samuel*[2], *Samuel*[1]), b. Dec. 8, 1841 ; m. Nov. 26, 1863, Martha A. C. Woodward.

Children, recorded at Carver, Mass. :

362.   I.   Albert E.[9], b. May 4, 1865.

232. JOSIAH W.[5] FULLER, (*James*[7], *James*[6], *Ezra*[5], *John*[4], *Samuel*[3], *Samuel*[2], *Samuel*[1]), b. Oct. 13, 1832, in Georgetown, Mass., m. Harriet Boynton.

Children ·

363.   I.   Edward B.[9], b. March 3, 1859.
364.   II.   Frank L.[9], b. Oct. 7, 1863.
365.   III. Frederick M[9], b. June 17, 1885. (F. A. Fuller MSS.)

234. EDWARD LITTLE[5] FULLER, (*Edward*[7], *James*[6], *Ezra*[5], *John*[4], *Samuel*[3], *Samuel*[2], *Samuel*[1]), b. April 11, 1841, at South Danvers, Mass., m. Dec. 22, 1864, Mary Cushing Doane of Brookline, Mass., b. Aug. 1, 1845, at Rocky Nook, Hingham, Mass.

Children ·

366.   I.   Elizabeth Lincoln[9], b. Sept. 21, 1865, in Brookline ; m. June 7, 1894, Rev. Henry North George Hall, of London, Eng.
367.   II.   Maybell Doane[9], b. May 3, 1868, in Boston ; d. there April 8, 1893.
368.   III. Margaret[9], b. Sept. 18, 1869 ; d. June 25, 1870, in South Framingham, Mass.
369.   IV.   Edward Abbott[9], b. Dec. 11, 1875, in Philadelphia, Pa., in business in Boston.

NINTH GENERATION.

239. ISAAC ARNALDO[9] FULLER, (*Edward*[8], *Isaac*[7], *Isaac*[6], *Issachar*[5], *John*[4], *Samuel*[3], *Samuel*[2], *Samuel*[1]), b. Feb. 12, 1837 ; d. Dec. 17, 1882 ; m. March 17, 1865, Sarah E. Smith, b. June 5, 1845, at North Turner, Me., d. Aug. 31, 1897, in Auburn, Me.

He was a shoemaker, and a veteran of the Civil war.

Their children were :

370.   ‡I.   Frank Arnaldo[10], b. Jan. 3, 1867 ; m. Helen May Dillingham.
371.   II.   Marie Adel[10], b. July 20, 1868, at North Turner ; m. May 22, 1886, Franklin H. Crafts, b. July 2,

1863, at West Auburn, Me , d. Sept. 2, 1895. Their son, Earl Franklin[11], was b. July 25, 1887, at Auburn.

372.   III.   Elizabeth Estelle[10], b. Aug. 22, 1872, at North Abington, Mass.

373.   IV.   Georgiana[10], b July 13, 1875, at Livermore, Me.; m. Sept. 12, 1893, Lester L Stevens, b. Oct. 18, 1873, at Auburn, Me.   Children, all b. at Auburn, are : Harold Elwood [11], b. Jan. 28, 1894 ; Hazel Electa[11], b. Jan. 28, 1895 ; Philip Haskell [11], b. June 27, 1901 , Eleanor Elizabeth[11], b. Feb 29, 1904, and Lester Leigh [11], b. Sept. 12, 1908

374   V.   Arnella Melvina[10], b. Sept 13, 1876, at Livermore, Me.; m. May 15, 1895, James E. Mitchell, b. Oct. 4, 1874, at Brunswick, Me.   They have : Leone Agnes [11], b. April 27, 1896, and James [11], b. June 26, 1900 ; both born in Auburn.

240. OCTAVUS WRIGHT[9] FULLER, (*Edward[8], Isaac[7], Isaac[6], Issachar[5], John[4], Samuel[3], Samuel[2], Samuel[1]* (deaf mute), b. Jan. 24, 1841 ; m. May 23, 1875, Omelia Jones (deaf mute) of Peeled Chestnut, Tenn., b. Nov. 30, 1849.

He was educated at the Institution for Deaf and Dumb in Connecticut ; has lived at South Paris, Me., for many years.

Children :

375.   I.   Edward Wright[10], b. June 13, 1877 ; d. Jan. 23, 1900

376.   II.   Alfred Elbridge [10], b. March 18, 1880.

246. HENRY W.[9] FULLER, (*Ezekiel[8], Isaac[7], Isaac[6], Issachar[5], John[4], Samuel[3], Samuel[2], Samuel[1]*), b. June 1, 1838, m. July 4, 1864, Huldah Reed Glover of Hartford, Me., b. Jan. 27, 1841, d. April 13, 1907, at their home near South Paris, Me.

Their children are .

377.   I.   Asenath A.[10], b. May 6, 1867 ; m. Nov. 11, 1893, Edson E. Spofford and has . Ethel Bernice [11], b. May 10, 1895, and Arthur Henry[11], b. June 4, 1903

378.   II.   Mary A.[10], b. Aug. 2, 1874 ; m. Oct. 18, 1902, Lysander J. Monk, and has . Eola Maude [11], b. April 19, 1906, and Ella Isabella[11], b. July 23, 1909.

249. ISAAC D.[9] FULLER, (*Ezekiel*[8], *Isaac*[7], *Isaac*[6], *Issachar*[5], *John*[4], *Samuel*[3], *Samuel*[2], *Samuel*[1]), b. March 8, 1846, m. Feb. 3, 1866, Olive A. Swallow, b. Sept. 4, 1846, d. May 19, 1893, at their home in North Buckfield, Me

He is a veteran of the Civil war. He met with a terrible misfortune at the celebration July 3, 1886, at Buckfield, Me, when both hands were blown off by the premature discharge of an anvil heavily loaded with powder.

Children :

379.	‡I.	Frank Eugene[10], b. Oct. 20, 1866; m. Carrie Ellen Rowe.
380.	II.	Florence A.[10], b Dec. 26, 1868; m. July 4, 1900, Lester F Champion of Brockton, Mass.
381.	III.	Flora D.[10], b. Oct. 31, 1870, m. Aug. 16, 1889, Frank Edson Smith, b. Feb. 12, 1866. Their children were. Madge Louise[11], b. Feb. 3, 1891; Arthur Bernard[11], b. Feb. 1, 1892, d. April 8, 1892, and Harry Lowell[11], b. Dec. 2, 1894.
382.	IV	Eva May[10], b. Sept 30, 1879; d. Sept. 5, 1905; m. Oct. 1, 1901, Edward E. Hammond. Their dau., Olive E.[11], was b. Aug. 23, 1905.

255. WELCOME F.[9] FULLER, (*Eland*[8], *Isaac*[7], *Isaac*[6], *Issachar*[5], *John*[4], *Samuel*[3], *Samuel*[2], *Samuel*[1]), b. Dec. 25, 1847; m. Dec. 4, 1881, Cora P. Boothby, b. May 12, 1859, at Livermore, Me.

In early life Mr. Fuller spent several years in the West, returning to Livermore in 1878 and opening a general merchandise store. He was Postmaster and Justice of the Peace for many years; was twice elected to town offices and then declined further honors; has been in business since 1906 in North Turner, Me.*

The children of Mr. and Mrs. Fuller were all born in Livermore :

383.	I.	Edna May[10], b. June 30, 1883.
384.	II.	Paul Stewart[10], b. July 19, 1890; d. Nov. 7, 1895.
385.	III.	Ralph Emerson[10], b. July 21, 1891.
386.	IV.	Elva Alberta[10], b. Jan. 25, 1895.

265. EDWIN E.[9] FULLER, (*Essec*[8], *Isaac*[7], *Iscac*[6], *Issachar*[5], *John*[4], *Samuel*[3], *Samuel*[5], *Samuel*[1]), b. Sept. 24, 1846; m. 1,

---

*It is to Mr. Welcome F. Fuller that the descendants of Isaac 7 Fuller and the compiler of this volume are greatly indebted for the practically complete genealogical data concerning the above-mentioned descendants.

Welcome F. Fuller.

Clinton Everett Fuller.

Henry Jones Fuller.

Edward Laton Fuller.

10, 1851, in Hawley, Pa.; d. Jan. 29, 1909, in Augusta, Ga., whither he had gone from his Scranton home accompanied by his physician. The immediate cause of death was apoplexy. He m. Sept. 28, 1876, Helen Maria Silkman of Scranton, b. Sept. 11, 1854.

Mr. Fuller received a common school education and entered the employment of a prominent mercantile house. Later he started in business for himself, but conditions and circumstances not being favorable his first adventures proved disastrous. He persevered nowever, and directing his attention to acquiring and operating coal properties, became recognized as one of the most capable and efficient individual operators. Later, he sold his collieries and organized the International Salt Company. He was also a railroad director and promoter, director Pennsylvania Casualty Co.; director Wyoming Shovel Works, treasurer Lackawanna Hospital; president board of trustees, Second Presbyterian Church; member Scranton Board of Trade, and of the Municipal League. Socially, Mr. Fuller was as active as in business, being a member of various local clubs, and also of the Maryland Club of Baltimore, the Buffalo Club of Buffalo, N. Y., of various New York clubs, and of the New England societies of both Scranton and New York. Mr. Fuller was not ostentatious. It was an article of his creed that wealth was a trust to be administered by its owner for the benefit of all whom it could wisely be made to reach, and that the trust should be discharged, as far as possible, personally and not by will. It was thoroughly characteristic of him and his wife that they chose as a method of celebrating their silver wedding the building of an addition to their church, in order that its activities might be widened and facilitated.

Mr. Fuller was deservedly popular. He possessed rare personal charms, manly vigor, a frank and open disposition, unusual conversational ability and unfailing cheerfulness. Perhaps his most striking quality was his dauntless courage. His spirit seemed to rise superior to every disaster and to take fresh impulse from multiplied obstacles. He was deeply loved by all who came most closely in contact with him, and his loss will be deeply felt by a country-wide circle of friends. (Gleanings from Scranton, Pa., Tribune, Jan. 30, 1909.)

Mrs. Fuller, who survives him, resides in Scranton.

They have one child, a son:

408.   ‡I.   Mortimer B.[10], b. Aug. 12, 1877, m. Kathryn
                Irvine Steel.

314. JAMES ALEXANDER[9] FULLER, (*Edward C.*[8], *Charles*[7],
Edward[6], *Issachar*[5], *John*[4], *Samuel*[3], *Samuel*[2], *Samuel*[1]), b. May
9, 1855, in Scranton, Pa., m. April 19, 1881, Eva Margaret Davis,
b. Dec. 24, 1855.

Resides in Geneseo, N. Y.

Children:

409.   I.   Bertha Davis[10], b. June 30, 1882.
410.   II.   Selia Jay[10], b. Jan. 22, 1884.

315. HARRY GRAFTON[9] FULLER, (*Edward C.*[8], *Charles*[7],
Edward[6], *Issachar*[5], *John*[4], *Samuel*[3], *Samuel*[2], *Samuel*[1]), b.
————, in Scranton, Pa.; m. Dec. 19, 1879, Ida Estelle Frink.

Children:

411.   ‡I.   Henry Grafton[10], b. Oct. 3, 1881; m. Lucy Claude.

323. JOHN DORRANCE[9] FULLER, (*John D.*[8], *Charles*[7], *Edward*[6],
Issachar[5], *John*[4], *Samuel*[3], *Samuel*[2], *Samuel*[1]), b. Feb. 6, 1875;
m. June 17, 1903, Ruth Jarvis, b. July 29, 1878.

He resides in Peckville, Pa.

Children:

412.   I.   Frances Mary[10], b. Oct. 23, 1906.

330. FRANCIS CARLING[9] FULLER, (*Isaac F.*[8], *George*[7], *Edward*[6],
Issachar[5], *John*[4], *Samuel*[3], *Samuel*[2], *Samuel*[1]), b. Oct. 12, 1875;
m. Bertha Lorine Powell.

Their children are:

413.   I.   Joseph Boies[10], b. April 25, 1903.
414   II.   Francis Wilmot[10], b. Feb. 4, 1905.
415.   III. Helen Powell[10], b. July 18, 1908.

337. THEODORE SEDGWICK[9] FULLER, (*Frederick*[8], *George*[7],
Edward[6], *Issachar*[5] *John*[4], *Samuel*[3], *Samuel*[2], *Samuel*[1]), b. Nov.
23, 1872, in Scranton, Pa.; m. Nov. 15, 1904, Margaret Stevens
Cissel, b. Jan. 17, 1878.

Children:

416.   I.   Katherine Barnard[10], b. Jan. 9, 1908.

CORRECTIONS AND ADDITIONS.

JCT 29 1910

Mr. Frederick Pardee Fuller, number 336 of the 5th Group in Vol. II of Fuller Genealogy, (see page 99), states in a letter dated at Yonkers, N Y., Oct 11, 1910, that he is the husband of Margaret Stevens (Cissel) Fuller, while Theodore S. Fuller, his brother, remains unmarried.

Mr. F. P. Fuller also gives the date of birth of his son, and states that the date of birth of his father, number 178 of said group, should be given as March 13, 1837, instead of May 13, 1837. Hence paragraphs attached to individual numbers 178, 336 and 337 of the 5th group need correcting in these particulars, and on page 108, substituting the individual number 336 for 337, the attached data should be as follows:

336. FREDERICK PARDEE[9] FULLER, (*Frederick*[8], *George*[7], *Edward*[6], *Issachar*[5], *John*[4], *Samuel*[3], *Samuel*[2], *Samuel*[1]), b. May 18, 1871, in Scranton, Pa.; m. Nov. 15, 1904, Margaret Stevens Cissel, b. Jan. 17, 1878.

Children :

416.   I.   Katherine Barnard[10], b. Jan. 9, 1908.
416*a*.   II.   Frederick Richard[10], b. Aug. 20, 1909.

The original data was taken from manuscript of the late C. R. Smith that was kindly loaned to me by Mrs. Nellie (Fuller) Smith, number 319 of the 5th Group, who died June 4, 1910.

Frederick E. Fuller.

339. ⁗Edward K.⁹ Fuller, (*Henry V.⁸, Henry⁷, Edward⁶, Issachar⁵, John⁴, Samuel³, Samuel², Samuel¹*), b. Oct. 21, 1877; m. May 18, 1900, ———.

Children:

417.   I.   Frederick W.¹⁰, b. March 22, 1903.
418.   II.   Blanche A.¹⁰, b. April 15, 1906.

351. Frederick E.⁹ Fuller, (*Isadas⁸, Ezra⁷, Consider⁶, Ezra⁵, John⁴, Samuel³, Samuel², Samuel¹*), b. Sept. 10, 1862, in East Bridgewater, Mass.; m. June 17, 1890, Mary Stanton Keith, b. Aug. 7, 1867, in East Bridgewater.

Mr. Fuller is a merchant residing in East Bridgewater; was a member of the Legislature in 1901 and 1902.

Their children, b. in East Bridgewater, are:

419.   I.   Marion Keith¹⁰, b. May 3, 1891.
420.   II.   Samuel¹⁰, b. Sept. 19, 1895.

359. Otis Granville⁹ Fuller, (*Ansel⁸, Smith⁷, Consider⁶, Ezra⁵, John⁴, Samuel³, Samuel², Samuel¹*), b. Aug. 18, 1869, at Middleboro, Mass.; m. Aug. 3, 1889, Lottie M. Wentworth.

Children:

421.   I.   Hazel Wentworth¹⁰,   b.   March   7,   1890,   at Middleboro.

360. Adelbert W.⁹ Fuller, (*Ansel⁸, Smith⁷, Consider⁶, Ezra⁵, John⁴, Samuel³, Samuel², Samuel¹*), b. Jan. 15, 1871, in Middleboro, Mass.; m. Feb. 24, 1892, Alice Doolan.

Children, all born in Middleboro:

422.   I.   Adelbert Otis¹⁰, b. Aug. 24, 1892.
423.   II.   Herman Mack¹⁰, b. May 24, 1894.
424.   III.   Granville Daniel¹⁰, b. Sept. 18, 1896.
425.   IV.   Agatha Thelma¹⁰, b. Sept. 30, 1903.

TENTH GENERATION.

370. Frank Arnaldo¹⁰ Fuller, (*Isaac A.⁹, Edward⁸, Isaac⁷, Isaac⁶, Issachar⁵, Samuel³, Samuel², Samuel¹*), b. Jan. 3, 1867; m. Jan. 26, 1889, Helen May Dillingham, b. July 8, 1869, in Lewiston, Me., d. June 20, 1905, leaving a daughter:

426.   I.   Sadie Marie¹¹, b. Nov. 6, 1890.

379. FRANK EUGENE[10] FULLER, (*Isaac D.[9], Ezekiel[8], Isaac[7], Isaac[6], Issachar[5], John[4], Samuel[3], Samuel[2], Samuel[1]*), b. Oct. 20, 1866; m. Dec. 10, 1893, Carrie Ellen Rowe, b. Nov. 12, 1874.

Their son ·

427.   I.   Lester Eugene[11], b. Nov. 13, 1895.

396. CHARLES L[10] FULLER, (*Albert H.[9], Charles T.[8], Consider[7], John[6], Issachar[5], John[4], Samuel[3], Samuel[2], Samuel[1]*), b. Jan. 15, 1877, in Brockton, Mass.; m. Sept. 30, 1903, Gertrude Walker.

They reside in Brockton, Mass.

Children :

428.   I.   Albert W.[11], b. Aug. 8, 1904.

408. MORTIMER BARTINE[10] FULLER, (*Edward L.[9], Edward C.[8], Charles[7], Edward[6], Issachar[5], John[4], Samuel[3], Samuel[2], Samuel[1]*), b. Aug. 12, 1877, in Scranton, Pa.; m. Feb. 16, 1904, Kathryn Irvine Steel, b. May 10, 1884.

Mr. Fuller was associated with his father in various industrial enterprises, one of the most important being the International Salt Co.

He resides in Scranton.

Their children are :

429.   I.   Edward Laton[11], b. Nov. 23, 1904.
430.   II.   Mortimer B.[11], b. July 23, 1907.

411. HENRY GRAFTON[10] FULLER, (*Harry G.[9], Edward C.[8], Charles[7], Edward[6], Issachar[5], John[4], Samuel[3], Samuel[2], Samuel[1]*), b. Oct. 3, 1881, m March 24, 1908, Lucy Claude.

He graduated Feb, 1906, from the U. S. Naval Academy with the rank of Ensign, and is now (1909) attached to U. S. S. Colorado.

Children :

431.   I.   John Wilkinson[11], b. March 20, 1909.

SIXTH GROUP.

FOURTH GENERATION.

JABEZ[4] FULLER, (*Samuel*[3]), AND SOME OF HIS DESCENDANTS.

20. JABEZ[4] FULLER, (*Samuel*[3], *Samuel*[2], *Samuel*[1]), b. June, 1701, in Plympton, Mass. (Plymouth Records); d. ———,1757, in Kingston, Mass. (Brainard's MSS.) ; m. 1, Nov. 12, 1724, by Rev. Isaac Cushman, to Deborah Soule (Plympton Records), who d. Jan. 24, 1724/5 (Gravestone Records in Mayflower Descendants Magazine, Vol. 10, p. 115) ; m. 2, Mercy Gray, b. Feb. 4, 1703/4 (Mayflower Desc., Vol. 1, p. 145), who "d. ——— 5, 1782, at Plymouth, in 79th year" (N. E. Register, Vol. X), "widow of Jabez Fuller."

Children, recorded at Kingston, Mass. :

1.	I.	Thomas[5], b. Aug. 31, 1734; d. April 2, 1738.
2.	II.	Joanna[5], b. March 31, 1736; m. May 3, 1762, Thomas Harlow.
3.	III.	James[5], b. Dec. 4, 1737; m. Hannah ———. Nothing further found.
4.	IV.	Jabez[5], b. Feb. 24, 1739; m. Ruth Wright. Nothing further found.
5.	‡V.	John[5], b. Sept. 29, 1741 ; m. Rebecca Robbins.
6.	VI.	Mercy[5], b. July 6, 1747; m. 1777, in Hardwick, Mass, Edmund Willis and removed to Woodstock, Vt. Letter to church there dated July 30, 1789 (Brainard's MSS.). Vermont Historical Gazetteer, Vol. 4, p 137, mentions "Nancy" (Mercy?) wife of Edward Willis — early settlers of Calais, Vt.

FIFTH GENERATION.

5. JOHN[5] FULLER, (*Jabez*[4], *Samuel*[3], *Samuel*[2], *Samuel*[1]), b.
Sept. 29, 1741, in Kingston, Mass.; d. Oct. 20, 1828; m. April 28,
1768, Rebecca Robbins of Carver, Mass., b. March 3, 1748, d. June
16, 1815, ae. 67 yrs.

Children, recorded at Kingston:

7.   I.   John[6], b. June 2, 1769, in Plymouth, Mass ;
             perhaps is the John Fuller of Kingston, who m.
             Sept. 16, 1792, Hannah Macomber at Middle-
             boro, Mass., and m. 2, March 23, 1806,
             "Elizabeth Donham, both of Kingston."

8.   II. Rebecca[6], b Aug. 12, 1771, in Plymouth; d. Dec.
             25, 1772.

9. ‡III.   James[6], b. Aug. 17, 1773, in Plymouth; m. Mary
             (Polly) Delano.

10.   IV. Mercy[6], b. Nov. 23, 1775, in Plymouth; d. Nov.
             25, 1775.

11.   V.   Mercy[6] 2d, b. Oct. 16, 1776, in Plymouth; m.
             Thaddeus Churchill. (Lewis, son of Thaddeus
             and Mercy Churchill, d. Sept. 22, 1835, ae.
             17 yrs.)

12.   VI. Rebecca[6] 2d, b. April 2, 1779; m. March 29, 1797,
             Joseph Rider of Plymouth.

13. ‡VII.   Eleazer Robbins[6], b. Nov. 22, 1784; m. Sarah
             (Sally) Drew

14.   VIII. Betsey[6], b. Sept. 2, 1787; m. May 10, 1804,
             Ephraim Patz.

SIXTH GENERATION.

9. JAMES[6] FULLER, (*John*[5], *Jabez*[4], *Samuel*[3], *Samuel*[2],
Samuel[1]), b. Aug. 17, 1773, in Plymouth, Mass.; d. June 22, 1859;
m. Feb. 15, 1799, Mary Delano, who d. Oct. 14, 1858.

He is called Capt. James Fuller.

Children:

15.   I.   Emily[7], b. Nov. 13, 1799; d. 1889; m. July 20,
             1820, Capt. Charles Robbins.

16.   II. Mary Chandler[7], b. Nov. 28, 1802; d. June 22,
             1829, at New Orleans, La.; m. Sept. 7, 1828,
             Capt. William Churchill.

17. ‡III.   James[7], b. Jan. 3, 1805; m. May 11, 1830, Asenath
             Delano Churchill.

18.   IV. Lucy Delano[7], b. July 27, 1807; d. May 5, 1816.

19.   V.   Matilda[7], b. ——— ; d. Sept. 29, 1817, ae. 3 y. 11 m.

13. ELEAZER ROBBINS[6] FULLER, (*John*[5], *Jabez*[4], *Samuel*[3], *Samuel*[2], *Samuel*[1]), b. Nov. 22, 1784, in Kingston, Mass.; d. Nov. 19, 1860; m. 1, Nov. 16, 1805, Sarah (Sally) Drew, b. 1786, d. Jan. 4, 1825, m. 2, March 1, 1835, Abigail Harlow of Plympton, Mass. Children, recorded in Kingston, Mass.:

20.	‡I.	Alexander[7], b. Sept. 1, 1806, m. Rebecca L. Spring.
21.	II.	Hannah D.[7], b. Dec. 2, 1807; m. Int. Pub. Nov. 24, 1833, with Philip Washburn.
22.	III.	Rebecca[7], b. Nov. 24, 1809; m. Oct. 15, 1843, John Battles.
23.	IV.	Eleazer[7], b. Dec. 22, 1811; d. July 20, 1834.
24.	V.	Samuel D.[7], b. May 7, 1813, d. June 23, 1906, in Kingston, aged 94 y. 1 m. 14 d.; married and lived in the West. Nothing more learned.
25.	VI.	Hiram[7], b. ——; d. Sept. 9, 1815, aged 22, days.*
26.	VII.	Sarah D.[7], b. Dec. 21, 1816; m. 1844, Thomas F. Staples.
27.	‡VIII.	Hiram[7] 2d, b. March 2, 1819, m. Emily ——.
28.	‡IX.	George[7], b. Jan. 1, 1821, m. Mary Thomas.

SEVENTH GENERATION.

17. JAMES[7] FULLER, (*James*[6], *John*[5], *Jabez*[4], *Samuel*[3], *Samuel*[2], *Samuel*[1]), b. Jan. 3, 1805; d. 1886; m. ——, Asenath Delano Churchill, b. 1805, d. 1885.

Children:

29.	I.	Mary Chandler[8], b. Aug. 8, 1831, in Kingston, Mass.; d. 1894, m. June 5, 1857, Capt. George Collingwood of Shaw's Flat, Tuolumne Co., Cal., and had. George[9], Mary E. C.[9], Beulah Orton[9], William C. C.[9] and Laura[9].
30.	II.	James Albert[8], b. July 29, 1833, in Kingston; d. March, 1905, in San Francisco, Cal., unmarried.
31.	‡III.	William Henry[8], b. Dec. 11, 1834; m. Clarinda H. Burns
32.	IV.	Lucia Churchill[8], b. Jan. 11, 1837, in Kingston; d. 1895, in Haverhill, Mass., m. July 3, 1867, in Boston, John Brown, and had: Chester F.[9], Arthur T.[9] and Asenath F.[9], all born in Haverhill.
33.	V.	Chester H.[8], b. July 14, 1838. Served 1½ years in

*The Kingston Records do not mention the birth of Hiram 1st, but give date of death as above.

18th Mass. Vols., and 3 years in the navy in the
Civil war, unmarried, resides in Kingston,
where he was born.

34.   VI.   Asenath Delano[5], b. July 30, 1840, in Kingston;
                d Feb. 17, 1868.

35.   VII.   Beulah Orton[8], b. March 7, 1843, in Kingston; d.
                Jan. 26, 1868.

36.   VIII. Arabella Johnson[8], b. Aug 21, 1847; d. Oct. 3,
                1905, in Haverhill, Mass.; m. Feb. 27, 1869,
                Horace L. Page and had: William Horace[9], b.
                Oct. 11, 1869, at Kingston, Beulah Asenath[9], b.
                Feb. 26, 1872, d. Dec. 14, 1879, Charles Ira[9], b.
                Dec. 20, 1877, at Haverhill; Henrietta Page[9],
                b. April 27, 1880, d. May 23, 1880; James
                Albert[9], b. April 16, 1881, in Haverhill; Florence
                Ella[9], b. June 29, 1888, m. July 2, 1906, George
                Frank Tift.

    20.   ALEXANDER[7] FULLER, (*Eleazer R.[6], John[5], Jabez[4], Samuel[3],
Samuel[2], Samuel[1]*), b. Sept. 1, 1806, in Kingston, Mass.;
d. —— ; m. Nov 14, 1832, in Sandwich, Mass., Rebecca L.
Spring of Sandwich, who d. Jan. 7, 1888. He was " of Sandwich "
at time of marriage.

    Children, b. in Sandwich.

37.   I.   Alexander[8], b. Dec. 28, 1838.

38.   II.   Sarah Elizabeth[8], b. Aug. 30, 1840; m. Nov. 30,
                1863, Oscar F. Wixon.

    27.   HIRAM[7] FULLER, (*Eleazer R.[6], John[5], Jabez[4], Samuel[3],
Samuel[2], Samuel[1]*), b. March 2, 1819, in Kingston, Mass.; d. July
21, 1877, m. ——, Emily ——, b. March 1, 1817, d. Dec. 10,
1852.

    Children :

39.   I.   Emma Ann[8], b. 1847, d. Aug. 11, 1848, aged
                11 m. 4 d. (From Kingston Cemetery Records.)

    28.   GEORGE[7] FULLER, (*Eleazer R.[6], John[5], Jabez[4], Samuel[3],
Samuel[2], Samuel[1]*), b. Jan 1, 1821, at Kingston, Mass.; m. May 26,
1845, Mary Thomas of Plymouth, Mass., who d. there Nov. 15,
1882.

    Children :

40.   I.   Mary[5], b. —— ; m. Oct. 4, 1866, Cornelius F.
                Bradford.

41.   ·   II.   Alice Drew[8], b. Nov. 27, 1854, in Plymouth.

EIGHTH GENERATION.

31. WILLIAM HENRY[8] FULLER, (*James*[7], *James*[6], *John*[5], *Jabez*[4], *Samuel*[3], *Samuel*[2], *Samuel*[1]), b. Dec. 11, 1834, in Kingston, Mass.; m. Dec. 24, 1867, in Kingston, Clarinda H. Burns of Boston, Mass., b. Aug. 3, 1849, d. Jan. 10, 1907.

Mr. Fuller was First Sergeant, Troop E, Second Cavalry, California Volunteers, Sept., 1861, to Oct., 1864. He now (1909) resides in Malden, Mass.

Children:

42.   I.   James Erskine[9], b. Sept. 25, 1868, in Kingston; d. May 29, 1875.

43.   II. Florence Taylor[9], b. Oct. 28, 1869, in Cambridge, Mass.; d. Jan. 9, 1888.

44.   III. Mary Asenath[9], b. Aug 6, 1871, in Arlington, Mass.; d. Sept. 18, 1896, m. Sept., 1894, Frederick Osborn of Cambridge and had Raymond[10], b. ———.

45.   IV. Hiram Chester[9], b June 20, 1873; d. Sept. 3, 1873.

46.   V.   Margaret Elizabeth[9], b. July 28, 187?; m. Dec. 25, 1898, Cyrus F. Lamb of Cambridge. Children: Margaret Hope[10] and Dorothy Bradford[10].

47.   VI. Clarinda Jessie[9], b. Sept. 2, 1876, in Cambridge; d. May 13, 1884.

48.   VII. William Thomas Maclin[9], b. Jan. 6, 1878; d. July 23, 1889.

49.   VIII. Agnes Jackson[9], b. Sept. 24, 1879, in Cambridge; d. Aug. 12, 1892.

50.   IX. Gertrude Aldine[9], b. Jan. 24, 1882, in Cambridge; d. Nov. 12, 1899; m. Sept., 1898, Frederick Savage of Cambridge.

51.   X.   Franklin Porter[9], b. April 26, 1885; resides in Malden, Mass.

SEVENTH GROUP.

FOURTH GENERATION.

JAMES⁴ FULLER, AND SOME OF HIS DESCENDANTS.

JAMES⁴ FULLER, (*Samuel³*, *Samuel²*, *Samuel¹*), b. Feb. 27, 1704 (Plymouth Records), d. ———, m 1, May 19, 1725, Judith Rickard, who d. Feb 23, 1726, m. 2, May 22, 1729, Mercy Perkins (Plympton Records).

Children:

        I.   Eleanah5, b Feb. 9, 1725/6. (Mayflower Descendant, vol. 1, p. 245.) H. W. Brainard's MSS. gives the name as Elkanah, and also gives:

"? II.   James5."

I have found nothing more concerning this family.

EIGHTH GROUP.

FOURTH GENERATION.

JOHN⁴ FULLER, (*John³*), AND SOME OF HIS DESCENDANTS.

23. JOHN⁴ FULLER, (*John³, Samuel², Samuel¹*), b. March 20, 1692, in Middleboro, Mass.; d. April 24, 1766, aged 74 years; m. 1, March 26, 1719, Hannan Thomas, who d. Sept 20, 1760, in 75th year; m. 2, April 27, 1762, Lydia (Alden) Eddy, who d. March 1, 1803, aged 92 years.

Children, born in Middleboro :

1.	I.	Hannah⁵, b. Feb. 7, 1720; "d. Nov. 18, 1769" (C. M. Thatcher).
2.	II.	Abigail⁵, b July 1, 1721; d. Oct. 17, 1723 (C. M. Thatcher).
3.	‡III.	John⁵, b Sept. 5, 1723; m. Joanna Tillson.
4.	IV.	Bathsheba⁵, b Jan. 19, 1726; m. Int. Pub. April 26, 1756, with Charles Ellis of Middleboro. (Churchill Gen.)

FIFTH GENERATION.

3. JOHN⁵ FULLER, (*John⁴, John³, Samuel², Samuel¹*), b. Sept. 5, 1723, in Middleboro, Mass.; d. ——— ; m. Dec. 27, 1743, Joanna Tillson. "Both of Halifax."

Children, recorded in Halifax ·

5.	‡I.	Ephraim,⁶, b. Nov. 1, 1744; m. Zerviah Thompson.
6.	‡II.	Thomas⁶, b. March 3, 1746; m. Hannah Ripley.
7.	III.	Abigail⁶, b. Nov. 26, 1747.

SIXTH GENERATION.

5. EPHRAIM[6] FULLER, (*John[5], John[4], John[3], Samuel[2], Samuel[1]*), b. Nov. 1, 1744, in Halifax, Mass.; d. ——— ; m. July 9, 1772, Zerviah Thompson. "Both of Halifax."

Children.

8.	‡I.	John[7], b. ——— , m. Hannah Cooper.
9.	‡II	Ephraim[7], b May 4, 1780, m. Zerviah Chandler.
10.	III.	Hannah[7], b. ———.
11.	IV.	Rebecca[7], b. ——— ; m. March 30, 1809, Ebenezer[7] Fuller (*Chipman[6], Ebenezer[5], Ebenezer[4], John[3], Samuel[2], Samuel[1].*)
12.	V.	Zerviah[7], b ——— ; m April 25, 1805, Isaiah Ripley Jr of Plympton, Mass. (Halifax Records.)

6. THOMAS[6] FULLER, (*John[5], John[4], John[3], Samuel[2], Samuel[1]*), b. March 3, 1746, at Halifax, Mass; d. Nov. 4, 1810, is probably the Thomas Fuller who m. May 25, 1769, Hannah Ripley, as given in Halifax Vital Records, "both of Halifax." It is to be noted that Sylvanus[7] named a son, Sylvanus *Ripley.*

Thomas Fuller is said to have served in the Revolutionary war.

Children :

13.	‡I.	Thomas[7], b. Aug. 6, 1778; m. Sally Sturtevant.
14.	‡II.	Cyrus[7], b. Aug. 22, 1780, m. Hannah Leonard.
15.	III.	Hannah[7], b. ——— ; m. Jan. 3, 1812, Consider Curtis of Hanover, Mass.
16.	‡IV.	Sylvanus[7], b. Feb. 20, 1783, m. Priscilla Sturtevant.
17.	V.	Wheelock[7], b. ———, 1787, d. July 8, 1854, aged 67 y. 21 d.
18.	VI.	Joanna[7], b. ——— ; m. April 27, 1809, Abiel White and had. Thomas F.[8], b. July 29, 1810; Frederick[8], b. Aug. 5, 1812; Lucy[8], b. Nov. 28, 1813; Cyrus[8], b. Sept. 6, 1814, and Albert[8], b. Jan. 29, 1816.

SEVENTH GENERATION.

5. JOHN[7] FULLER, (*Ephraim[6], John[5], John[4], John[3], Samuel[2], Samuel[1]*), b. May 3, 1774, in Halifax, Mass., d. there Nov. 26, 1857, aged 83 y. 6 m. 23 d.; m. May 16, 1811, Hannah Cooper of Plympton, who d. Nov. 19, 1868, aged 82 y. 11 m. 24 d.

Children :

| 19. | ‡I. | Ephraim[8], b. ———, 1813; m. Rebecca Fuller. |

20. II. John[8], b. ——, 1819, d. Sept. 13, 1891;
          unmarried.
21. ‡III. James D[8], b ——, 1822, m. Dorcas Soule.

9. EPHRAIM[7] FULLFR, (*Ephraim*[6], *John*[5], *John*[4], *John*[3],
Samuel[2], *Samuel*[1]), b. May 4, 1780, in Halifax, Mass.; d. Aug. 10,
1847, in Plympton, Mass. (Plympton Records); m. Aug. 29, 1808,
Zerviah Chandler of Plympton (Halifax Records), who d. March 30,
1872, in Plympton, aged 80 y. 5 m 22 d. (Plympton Rec.)
    Children, recorded in Plympton :
22. I. Zerviah Thompson[8], b. Feb. 28, 1809, d. May 5,
          1874; m. May 25, 1828, Ira May, b. April 15,
          1807, d. Jan. 8, 1900. Children: Bradford
          Richmond[9], b. Sept. 1, 1829; Rozilla Ellen[9], b.
          March 18, 1836, and Ira William[9], b. March 21,
          1843.
23. II. Clara[8], b. Dec. 19, 1810, d Jan. 13, 1840.
24. ‡III. Solomon[8], b. Nov. 13, 1812, m. 1, Mary Soule;
          m. 2, Catherine Gibbs.
25. IV. Hannah[8], b. April 26, 1815; d. Oct. 14, 1868; m.
          Feb. 1, 1834, George W. May, b. Feb. 1, 1813,
          d Jan. 6, 1883; daughter, Clara F.[9], was b.
          March 1, 1841.
26. ‡V. Ephraim[8], b. Dec. 18, 1817, m. Mary B. Nye.
27. ‡VI. Zebedee Chandler[8], b. July 22, 1821; m. Mary
          Martin Perkins.
28. VII. Earl[8], b. Oct. 1, 1823, d. Jan. 28, 1900;
          unmarried.
29. ‡VIII. Marcus[8], b. Oct. 30, 1826, m. June 4, 1850,
          Deborah C. Sherman.
30. IX. Eliza Chandler[8], b. Dec. 5, 1830; d. Nov. 14,
          1893; m. Martin Smith. They had no children.

13. THOMAS[7] FULLER, (*Thomas*[6], *John*[5], *John*[4], *John*[3], *Samuel*[2],
Samuel[1]), b. Aug. 6, 1778, in Halifax, Mass.; d. there Oct. 15,
1845; m. Nov. 11, 1811, Sally Sturtevant, b. May 25, 1793, d. Dec.
23, 1845.
    Children :
31. I. Thomas[8], b. Dec. 3, 1812; d. Feb. 7, 1821.
32. ‡II. Hiram[8], b. Sept. 6, 1814; m. Emily Louise
          Delaplaine.
33. III. Darius[8], b. May 5, 1816; d. Feb. 6, 1821.
3₁ IV. Sophronia[8], b. April 21, 1818; d. Feb. 4, 1821.

35.   ‡V.   Elbridge Gerry⁸, b. May 12, 1821, m. Mary
              Phillips Fish.
36.   VI.   Miranda⁸, b. June 15, 1823; d. May 24, 1847.
37.   ‡VII. Orlando⁸, (name changed to Richard Henry⁸), b.
              Aug. 13, 1825.
38.   VIII. Sarah Thomas⁸, b. Feb. 9, 1831; resides N. Y.
              City.

    14.   CYRUS⁷ FULLER, (*Thomas⁶, John⁵, John⁴, John³, Samuel²,
Samuel¹*), b. Aug. 22, 1780, in Halifax, Mass.; d. Feb. 23, 1816,
aged 35 years, m. May 24, 1807, Hannah Leonard, who d. March
26, 1862.
    Children:
39.   I.   Abigail⁸, b. ——, 1807; d. Dec. 16, 1865, aged
                 58 y. 9 m 29 d.
40.   ‡II.   Cyrus⁸, b. ——, 1813, m. Mary F. Thompson.
41.   ‡III.   Josiah Kingman⁸, b. Oct. 7, 1815; m. Sarah K.
                 Blanchard.

    16.   SYLVANUS⁷ FULLER, (*Thomas⁶, John⁵, John⁴, John³,
Samuel², Samuel¹*), b. Feb. 20, 1783, d. Nov. 10, 1851, aged 68 y.
8 m. 21 d, in Halifax, Mass., m. March 27, 1811, Priscilla
Sturtevant, who d July 16, 1860, aged 74 y. 5 d.
    Children, all b. in Halifax:
42.   ‡I.   Sylvanus Ripley⁸, b. May 15, 1813.
43.   II.   George⁸, b. Feb 2, 1815 *
44   ‡III. Charles⁸, b Nov. 16, 1816; m Susan A. Pope.
45.   IV.   Hannah⁸, b Dec. 14, 1818; d. Sept. 25, 1843.
46   V.   Joshua Thomas⁸, b. Nov. 23, 1820; d. Oct. 25,
              1842.
47.   VI.   Lydia⁸, b March 22, 1824; m. Charles
              McCammon of Albany, N. Y.
48.   ‡VII. Francis⁸, b. March 23, 1826; m. Patience Bryant.

EIGHTH GENERATION.

    19.   EPHRAIM⁸ FULLER, (*John⁷, Ephraim⁶, John⁵, John⁴, John³,
Samuel², Samuel¹*), b. ——, 1813, in Halifax, Mass.; d. there
Dec. 11, 1843, aged 30 years; m. Int Pub. April 2, 1836, with
Rebecca⁸ Fuller (*Ebenezer⁷, Chipman⁶, Ebenezer⁵, Ebenezer⁴,
John³, Samuel², Samuel¹*).

——————
    * The m Int of a George Fuller of Middleboro and Lucy Ann Harrington were
published in Middleboro April 8, 1851.

Children:

49. I. William Harwood[9], b July 11, 1842, d. June 27, 1862.

21. JAMES D.[8] FULLER, (*John[7], Ephraim[6], John[5], John[4], John[3], Samuel[2], Samuel[1]*), b 1822, d. June 13, 1864, in Halifax, Mass.; m. 1, April 8, 1849, Dorcas Soule, who d. April 16, 1850; m. 2, ———, Betsey ·——· .

Children.

50. ‡I. James Thomas[9], b. March 28, 1850; m. Gustava O. Swenson.

51. II John E[9], b April 3, 1862 Resides in Mansfield, Mass.

24. SOLOMON[8] FULLER, (*Ephraim[7], Ephraim[6], John[5], John[4], John[3], Samuel[2], Samuel[1]*), b. Nov. 13, 1812, in Plympton, Mass.; d. there Aug. 22, 1896, m. 1, May 9, 1841, Mary Soule, who d. March 15, 1850; m 2, Catherine Gibbs, who d. May 18, 1887.

Children, recorded in Plympton .

52. I. Elizabeth[9], b. Sept 18, 1842, m. June 26, 1870, George W. Randall

53 II. Susan Frances[9], b. June 26, 1846

54. III. Henry Solomon[9], b Dec. 10, 1849; d. Oct. 8, 1851.

55. IV. Lauretta Gibbs[9], b. Jan 10, 1853; m. Dec. 27, 1874, George S Sylvester

56. V. Henry Allen[9], b Aug. 27, 1855.

57. VI. Ella F.[9], b. ——— ; m. Dec. 30, 1883, Walter F. Nesmith.

26. EPHRAIM[8] FULLER, (*Ephraim[7], Ephraim[6], John[5], John[4], John[3], Samuel[2], Samuel[1]*), b Dec. 18, 1817, in Plympton, Mass.; d. there Sept. 29, 1897; m. April 10, 1842, Mary B Nye, who d. Dec. 20, 1906, aged 82 y. 1 m. 9 d.

Children:

58. I Elvira Lincoln[9], b. May 1, 1844: d. Aug. 9, 1844.

59. II. Mary Ellen[9], b. July 1, 1846, m. Nov. 20, 1872, Charles W. Humphrey.

60. III. George Frederick[9], b Sept. 15, 1849; d. Jan. 3, 1887.

61. IV. Ephraim[9], b March 16, 1858; m. Nov. 26, 1885, Lucy F. Godfrey, b. in Taunton, Mass.

62. V. Martha S.[9], b. Jan. 8, 1861; m. Nov. 27, 1884, James W. Hunt.

63. VI. John[9], b. ——— , m. July 2, 1901, Mary A. Reed.

27. ZEBEDEE CHANDLER[5] FULLER, (*Ephraim*[7], *Ephraim*[6], *John*[5], *John*[4], *John*[3], *Samuel*[2], *Samuel*[1]), b. July 22, 1821, in Plympton, Mass , d. there Oct 31, 1875 , m. Sept. 22, 1844, Mary Martha Perkins, b. in Plympton, April 28, 1825, now (1910) living there.

He always resided in Plympton.

Their children were :

64.	I.	Clara L.[9], b Nov. 16, 1849 , resides in Plympton.
65.	II.	Mary Lillian[9], b Nov 7, 1857 ; d Feb 18, 1910 in Plympton.
66.	III.	Franklin Alton[9], b. June 6, 1861 ; resides in Plympton.
67.	‡IV.	Josiah Chandler[9], b. May 28, 1869 ; m. Ellen LaCroix Hull.

29. MARCUS[8] FULLER, (*Ephraim*[7], *Ephraim*[6], *John*[5], *John*[4], *John*[3], *Samuel*[2], *Samuel*[1]), b Oct 30, 1826, in Plympton, Mass., d. June 10, 1877 , m June 4, 1850, Deborah Cobb Sherman.

Their children were .

68.	I	Juliet Inez[9], b March 13, 1854 , d. Aug. 20, 1854.
69.	II	Ettie Frances[9], b. Oct. 30, 1858 , m. Jan. 3, 1883, John E. Herne Reside in Middleboro, Mass.
70.	III.	Alice Martin[9], b. Feb. 28, 1872.

32. HIRAM[8] FULLER, (*Thomas*[7], *Thomas*[6], *John*[5], *John*[4], *John*[3], *Samuel*[2], *Samuel*[1]), b Sept. 6, 1814, in Halifax, Mass.; d. 1880, in Paris, France , m Oct, 1844, Emilie Louise Delaplaine, dau. of John B. Delaplaine of New York.

Quoting from a publication of the Rhode Island Historical Society, a correspondent says . "In 1843 he joined N. P. Willis and George P. Morris in publishing the N. Y. Mirror and eventually became sole proprietor. He wrote for it a series of piquant society letters · "Belle Brittan on a Tour," "At Newport," "Here and There ," also published "The Groton Letters," 1845 ; " Sparks from a Locomotive," 1849 ; and "Glimpses of Home after Thirteen Years Abroad," 1875.

Espousing the cause of the Southern Confederacy, he went to London, Eng., and established "The Cosmopolitan," devoted to the advocacy of the Southern question. Later he removed to Paris, where he died. One night in 1883, after Mr. Fuller's death, the invalid wife disappeared from a steamboat on the Hudson River and the body never was found."

They had no children, but had an adopted daughter, who married, had several children, and resides in New York City.

35. ELBRIDGE GERRY[8] FULLER, (*Thomas[7], Thomas[6], John[5], John[4], John[3], Samuel[2], Samuel[1]*), b. May 12, 1821, in Halifax, Mass.; d. Oct. 18, 1887, in Pembroke, Mass ; m. Nov. 24, 1844, Mary Phillips Fish of Pembroke, who d May 9, 1908, at Newton Centre, aged 83.

Children :

71. ‡I. Thomas G [9], b. Nov. 12, 1845 ; m. 1, Etta P. Cook ; m. 2, Mary E. Briggs; m. 3, Mary E Wheeler.

72. II. Mary Frances[9], b Dec. 27, 1847, d. March 7, 1906 ; m. Oct. 6, 1864, John Foster and had : Edgar Martin[10], b. March 17, 1865, d. Oct. 1, 1868 , Elwyn Norwood[10], b. June 20, 1871, d. Dec , 1892.

73. III. Emma Louise[9], b. March 6, 1851 ; m. Nov. 24, 1870, H. Waldo Foster and had: Clifford Waldo[10], b. Sept. 30, 1874, d. June 10, 1892.

74. IV. Miranda W [9], b. March 3, 1857, in South Hanson, Mass., d. Aug. 25, 1875.

37. RICHARD HENRY[8] FULLER, (*Thomas[7], Thomas[6], John[5], John[4], John[3], Samuel[2], Samuel[1]*), b Aug. 13, 1825 , d. Aug 16, 1896, at Halifax, Mass., m. May 15, 1859, Frances Williams Bonney, who d. Jan. 25, 1872

Children :

75. I. Edwin Francis, ⎫ twins ⎰ b. April 1, 1861 ; living in
76. II. Edgar Allen, ⎬   ⎱ Brockton ; unmarried.

40. CYRUS[8] FULLER, (*Cyrus[7], Thomas[6], John[5], John[4], John[3], Samuel[2], Samuel[1]*), b. ———, 1813 ; d. Feb. 22, 1892, in Middleboro, Mass , m. Nov. 28, 1841, Mary F Thompson of Middleboro.

Children, recorded in Halifax ·

77. I. A dau., b. Sept. 1, 1842.
78. II. A dau., b. Feb. 24, 1845.

41. JOSIAH KINGMAN[8] FULLER, (*Cyrus[7], Thomas[6], John[5], John[4], John[3], Samuel[2], Samuel[1]*), b. Oct. 7, 1815, in Halifax, Mass.; m. June 9, 1839, Sarah K. Blanchard.

Children :

79. I. Henrietta Arlington[9], b. ——— .

80.   ‡II.   Henry Eustis⁹, b. July 30, 1843; m. Lydia
                 Sylvester.
81.   III.   Sarah Emeline⁹, b. ———— .
82.   IV.   John Francis⁹, b ———— .
83.   V.   Elizabeth Florence⁹, b. ———— .

42. SYLVANUS RIPLEY⁸ FULLER, (*Sylvanus⁷, Thomas⁶, John⁵,
John⁴, John³, Samuel², Samuel¹), b May 15, 1813, in Halifax,
Mass ; d. Feb. 17, 1876 (Plymouth Rec.) ; m 1, March 26, 1844,
in Halifax, Sarah S Barden of Middleboro, Mass, who d. May 5,
1845 , m. 2, April 23, 1848, Julia R. Barden, who d. Oct. 28, 1854 ,
m. 3, June 21, 1863, Maria Porter Thompson, who d. July 2, 1886.
    Children .
84.   I.   Sarah Barden⁹, b March 1, 1845, m Nov. 18,
                 1869. Joseph C. Holmes
85.   ‡II   George E.⁹, b Sept. 26, 1852 , m. 1, Marion P.
                 ———— : m. 2, Mary E. Chase.
86.   III.   Charlotte M⁹, b. Sept. 24, 1865 ; m Dec. 27, 1892,
                 Irvin W. Davis.
87.   IV.   Anne L⁹, b. Nov. 29, 1867, m. June 5, 1895,
                 Wallace E. Reed.
88.   V.   Charles F.⁹, b. March 8, 1870, in Plymouth, Mass.

44. CHARLES⁸ FULLER, (*Sylvanus⁷, Thomas⁶, John⁵, John⁴,
John³, Samuel², Samuel¹), b. Nov. 16, 1816, in Halifax, Mass.; d.
there March 10, 1863 , in 1, Dec 21, 1851, Susan A Pope, who d.
Oct. 5, 1857 ; m. 2, Ella M. ————, b in Damariscotta, Me.
    Children .
89.   I.   Augusta⁹, b Nov. 30, 1852, in Halifax, Mass.
90.   II.   Susan A⁹, b. Sept. 26, 1857, in Kingston, Mass.,
                 d. April 15, 1858.
91.   III.   Ella Margaret⁹, b. Jan. 22, 1863, in Kingston.

48. FRANCIS⁸ FULLER, (*Sylvanus⁷, Thomas⁶, John⁵, John⁴,
John³, Samuel², Samuel¹), b. March 23, 1826, in Halifax, Mass.;
d. Sept. 1, 1886; m. Int. Pub. April 23, 1852, with Patience S.
Bryant of Kingston, Mass., who d. there July 26, 1895, aged 64 y.
4 m. 21 d.
    Children :
92.   I.   Edgar Frank⁹, b July 1, 1853, in Kingston ; d. Oct.
                 16, 1853, in Halifax.
93.   II.   Ida May⁹, b. 1854 , d. Aug. 26, 1877. (Kingston
                 G. S. Rec.)

NINTH GENERATION.

50. JAMES THOMAS[9] FULLER, (*James D.[8], John[7], Ephraim[6], John[5], John[4], John[3], Samuel[2], Samuel[1]*), b March 28, 1850, in Halifax, Mass , m Nov. 8, 1883, Gustava O Swenson, b. in Sweden. Resides in Bryantville, Mass.

Children:

94. I. James Oscar[10], b. Sept. 12, 1884, in Brockton, Mass ; d. Sept 27, 1908, in Pembroke, Mass.
95. II. John Davis[9], b. July 12, 1887.
96. III. Charles A. F.[9], b. Nov. 1, 1896.

67. JOSIAH CHANDLER[9] FULLER, (*Zebedee C.[8], Ephraim[7], Ephraim[6], John[5], John[4], John[3], Samuel[2], Samuel[1]*), b. May 28, 1869, in Plympton, Mass.; m. Aug. 6, 1895, Ellen LaCroix Hull, b. May 26, 1869.

He resides at Atlantic, Mass.

Children:

97. I. Bertha LaCroix[10], b. May 13, 1896

71. THOMAS GILMAN[9] FULLER, (*Elbridge G.[8], Thomas[7], Thomas[6], John[5], John[4], John[3], Samuel[2], Samuel[1]*), b. Nov. 12, 1845, in Halifax, Mass., m. 1, May 9, 1864, Etta P. Cook; divorced 1871, m. 2, 1872, Mary E. Briggs; divorced 1906; m. 3, Mary B Wheeler

Mr. Fuller is a builder residing at Newton Center, Mass.

Children by second wife:

98. I. Grace Gilman[10], b. Oct. 16, 1873; d. Oct. 18, 1877.
99. II. Nettie Miller[10], b. March 1, 1875, d. June, 1875.
100. III. George Edward[10], b. Aug. 27, 1876, living at South Hanson.
101. ‡IV. Frederick Gilman[10], b. Nov. 30, 1878; m. Cassie Stevenson.
102. V. Mary Louise[10], b Jan. 7, 1880; m. Feb. 2, 1907, Charles Simmons. No children. Reside at South Hanson.
103. VI. Blanche[10], b. July 6, 1883; m Oct. 7, 1903, Merlin M. Foster and has: Dorris Louise[11], b. Jan. 13, 1904; Ernestine Francis[11], b. March 12, 1907, and Presley Eugene[11], b. July 4, 1908. Resides at Bridgewater, Mass.

104.   VII.   Herbert Thomas[10], b. Aug. 7, 1886; m. Dec. 9, 1908, Lillie Provost.   Resides at Newton Center.
105.   VIII.   Frank[10], b. June 14, 1888, d. Sept. 18, 1888.

80. HENRY EUSTIS[9] FULLER, (*Josiah K.[8], Cyrus[7], Thomas[6], John[5], John[4], John[3], Samuel[2], Samuel[1]*), b. July 30, 1843, in East Abington (now Rockland), Mass., m. Dec. 1, 1867, Lydia Sylvester of Hanover, Mass.

He resides at Rockland, Mass.

Children :

106.   I.   Frederic Henry[10], b. March 19, 1871; m. Sept. 28, 1904, Florence M. Look of Farmington, Me.
107.   II.   Mabel Sylvester[10], b. May 3, 1875, m. Oct. 3, 1903, Charles B. Perry of Holyoke, Mass.

85. GEORGE E.[9] FULLER, (*Sylvanus R.[8], Sylvanus[7], Thomas[6], John[5], John[4], John[3], Samuel[2], Samuel[1]*), b. Sept. 26, 1852, in Halifax, Mass.; m. 1, Marion P. ——— ; m. 2, Nov. 11, 1886, Mary E. Chase, b. Fall River, Mass.

Children ·

108.   I.   Edwin P.[10], b. Sept. 26, 1876.

TENTH GENERATION.

101. FREDERICK GILMAN[10] FULLER, (*Thomas G.[9], Elbridge G.[8], Thomas[7], Thomas[6], John[5], John[4], John[3], Samuel[2], Samuel[1]*), b. Nov. 30, 1878; m. May 20, 1900, Cassie Stevenson.   They reside at Newton Center, Mass.

Their children are :

109.   I.   Frederic Thomas[11], b. Aug. 6, 1901.
110.   II.   Edwin Herbert[11], b March 17, 1903.
111.   III.   Walter Elbridge[11], b. Aug. 15, 1905.
112.   IV.   Margaret Elizabeth[11], b. Oct. 2, 1906.
113.   V.   Lawrence Gilman[11], b. Dec. 29, 1907.

NINCH GROUP.

FOURTH GENERATION.

EBENEZER⁴ FULLER, (*John³*), AND SOME OF HIS DESCENDANTS.

26. EBENEZER⁴ FULLFR, (*John³, Samuel², Samuel¹*), b. Nov. 1, 1697, probably in Halifax, Mass; d. there "November ye 12th 1794. His age was 97 years and 12 days old when he Died" (Halifax Records), m. ——, 1715, Elizabeth Short.
Children, recorded at Middleboro, Mass. ·

1.	I.	Susannah⁵, b Dec. 7, 1716; m. —— Murdock.
2.	II.	Ruth⁵, b. April 18, 1719; d. Jan. 24, 1743; m. Nov. 5, 1741, Joseph Bosworth and had James⁶, b. Jan. 16, 1743.
3.	‡III.	Ebenezer⁵, b. Oct. 18, 1721; m. 1, Lydia Chipman; m 2, Deborah (Fuller) Eaton.
4.	‡IV.	Nathan⁵, b. April 22, 1725; m Mary Parlow.
5.	V.	Elizabeth⁵, b. Aug. 5, 1729; m. John Thompson, both of Halifax.
6.	VI.	Noah⁵, b. Sept. 7, 1732; d. April 22, 1749, in his 17th year. (Charles M. Thatcher's cemetery inscriptions.) (Brainard's MSS. says d. July 4, 1776, by "bursting of a cannon.")
7.	VII.	Lois⁵, b. July 22, 1740. (Halifax Vital Records.)

FIFTH GENERATION.

3. EBENEZER⁵ FULLFR, (*Ebenezer⁴, John³, Samuel², Samuel¹*), b. Oct. 18, 1721 (Middleboro Records); d. Dec. 22, 1769, in his 49th year (C. M. Thatcher); m. 1, Jan. 6, 1746, Lydia Chipman; m. 2, April 7, 1768, Mrs. Deborah (Fuller) Eaton, probably the daughter of Jabez[1] Fuller, (*John*[3], *Samuel*[2], *Samuel*[1]). She was b. Nov. 23, 1727, at Plympton, Mass. The Kingston Burial Ground Records (Vol 7 Mayflower Descendants) gives the date of death of Deborah Fuller, widow of Ebenezer, formerly wife of David Eaton, as July 25, 1809, aged 81 years.

Children, b. in Halifax (Brainard's MSS) :

8.	I.	Lydia[6], b. 1747 ; d unmarried
9.	II.	Priscilla[6], b. 1749 , m. Ezekiel Ripley.
10.	III.	Eunice[6], b. 1753 ; m. Joel Perkins; removed to Pittsfield, Mass.
11.	‡IV.	Chipman[6], b. 1755 ; m. Thankful Wright.
12.	V	Ruth[6], b 1751 , m. July 10, 1771, Elijah Leach Jr. and had . Ebenezer[7], b. Dec. 11, 1772 , Lucy[7], b. Jan 31, 1775, and Lois[7], b May 10, 1777.
13.	VI.	Ichabod[6], b ———. (Chipman's MSS. says Ichabod died young)

4. NATHAN[5] FULLER, (*Ebenezer*[4], *John*[3], *Samuel*[2], *Samuel*[1]), b. April 22, 1725 (Middleboro Record) , date of death not found , m. Sept. 19, 1749, Mary Purlow at Middleboro , published June 3, 1749, in Halifax, Mass , as Mary Parlour (Halifax Vital Records).

He resided at Halifax.

His children, according to Davis ("Ancient Landmarks of Plymouth)", were .

14.	I.	Noah[6], b. ——— .
15.	II.	Chipman[6], b. ———
16.	III.	Hannah[6], b. ——— .
17.	IV.	Asenath[6], b. ——— ; m. John Kelman of Pittsfield, Mass.
18.	V.	Thomas[6], b. ——— .
19.	VI.	Susanna[6], b. ——— , m. Oct. 21, 1779, William Wood of Middleboro, and removed to Pittsfield, Mass.

SIXTH GENERATION.

11. CHIPMAN[6] FULLER, (*Ebenezer*[5], *Ebenezer*[4], *John*[3], *Samuel*[2], *Samuel*[1],) b. 1755, in Halifax, Mass. , date of death not found ; m. Dec. 9, 1779, Thankful Wright of Plympton, Mass.

He resided in Halifax.

Children, recorded in Halifax :

| 20. | I | Ruth[7], b. Oct. 23, 1780 ; m. Nov. 14, 1805, Isaac Soule of Middleboro, Mass. |

21. ‡II. Ebenezer⁷, b. Nov. 26, 1782 ; m. 1, Rebecca Fuller ;
m. 2, Abigail Sampson.
22. ‡III. Nathan⁷, b. Feb. 23, 1785 ; m. Faith Soule.
23. IV. Priscilla⁷, b. Nov. 29, 1787 ; m. Oct. 22, 1808,
Noah Bosworth
24. V. Nancy⁷, b. June 25, 1795.

By U. S. census 1790 there were 8 persons in Chipman Fuller's
family.

SEVENTH GENERATION.

21. EBENEZER⁷ FULLER, (*Chipman⁶, Ebenezer⁵, Ebenezer⁴,
John³, Samuel², Samuel¹*), b. Nov. 26, 1782, in Halifax, Mass.; d.
there Feb. 20, 1844, m. 1, March 30, 1809, Rebecca⁷ Fuller,
(*Ephraim⁶, John⁵, John⁴, John³, Samuel², Samuel¹*) ; m. 2, Dec. 4,
1817, Abigail Sampson of Plympton, Mass., who d. March 1, 1859.
Children :
25. I. Zerviah Nelson⁸, b. July 3, 1811 ; m. July 1, 1833,
Calvin Gammon of Rochester, Mass.
26. II. Rebecca⁸, b ———, 1819 ; m Int. Pub April 2,
1836, with Ephraim⁸ Fuller, (*John⁷, Ephraim⁶,
John⁵, John⁴, John³, Samuel², Samuel¹*).
27. ‡III Ebenezer⁸, b Sept 18, 1821 ; m. May 22, 1842, in
Middleboro, Mass., Mary Ann Colwell.

22. NATHAN⁷ FULLER, (*Chipman⁶, Ebenezer⁵, Ebenezer⁴, John³,
Samuel², Samuel¹*), b. Feb. 23, 1785, in Halifax, Mass.; d. there
Jan. 7, 1875 , m. April 23, 1809, Faith Soule, who d. Nov. 11, 1864.
Children, born in Halifax :
28. ‡I. Chipman⁸, b. March 22, 1810 ; m. Hannah Fuller.
29. ‡II. Nathan⁸, b. Dec. 21, 1813 , m. Sarah Fuller.
30. ‡III Alfred⁸, b. April 21, 1817 , m. Int. Pub. April 8,
1837, with Mary P. Mitchell.

EIGHTH GENERATION.

27. EBENEZER⁸ FULLER, (*Ebenezer⁷, Chipman⁶, Ebenezer⁵,
Ebenezer⁴, John³, Samuel², Samuel¹*), b. Sept. 18, 1821 ; d. 1910,
in Brockton, Mass. , m. May 22, 1842, in Middleboro, Mass., Mary
Ann Colwell.
Children, born in Halifax, Mass. :
31. I. Nelson Haywood⁹, b. Aug. 14, 1843 ; m. Sept. 3,
1866, Sarah E. Lucas.

32.   II.   Frederick[9], b. Aug. 30, 1845, d. Dec. 1, 1862, in
              Halifax.
33.   III.   Charlotte[9], Nov. 3, 1849; m. and resides in
              Brockton, Mass.
34.   IV.   Frank[9], b. ———— .
35.   V.   Elbertice[9], b. ———— .

28. CHIPMAN[5] FULLER, (*Nathan[7], Chipman[6], Ebenezer[5],
Ebenezer[4], John[3], Samuel[2], Samuel[1]*), b. March 22, 1810, in
Halifax, Mass.; d. Nov. 27, 1896; m. 1, April 1, 1836, Hannah
Fuller, who d. Oct. 16, 1874; m. 2, Dec. 16, 1877, Hannah M.
(Weston) Washburn, who d. March 2, 1889.
      Children, born in Halifax

36.   I.   Granville C.[9], b. ————, 1842, d. July 6, 1893;
              m. April 30, 1874, Adaline M. Westgate, who d.
              July 11, 1887.
37.   II.   Ephraim[9], b. July 4, 1847; d. Sept. 12, 1847.

29. NATHAN[5] FULLER, (*Nathan[7], Chipman[6], Ebenezer[5],
Ebenezer[4], John[3], Samuel[2], Samuel[1]*), b. Dec. 21, 1813, in Halifax,
Mass.; d. there May 5, 1886; m. Dec. 18, 1842, Sarah S.[8] Fuller
(*Consider[7], John[6], Issachar[5], John[4], Samuel[3], Samuel[2], Samuel[1]*),
who d. Dec. 20, 1898.
      Children, born in Halifax :

38.   I.   Emily French[9], b. Dec. 21, 1843, m. Nov. 25,
              1865, Silas Pratt, 1st wife.
39.   II.   Laverta N.[9], b. March 8, 1846; m. Nov. 6, 1873,
              Silas Pratt, 2d wife.
40.   ‡III.   Edmund Herbert[9], b. June 13, 1848; m. Almeda
              Freeman.

30. ALFRED[8] FULLER, (*Nathan[7], Chipman[6], Ebenezer[5],
Ebenezer[4], John[3], Samuel[2], Samuel[1]*), b April 21, 1817, in Halifax,
Mass.; m. April 16, 1837, Mary P. Mitchell, who d. May 30, 1886.
      Children :

41.   I.   Nancy[9], b. ————, 1838; m. Aug. 11, 1859, Wm.
              H Bosworth.
42.   II.   Jane[9], b. ————, 1840, m. May 3, 1857, Sylvanus
              Pratt.
43.   III.   Mary[9], b. ————, 1845; m. Sept. 7, 1878, Wm. W.
              Atwood.
44.   IV.   Elizabeth[9], b. ————, 1850; d. Aug. 26, 1868.

NINTH GENERATION.

40. EDMUND HERBERT[9] FULLER, (*Nathan*[8], *Nathan*[7], *Chipman*[6], *Ebenezer*[5], *Ebenezer*[4], *John*[3], *Samuel*[2], *Samuel*[1]), b. June 13, 1848, in Halifax, Mass.; m. March 30, 1877, Almeda Freeman. (Pembroke Rec.)

Children :

45.   I. Chester Freeman[10], b. Sept. 11, 1881.

46.   II. Andrew Burton[10], b. Dec. 26, 1882; d. Dec. 6, 1884.

TENTH GROUP.

FOURTH GENERATION.

JABEZ⁴ FULLER, (*John³*), AND SOME OF HIS DESCENDANTS.

27. JABEZ⁴ FULLER, (*John³, Samuel², Samuel¹*), b. ———,
1698. d. Oct. 14, 1728, in Plympton, Mass., m. Jan. 12, 1726/7,
Priscilla Sampson (Plympton Records). Records at Plymouth,
Mass., show that Jabez Fuller, who married Priscilla, died intestate,
and that his brother, Ebenezer Fuller, was appointed administrator
April 13, 1729.

Children :

<table>
<tr><td>1.</td><td>I.</td><td>Deborah5, b. Nov. 23, 1727, at Plympton. Perhaps this is the Deborah Fuller who m. Nov 25, 1743, David Eaton, "both of Kingston," and m. 2, April 7, 1768, her cousin, Ebenezer5 Fuller, (*Ebenezer4, John3, Samuel2, Samuel1*), and died July 25, 1809, aged 81. The Eaton children were : Lot6, b. May 18, 1744 ; Jabez6, b. Aug. 2, 1746, Job6, b. Oct. 26, 1749 ; Consider6, b. March 1, 1752 ; Joshua6, b. July 12, 1755, and Eunice6, b. April 12, 1759.</td></tr>
</table>

ELEVENTH GROUP.

FOURTH GENERATION.

SAMUEL[4] FULLER, (*John*[1]) AND SOME OF HIS DESCENDANTS.

29. SAMUEL[4] FULLER, (*John*[3], *Samuel*[2], *Samuel*[1]), b. ———, 1704, in Halifax or Middleboro; (date and place of death not learned) ; m. Nov. 14, 1726, Silence Short.

Resided in Bridgewater, Mass.

Children :

1.	I.	Sarah[5], b. ———, 1730; d. Nov., 1794, aged 64; m. 1751, Samuel Pratt. (Pratt Genealogy and F. A. Fuller's MSS)
2.	‡II.	Samuel[5], b. ———, m. Deborah ———.
3.	III.	Mercy[5], b. Feb. 3, 1737.
4.	‡IV.	William[5], b March 16, 1739, m. Deborah Rider.
5.	V.	Simeon[5], b. Sept. 13, 1741, m. Int. Pub. Oct. 6, 1764, with Anna Blackmer. (C. M. Thatcher.)

FIFTH GENERATION.

2. SAMUEL[5] FULLER, (*Samuel*[4], *John*[3], *Samuel*[2], *Samuel*[1]), b. ———; d. ———, m. ———, Deborah ———.

Children :

6.	I.	Jabez[6], b. 1764, d. 1788.
7.	II.	William[6], b. 1769; m. 1801, Tabitha Benson of Plymouth, Mass.
8.	III.	Silence[6], b. 1770; m. 1792, Samuel Hardin.
9.	IV.	Versalla[6], b. ———. (Brainard's MSS.)

4. WILLIAM[5] FULLER, (*Samuel*[4], *John*[3], *Samuel*[2], *Samuel*[1]), b. March 16, 1739, in Bridgewater, Mass.; d. ———; m. Jan. 14, 1762, Deborah Rider.

Children :

10.	I.	Samuel[6], b. Oct. 27, 1762. (Charles M. Thatcher.)

TWELFTH GROUP.

FOURTH GENERATION.

ISAAC⁴ FULLER AND SOME OF HIS DESCENDANTS.

32. ISAAC⁴ FULLER, (*Isaac³, Samuel², Samuel¹*), b. Sept. 24, 1712, at Halifax, Mass., m ———, 1737, Sarah Packard and settled in North Bridgewater, Mass., about 1736.

Isaac Fuller was described by Lemuel⁶, (Isaac⁵, Isaac⁴), as "a tall slender man with light complexion and blue eyes, and his wife as a short black-eyed woman Isaac owned a good farm and had a good stock of cattle, he died aged between 70 and 80; his parents were people of property." (Linus E. Fuller.) Isaac and son Benjamin removed to Winchester, N. H, after 1777.

Children, b. at North Bridgewater:

1.	‡I.	Isaac ⁵, b. Dec. 5, 1738, m Mary Alden.
2.	II.	Olive⁵, b Oct 14, 1740; m. Oct. 21, 1765, Daniel Edson.
3.	III.	Lemuel⁵, b. Sept. 29, 1742; d. May 20, 1762, in the army.
4.	‡IV.	Isaiah⁵, b July 7, 1744, m Mary Keyser.
5.	V.	Sarah⁵, b March 22, 1746, m. Jan. 24, 1764/5, John Freelove.
6.	VI.	Susannah⁵, b. Nov. 27, 1748; m. April 12, 1770, Ashley Curtis.
7.	VII.	Lois ⁵, b Oct. 13, 1751, m. Nov. 12, 1772, Samuel Dike. (Lemuel⁶ says Louisa and husband Anthony Dike, describes her as a "medium sized woman with black eyes, light hair and complexion")
8.	‡VIII.	Benjamin⁵, b. Sept. 22, 1754, m. Sarah Ames.

9. IX. Reliance[5], b. Dec. 22, 1756, m. April 2, 1777,
Josiah Edson, described as a slender woman
with black eyes and hair, lived at Bridgewater.
Their children were: Zilpah[6], b. March 22,
1778, Susannah[6], b. March 3, 1780; Sarah[6], b.
Nov. 17, 1783, Barnabas[6], b. March 5, 1786;
Esther[6], b. July 2, 1788; Reliance[6], b. Feb. 9,
1792, and Olive[6], b. May 5, 1795.

FIFTH GENERATION.

1. ISAAC[5] FULLER, (*Isaac[4], Isaac[3], Samuel[2], Samuel[1]*), b. Dec.
15, 1738, in North Bridgewater, Mass.; d. Aug. 22, 1803, at Easton,
Mass.; m. Sept. 15, 1764, Mary Alden, b. Aug. 5, 1745, at Bridgewater, d. Sept. 10, 1818, at East Mansfield, dau. of Daniel and
Abigail (Shaw) Alden, and granddaughter of John Alden and
Priscilla. Mary described as being "short and fleshy with blue eyes
and dark hair."

"Isaac Fuller was a man six feet tall, spare but broad shouldered,
with dark complexion, dark eyes and hair. He served in the Indian
and French wars, was at the battle of Lak George; was at the
defeat suffered at Ticonderoga, served at Bunker Hill; was a
Corporal at the battle of Lexington, served at White Plains,
Monmouth, and at Germantown as Lieutenant, was also one of the
bodyguards to escort Washington to Mt. Vernon. He lived at
Bridgewater, Mass., and Kent, Ct. He died in Easton, Mass., at
what is known as the "Fuller place." He died out under the
apple trees, where he had begged to be taken to see the sun set
once more." (F. A. Fuller's MSS.)

Children:

10.   I. Polly[6], b. Oct. 15, 1766; d. at 12 years.
11. ‡II. Lemuel[6], b. May 12, 1768, m. Fanny Briggs.
12. ‡III. Isaac[6], b. Dec. 15, 1769; m. Anna Boggs
13. ‡IV. Barzillai[6], b. June 29, 1772; m. Betsey Tisdale.
14. ‡V. Alden[6], b Aug. 16, 1773, m. Abigail White.
15. ‡VI. Hosea[6], b. March 23, 1775, m. 1, Int. Pub. with
Lydia Crane; m. 2, Catherine Washburn; m. 3,
Mrs. Sarah Smith.
16.   VII. Eunice[6], b. May 23, 1778; d. ———; m. Oct. 24,
1805, Simeon Drake and had: Simeon Alden[7],
b. May 11, 1806; Horatio Nelson[7], b. Dec. 20,
1807; Eunice Fuller[7], b. Feb. 1, 1810; Clement
Briggs[7], b. June 29, 1812, m. Rinda May Fuller;

Charles Hewitt[7], b. Dec. 13, 1814, and Mary Ann W.[7], b. Dec. 3, 1818. (Drake Family Genealogy.)

17.   ‡VIII.   Alpheus[6], b. Dec. 3, 1779, m. 1, Amy Leverett; m. 2, Barbara Bostwick.

18.   ‡IX   Rufus[6], b. Nov. 27, 1781, m. 1, —— Fenn, m 2, Elizabeth Drake.

19   ‡X.   Otis[6], b. Sept. 29, 1785, m. 1, Minerva Curtis, m. 2, Laura Wiley.

4. ISAIAH[5] FULLER, (*Isaac[4], Isaac[3], Samuel[2], Samuel[1]*), b. July 7, 1744, in North Bridgewater, Mass., then a part of Duxbury, later a part of Bridgewater, and now known as Brockton, d. March 10, 1809, in Warwick, Mass, m Sept. 30, 1768, Mary Keyser, who d. Sept 2, 1831, in Warwick, aged 80 years.

In answer to inquiries concerning Isaiah's family, the Brockton City Clerk states that Jacob, born in 1776, is the only child of Isaiah's mentioned in Mitchell's or Kingman's Histories of Bridgewater and North Bridgewater, apparently assuming that these histories contain all the information the vital records of those towns contain regarding him The U. S. census for 1790 mentions Isaiah in Bridgewater with six persons in his family, and also in Warwick with the same number. The volumes of "Massachusetts Soldiers and Sailors of the Revolution" credit Isaiah Fuller of Bridgewater with service in the Revolutionary war. The "History of Warwick" mentions Isaiah Fuller in a list of house owners in Warwick in 1798. The vital records of the town of Warwick, according to the town clerk, contain no mention of Isaiah Fuller.

Mr. Linus E. Fuller (No. 116 of this Group) states that Isaiah Fuller was described by Lemuel[6] (No. 11 of this Group) to a nephew as a man of middle size with blue eyes and dark hair, and his wife as a beautiful woman of a very respectable Bridgewater family. Mr L. E Fuller has visited the Warwick and Winchester cemeteries, but thinks that Isaiah, Isaiah's widow, and Isaiah's father, Isaac, are buried in a small graveyard near the northeast corner of Warwick which he had not time to visit.

The children of Isaiah and Mary, according to descendants and others, were :

20.   I.   "John[6], the oldest, went to sea and was never heard from."?

21. ‡II Jacob⁶, b 1776, m. Abigail Leonard
22. III. A dau., b. ——, m. ——, probably removed West.
23. ‡IV. Henry⁶, b. 1780, m Hannah Cobb.
24. ‡V. Seth⁶, b. 1782; m. 1, ——, m. 2, Pruda Cutter.
25. VI. Samuel⁶, b. ——.
26. ‡VII. James⁶, b. 1793, m. Nancy Lesuie.

Information about John and date of birth of James came from Mr. Hoyt E. Fuller (No. 202 of this Group) ; that about Jacob from the Brainard MSS. and Brockton city clerk. The names of Henry, Seth, Samuel and James, and information in regard to their sister, from Mrs Augustus Fuller, widow of No. 99 of this Group, who thinks Seth and Samuel were in business together in Boston as bell-hange.s. Mr. H. D. Iearnard of Boston furnished date of death of Mary (Keyser) Fuller, and genealogical data regarding Seth, and the town clerk of Warwick the names, etc , of children of Henry and James.

8. BENJAMIN⁵ FULLER, (*Isaac⁴, Isaac³, Samuel², Samuel¹*), b. Sept. 22, 1754, in North Bridgewater, Mass.; d ——; m. Sept., 1777, Sarah Ames, who d. April 1, 1812, aged 58 years, dau. of Daniel Ames.

Benjamin Fuller removed after 1777 to Winchester, N. H. He has been described as a tall man with light hair and blue eyes, and it is said was possessed of a handsome property

His children were :

27. I. Daniel⁶, b. July 24, 1779 (also given July 1).
28. II. Lois⁶, b. Feb. 4, 1782 (also given Feb. 1) ; d. Oct. 26, 1863, aged 82 ; unmarried. (Gravestone Record.)
29. III. Phebe⁶, b. April 18, 1787 ; d. Nov. 13, 1837 ; m. 1804, Daniel Holman and had nine children.
30. IV. Mehitabel⁶, b. May 5, 1789 ; d June 12, 1836 ; unmarried.
31. V. Sally⁶, b. March 27, 1791 (also given Feb. 27) ; d. Nov. 2, 1838 ; m. —— Clark and removed to Ohio ; had seven children.
32. ‡VI. Benjamin⁶, b. Dec. 4, 1792 (also given Dec. 1) ; m. Dorothy Bliss.

SIXTH GENERATION.

11. LEMUEL[6] FULLER, (*Isaac[5], Isaac[4], Isaac[3], Samuel[2], Samuel[1]*), b. May 12, 1768, at Bridgewater, Mass.; d. Feb. 23, 1851, at Bennington Falls, Bennington, Vt., m. Feb. 4, 1796, at Norton, Mass., Fanny Briggs (Norton Vital Records), dau. of Stephen and Sarah (Pratt) Briggs, b at Norton, Oct. 17, 1766, d. Feb. 14, 1831, at Dalton, Mass. (Linus E. Fuller.)

Children :

33.   I.   Fanny[7], b. 1796, d. 1880, m 1820, Jarvis Glover. Removed to Springfield, Mass., about 1826. Children: Martha M.[8], Mary E.[8], Fanny M.[8], George H.[8], Samuel J.[8] and Frank W.[8]

34.   II.   Mary[7], b. June 7, 1798, in Easton, Mass , d Aug 15, 1876, m. May 19, 1824, Timothy Allen of Springfield, Mass., and had : Martha J.[8], and Sarah Frances[8].

35.   III.   Persis[7], b. March 11, 1800, in Dalton, Mass., d. Aug. 18, 1879, in Lee, Mass.; m. Sept. 3, 1819, William M. Black. Children : James[8], b. May 17, 1820, in Dalton , William M [8], b. Sept. 17, 1821, in Lee, Mass , Mary[8], b March 5, 1823 , Jane[8], b. Feb. 18, 1825 , John[8], b. March 4, 1829 , George Nelson[8], b. March 15, 1833; Julia Maria[8], b. June 10, 1834, and Alexander M [8], b. Feb. 22, 1836.

36.   IV.   Abigail Maria[7], b. Jan. 17, 1804, in Dalton, Mass , d. Aug. 24, 1875, in Geneva, Ill., m. in Lee, Mass, Gurdon J. Hollister and removed to Geneva 1846. Children, all born in Lee : Edward P.[8], b. March 25, 1828 , George L.[8], b. Aug. 3, 1829; Mary A.[8], b. Sept. 12, 1832 , James B.[8], b. July 4, 1837, and William J.[8], b. Aug. 6, 1840.

37.   ‡V.   Lemuel[7], b. Feb. 14, 1807 ; m. 1, Lucy Putnam ; m. 2, Sophronia Lyon , m. 3, Anna E. Potter.

38.   VI.   Caroline Elvira[7], b. Aug. 11, 1811 ; d. March 2, 1872, in Hartford, Ct.; m. Lewis Lamb of Springfield, Mass. Children . John Jerome[8] and Mary F.[8]

39   VII.   William Nelson[7], b. April 22, 1815 ; m. 1, Harriet N. Comstock , m. 2, Caroline L. Nelson.

12. ISAAC[6] FULLER, (*Isaac[5], Isaac[4], Isaac[3], Samuel[2], Samuel[1]*), b. Dec. 15, 1769, in Easton, Mass.; d. Feb. 26, 1841, in Warren, Me.; m. Anna Boggs.

They resided in Warren:

Their children were:

40.   I. Ephraim[7], b. Sept. 8, 1789, d. Feb. 26, 1862; unmarried.

41. ‡II. James[7], b. Jan. 10, 1791; m. Melinda Cummings.

42.   III. Mary[7], b. May 2, 1795; d Oct. 13, 1825; m. John Jameson and had. Isaac F.[5], b. Dec. 20, 1814, Gilbert[5], b. Aug. 10, 1816, Sarah Ann[5], b. Sept. 27, 1818, Rufus[5] b. April 18, 1820; Arthur[5], b. May 19, 1822, and George[5], b Aug. 26, 1824. Charles A. Jameson of Great Works, Me., is son of Arthur[5].

43.   IV. Susan[7], b. Sept. 29, 1797; d. June 10, 1874; m. Nov. 12, 1820, Ebenezer Blunt of Union, Me., and had: Henry[5], b. Sept. 4, 1821, Eliza[5], b. Nov. 5, 1822; Thomas J.[5], b. Oct. 22, 1824; Isaac[5], b. June 19, 1826; Arthur C.[5], b. April 4, 1828, Mary Ann[5], b. April 7, 1830, Martha[5], b. Aug. 13, 1832, Betsey[5], b. April 20, 1834; Sarah[8], b April 15, 1838, and Oscar[5], b. Aug. 25, 1842, living at Thomaston, Me.

44. ‡V. Given[7], b. Jan. 7, 1800; m. Widow Melinda (Cummings) Fuller.

45. ‡VI. Isaac[7], b. Feb. 22, 1803; m. 1, Avis Cummings; m. 2, Thankful Williams.

46. ‡VII. Prince Ford[7], b. April 5, 1807; m. Miriam B. Hart.

13. BARZILLAI[6] FULLER, (*Isaac[5], Isaac[4], Isaac[3], Samuel[2], Samuel[1]*), b. June 29, 1772, probably in Easton, Mass.; d. there March 24, 1845, aged 73 years; m. Nov. 11, 1792, Betsey Tisdale. Children, recorded at Easton:

47.   I. Barzillai[7], b. March 15, 1793; m. Dec. 29, 1819, Patience Beals.

48. ‡II. Tisdale[7], b. June 29, 1796; m. 1, Harriet Goward; m. 2, Betsey Snow.

49.   III. Betsey[7], b. May 11, 1798.

50.   IV. Ruth[7], b. March 20, 1800.

14. ALDEN[6] FULLER, (*Isaac[5], Isaac[4], Isaac[3], Samuel[2], Samuel[1]*), b. Aug. 16, 1773, in Easton, Mass.; d. Jan. 14, 1836;

probably the Alden Fuller who m. Sept. 17, 1795, Abigail Wnite,
"both of Mansfield, Mass."

Children :

51.	‡I.	Harrison⁷, b. March 24, 1810 ; m. Mary P. Morse.
52.	II.	Alden⁷, b. 1812 ; d. Sept. 16, 1891 ; m. Oct. 31, 1876. ——.
53.	III.	Harriet⁷, b. 1816, d. ——, 1840.
54.	IV.	Albert⁷, b 1820, d. June 20, 1843.

15. HOSIA⁶ FULLER, (*Isaac⁵, Isaac⁴, Isaac³, Samuel², Samuel¹*),
b. March 23, 1775, at Easton, Mass., d. May 10, 1866, at Water-
vliet (Shakers P. O , West Albany, N. Y.) , m. Int. Pub. July 1,
1810, with Lucia Crine (Hinsdale, Mass., Vital Records) , m. 2,
said to have married at Dalton, Mass., Mrs. Sarah Smith, who d. at
Cheshire, Mass, in 1824 , m 3, Aug. 17, 1834, Catherine Washburn
(Easton, Mass , Town Records).

Children :

55.	I.	Lucy⁷, b. Sept 15, 1813 ; d. at the Shakers April 16, 1875. She had been with the Shakers since she was a child and was much respected and beloved. She was at the head of the Society, and brought her father there to live about 1850.
56	II.	Eunice⁷, b. May 18, 1815 ; d. about 1834 or 1835, in Albany , was with the Shakers but left them and married in Albany, Truman Hibbard , had a son William, who resides in Ohio.
57.	‡III.	Waldo C.⁷, b. Aug. 5, 1817, m. 1, Henrietta Stocking , m. 2, Jane C. Hall.

17. ALPHEUS⁶ FULLER, (*Isaac⁵, Isaac⁴, Isaac³, Samuel²,
Samuel¹*), b Dec. 3, 1779, at Easton, Mass.; d. March 11, 1865, in
Kent, Ct.; m. April 16, 1807, Amy Turrill, b. July 26, 1784, at
Kent, d. there Nov. 14, 1815, dau. Abel and Jerusha (Peet)
Turrill, m. 2, Dec. 23, 1817, at New Milford, Ct., Barbara Bostwick,
b. there June 11, 1786, d. July 10, 1865, at Kent, dau. of Ichabod
Bostwick.

Children :

| 58. | I. | Jerome B.⁷, b. Jan. 26, 1808, m. Oct. 27, 1834, Lucy A. Pratt. |
| 59. | II. | Lucy⁷, b Dec. 21, 1809 ; d. March 17, 1900, at New Haven, Ct.; m. Abraham Swift, son of John H. Swift and Lydia⁶ Fuller (Abraham⁵, Joseph⁴, |

John[3], Samuel[2], Edward[1]) ; had dau. Josephine[5], who m. Clark B. Bryant.

60.   III. A dau., b Feb 10, 1812

61.   IV. Henry Ichabod[7], b March 26, 1822; d. July 7, 1851, at Hartford, Ct.

62.   V. Charles Isaac[7], b. Sept. 21, 1823, d. March 31, 1867.

18. RUFUS[6] FULLER, (*Isaac[5], Isaac[4], Isaac[3], Samuel[2], Samuel[1]*), b. Nov. 29, 1781, at Easton, Mass.; d Sept. 13, 1850, at Kent, Ct.; m. 1, March 2, 1806, Bede Fenn, b Jan. 10, 1786, at Plymouth, Ct., d. March 18, 1817, at Kent, m. 2, Feb 1, 1821, Elizabeth Drake, b. Dec. 27, 1792, at Easton, Mass, d March 23, 1876, at Kent.

Children :

63.   ‡I. Linus Fenn[7], b. Feb. 15, 1807 ; m. Catherine Sophia Whiteside.

64.   II. Julia Ann[7], b Sept. 1, 1808, at Red Hook, N. Y.; m. Nov. 8, 1827, Matthew Barnum. No issue.

65.   ‡III. Rufus[7], b. Nov. 13, 1810, m. ———.

66.   IV Eliza[7], b. Dec. 10, 1812 ; d. Dec. 14, 1816, at Plymouth, Ct.

67.   V. Bede Ann Eliza[7], b. Feb. 11, 1822, at Kent; d. there Dec. 10, 1897, m. Oct. 28, 1843, George Hopson and had · Morton[8], William[8], Mary[8], and two that died young.

19. OTIS[6] FULLER, (*Isaac[5], Isaac[4], Isaac[3], Samuel[2], Samuel[1]*), b. Sept. 29, 1785 (Brainard MSS), or Sept 13, 1785 (L. E. Fuller MSS), at Easton, Mass.; d Aug 31, 1862, at Naples, N. Y ; m. 1, May 7, 1809, at Hinsdale, Mass, Minerva Curtis, b. Dec. 30, 1790, at Cummington, Mass., d. Nov. 2, 1818, at Naples, m 2, Nov. 2, 1819, at Naples, Laura Wiley, b. Jan. 2, 1790, at Dalton, Mass., d. at Naples April 10, 1877, dau. of Robert Wiley.

Otis Fuller was a physician with an extensive practice. He was a critical student of English literature. He was kind and jovial in disposition and generous to the poor.

His children, born at Naples, were :

68.   I. Minerva[7], b Aug. 1, 1811 ; d July, 1877.

69.   II. Otis[7], b. 1815, d. July 22, 1815.

70.   III. Eliza Ann[7], b. March 17, 1817 ; d. Sept. 4, 1860, at Mondovi, Wis.; m. June 29, 1836, Elijah Warren and had : Augustus[8], b. Aug. 9, 1837 ; Otis F.[8], b. July 7, 1839 ; Mary Minerva[8], b. May

27, 1841; Ann Eliza[8], b. Oct. 29, 1843; Laura Augusta[8], b. Dec. 1, 1845, Martha Augusta[8], b. July 9, 1847, Jay[8], b. July 24, 1849; Elijah[8], b. Oct. 28, 1852; Eunice F[8], b. Nov. 15, 1854; Ann Josephine[8], b. July 6, 1857, and Ella[8], b. Sept. 4, 1860.

71.   ‡IV.   Lorenzo Dow[7], b. Aug. 15, 1820; m. Mary M. Cleveland.

72.   V.   Laura Sprague[7], b. April 14, 1822; d. March 6, 1904, m. 1, Aug. 8, 1853, Orrin W. Dowd, b. May 14, 1826, d. Jan. 21, 1857; no children; m 2, July 5, 1859, Charles S. Long, who d. in 1867. They had two children, a son and a dau., Cora, b. May 1, 1860, the son d May 2, 1860, and Cora d. Aug. 19, 1861. Laura S. m. 3, Henry White Curtis, Dec. 21, 1876, at Naples, N. Y., who was living in Hinsdale, Mass, in 1908.

73.   VI.   De Witt Clinton[7], b. Feb. 17, 1824; m. Augusta Wells in Michigan.

74.   VII.   Mary Alden[7], b. Oct. 13, 1826; d. April 19, 1829.

75.   ‡VIII.   Jerome Bonaparte[7], b. Jan. 8, 1829; m. Elizabeth Mercy Wells.

21. JACOB[6] FULLER, (*Isaiah[5], Isaac[4], Isaac[3], Samuel[2], Samuel[1]*), b. 1776, at Bridgewater, Mass.; d. ------; m. 1, ------, 1800, Abigail Leonard, who d. 1805, m. 2, Sept. 9, 1806, Hannah Orcutt, who d. 1828, m. 3, May 24, 1829, Mary Edson.

He resided at Campello, Mass.

His children were.

76.   I.   Betsey[7], b. April 16, 1801, m. 1824, Francis Packard.

77.   II.   Josiah[7], b. Sept 3, 1803; m. Almira Holbrook.

78.   III.   Nabby[7], b. May 9, 1807, m. Jan. 7, 1834, Joseph D. Corkins

79.   ‡IV.   Leonard Orcutt[7], b. Sept. 18, 1809, m. Susan Ann Thayer.

80.   V.   Mary Flagg[7], b April 14, 1814.

81.   VI.   Hannah[7], b. Sept. 28, 1820; d. 21 months of age.

23. HENRY[6] FULLER, (*Isaiah[5], Isaac[4], Isaac[3], Samuel[2], Samuel[1]*), b. 1780, probably in Warwick, Mass.; d. there April 29, 1835, m. Oct. 26, 1802, Hannah Cobb, both of Warwick; she d. May 9, 1849.

Children, b. in Warwick:

82.   I.   Esther[7], b. Jan 9, 1802 ; d. March 31, 1871 ;
                  unmarried
83.   II. Fanny[7], b. Feb 25, 1804, m. Jan. 15, 1826,
                  William Frye of Boston.
84.   III. Mary[7], b June 11, 1805 ; d. May 10, 1829.
85.   IV. Henry[7], b. April 9, 1807, d. Oct. 16, 1830.
- 86   V.   Hannah[7], b. Nov 4, 1808, d. May 11, 1831.
87.   VI. Harris[7], b. Jan. 28, 1810 ; d. Jan. 1, 1837.

Mrs. Augustus Fuller (Widow of No 99 of this group) mentions
another son, A. Baker Fuller, probably :

88.   ‡VII.   Artemas B.[7], of the Town Clerk's report, who m. 1,
                Ophelia P. Packard, and m. 2, Caroline W.
                Williams, all of Warwick.

24.   SETH[6] FULLER, (*Isaiah*[5], *Isaac*[4], *Isaac*[3], *Samuel*[2], *Samuel*[1]),
b. 1782, in Warwick?, Mass. ; d. Sept. 27, 1846, in Boston, Mass. ;
m. 1, ——— ; m. 2, Pruda Cutter of Sudbury, Mass., May 7, 1809.
     Children :

89.   I.   Adeline[7], b. ——— ; m. Robert Fletcher.
90.   II   Almira[7], b. ———, m. John L. Stodder.
91.   ‡III.   Joseph[7], b. ———, m Mary Hall.
92.   ‡IV.   Seth Wyman[7], b ———, m. Ann Dewitt Cross.
93.   V.   Harriet[7], b.———, unmarried
94.   VI. Elizabeth[7], ——— ; m. Jesse Kingsbury.

26.   JAMES[6] FULLER, (*Isaiah*[5], Isaac[4], *Isaac*[3], *Samuel*[2], *Samuel*[1]),
b. June 30, 1793, in Warwick, Mass., d. there June 22, 1851 ; m.
Feb. 15, 1816, Nancy Lesure, who d. June 4, 1864, aged 68 years.
     They reside in Warwick.
     Children, recorded in Warwick:

95.   I.   James Dwight[7], b. Aug. 5, 1816 ; d. April 24, 1833.
96.   II. Lucy Maria[7], b Jan 10, 1819, d March 28, 1900 ;
                  m April 23, 1837, Calvin W. Delva of Warwick,
                  and had · James[8], Emeline[8], Ellen[8], Annette[8],
                  Susan[8], Bessie[8], Anna[8], Nellie[8] and Frank.[8]
97.   ‡III.   Benjamin F.[7], b. Aug. 26, 1821 ; m. Mary Emeline
                  Green.
98.   IV. Sophia[7], b. Aug. 17, 1823 ; d. Oct. 29, 1823.
99.   ‡V.   Augustus[7], b. March 4, 1825 ; m. Almira Jane
                  Brooks.
100.   ‡VI.   Henry Martin[7], b. May 3, 1828, m. Mary B. Wilson.
101.   ‡VII.   Dwight[7], b. Dec. 13, 1832 ; m. Sarah Jane Johnson.

102.   ‡VIII.   James E.[7], b. Oct. 5, 1836 ; m. Clara Gould.
103.   ‡IX.   Franci, L.[7], b Dec. 9, 1839 ; m. Hattie Whitney.

32.   BENJAMIN[6] FULLER, (*Benjamin*[5], *Isaac*[4], *Isaac*[3], *Samuel*[2], *Samuel*[1]), b. Dec. 4, 1792, probably in Winchester, N. H.; d. March 6, 1860; m. July 3, 1817, Dorothy Bliss, who d. Oct. 30, 1839.

Children, all born at Winchester, N. H. :

104.   I.   Susah Bliss[7], b. April 13, 1818, d. July 25, 1836 ; unmarried
105.   II.   Elmina Tamajen[7], b. March 25, 1820, m. Feb. 11, 1840, in Warwick, Mass., Samuel Davis Wheaton, and had · Julius Davis[8], b. Jan. 10, 1841, d. Sept 30, 1895, unmarried ; Junius Levi[8], b. July 19, 1842, d. Dec 19, 1843 ; Julia Elmina[8], b. June 3, 1844, d June 26, 1900, m. Nov. 30, 1867, Nathan P. Peck of Woodbridge, Ct. ; Sarah[8], b. Aug. 4, 1846, d. May 24, 1890, in Westville, Ct., unmarried ; Christopher C.[8], b. July, 1848, d. Nov. 8, 1897 ; Hattie Elizabeth[8], b. Feb. 14, 1851 ; Williston Wayland[8], b. April 18, 1856, d. Feb. 14, 1861, in Warwick.
106.   ‡III. Emery Goddard[7], b. July 1, 1822 ; m. H. Eliza Hale.
107.   IV.   Hattie Bliss[7], b. Oct. 15, 1824, d. Feb. 21, 1879 ; m. June 20, 1872, in Watsonville, Cal., Thomas Fuller, b. in England, who removed to Mexico after the death of his wife in Tecopa, Cal. No children.
108   V.   Miranda Elizabeth[7], b. Jan. 21, 1828, d. Sept. 5, 1851, unmarried.
109   VI.   Caroline H.[7], b. Feb. 27, 1831, d. Aug. 16, 1832.
110   ‡VII. Lucius Ames[7], b. Nov. 12, 1833 ; m. Ellen Calista Bennett
111.   VIII. Caroline W.[7], b. Oct 12, 1837, d. Nov. 25, 1897 ; m. Feb. 15, 1858, Wells Beecher of Woodbridge, Ct, and had : Frank W., b. June, 1861, d. Oct., 1861, and Edward W., b. Nov. 30, 1859. Resides in Wallingford, Ct.

SEVENTH GENERATION.

37.   LEMUEL[7] FULLER, (*Lemuel*[6], *Isaac*[5], *Isaac*[4], *Isaac*[3], *Samuel*[2], *Samuel*[1]) b. Feb. 14, 1807, at Pittsfield, Mass.; d. Jan. 1, 1893, at Bennington Falls, Bennington, Vt.; m. 1, Nov. 18, 1828,

in Lebanon, N. Y., Lucy Putnam, b. 1804, at Becket, Mass., who d. Aug. 13, 1841, at Bennington Falls; m. 2, Jan. 1, 1842, Sophronia Lyon, b. April 26, 1823, at Woodford, Vt., who d. Sept. 16, 1860, at Bennington Falls, m. 3, April 25, 1863, Anna E. Potter.

Children:

112.   I. Caroline Elvira[8], b. Dec. 20, 1829, in Dalton, Mass.; d. March 31, 1871, at Bennington Falls; m. there Jan. 30, 1850, Salem White. Their children, born at Bennington Falls, were: Caroline[9], b. April 7, 1851; Willard[9], b. Jan. 20, 1852, Frank H.[9], b. Nov. 26, 1854, Frederick[9], b. Sept. 14, 1856; Kittie[9], b. Feb. 14, 1858; Libbie G.[9], b. March 15, 1861; Salem H.[9], b. Dec. 26, 1862, Lucy[9], b. March 29, 1864; Linus[9], b. Aug. 20, 1867, and Nettie E.[9], b. Aug. 15, 1868.

113.   II. A son, b. ————, died young.

114.   III. Emily J.[8], b. Oct. 20, 1836, at Bennington Falls; m. Oct. 6, 1858, Henry D. Rouse, who d. Jan. 6, 1905, at West Philadelphia, Pa. They had: Ada M.[9], b. Nov. 26, 1864, Frederick F.[9], b. Nov. 28, 1866, at Rutland, Vt., and Henry D.[9], b. at Philadelphia.

115.   IV. Lucy P.[8], b. Aug. 13, 1841, at Bennington Falls; m. Dec. 22, 1862, Eli B. Hicks. Reside at North Adams, Mass. Children: Mary[9], b. Nov. 21, 1863, Charles H.[9], b. Oct. 29, 1865, Harry[9], b. March 24, 1868; twins, b. Dec. 24, 1869, died young, Viva C.[9], b. Jan. 10, 1871; Elmira M.[9], b. April 16, 1873; Frederick[9] and Frank[9], twins, b. Aug. 2, 1875; Anna F.[9], b. April 5, 1877; Walter[9], b. April 12, 1880, and Ada Amelia[9], b. Aug. 9, 1884.

116.   V. Linus E.[8], b. May 2, 1844; m. Oct. 17, 1866, Amelia J. Landon. Resides in New York City. No children.

39. WILLIAM NELSON[7] FULLER, (*Lemuel[6]*, *Isaac[5]*, *Isaac[4]*, *Isaac[3]*, *Samuel[2]*, *Samuel[1]*), b. April 22, 1815, in Dalton, Mass.; d. Nov. 23, 1887, at Oconee, Ill.; m. 1, April 15, 1834, Harriet Newell Comstock in Dalton, who d. May 17, 1843, aged 29; m. 2, Nov. 29, 1843, Caroline Lovina Nelson, who d. Jan. 22, 1879, at Ramsey, Ill.

Children, all but the youngest child b. in Dalton:

117.   I. William Nelson[8], b. Feb. 3, 1835; d. Sept. 19, 1837.

118.   ‡II.   Nelson William[8], b. July 29, 1838; m. Elizabeth J.
                    Craig.
119.   III.   George Newell[8], b. Dec. 11, 1840; d. Aug. 16,
                    1846.
120.   IV.   Harriet Newell[8], b. April 14, 1843; m. April 19,
                    1865, George E. Hagar. Children: Kate[9], b.
                    June 17, 1867; Susie B.[9], b. Dec. 10, 1869;
                    Harriet W[9], b Aug. 20, 1872, George S.[9], b.
                    Dec. 1, 1876; Lucy G.[9], b. Nov. 11, 1879;
                    James W[9], b. Jan. 5, 1883, and Catherine O.[9], b.
                    Jan. 17, 1886.
121.   V.   Matthias G. L.[8], b. Aug. 22, 1847; m. Jennie
                    Wheeler; no issue. Reside Oconee, Ill.
122.   VI.   Caroline Lovinia[8], b. July 2, 1849; m. Dec. 17,
                    1868, in Decatur, Ill., Henry McKnight. Reside
                    at Caldwell, Kan. (1896). Children, all b. at
                    Ramsey, Ill.: Beatrice B.[9], b. Jan. 15, 1873;
                    Roma R.[9], b. Nov. 16, 1874; Louis E.[9], b. March
                    11, 1876; Fanny M.[9], b. May 12, 1878; Chad
                    C.[9], b Aug. 6, 1884.
123.   VII.   Fanny Briggs[8], b. March 22, 1852; m. Dec. 28,
                    1876, Chadwick Gale. They reside (1896)
                    Oconee, Ill. Their children, all b. in Oconee,
                    are: Lottie L.[9], b. May 12, 1878, Bessie C.[9], b.
                    Sept. 5, 1879; Charles C.[9], b. June 28, 1886;
                    Gertrude F.[9], b. June 25, 1889, and George N.[9],
                    b. March 20, 1891.
124   VIII.   Jerome Minot[8], b. Sept. 7, 1855; d. Jan. 27, 1856.
125.   IX.   Mary Maria[8], b Dec. 25, 1859, at Ramsey, Ill.; m.
                    June 4, 1890, George Burr. Children: Mabel
                    A.[9], b April 27, 1891, and Guy F.[9], b. June 15,
                    1895

    41. JAMES[7] FULLER, (*Isaac[6]*, *Isaac[5]*, *Isaac[4]*, *Isaac[3]*, *Samuel[2]*,
Samuel[1]), b Jan. 10, 1791, in Warren, Me.; d. there Nov. 10,
1826, m. Dec., 1816, Melinda Cummings.
    Lived at Thomaston, Me.
    Children born to them were:
126.   I.   Elizabeth[8], b. ———; m. Reuben Weeks of
                    Roxbury, Mass. Children: William[9], Charles[9],
                    Ruskin[9] and Reuben[9].
127.   ‡II.   James[8], b. ———, m. Ellen M. Robinson.
128.   III.   Mary Jane[8], b. ———; m. David Hardecar of
                    Roxbury, Mass., where she lived and died.

44. GIVEN[7] FULLER, (*Isaac*[6], *Isaac*[5], *Isaac*[4], *Isaac*[3], *Samuel*[2], *Samuel*[1]), b. Jan. 7, 1800, in Warren, Me.; d. April 13, 1847; m. Mrs. Melinda Cummings, widow of his brother James.

Resided at Thomaston, Me.

Children:
129.   ‡I.   Charles[8], b. ——, m. ——.
130.   ‡II. George[8], b. ——; m. ——.

45. ISAAC[7] FULLER, (*Isaac*[6], *Isaac*[5], *Isaac*[4], *Isaac*[3], *Samuel*[2], *Samuel*[1]), b. Feb. 22, 1803, in Warren, Me.; d. April 9, 1873; m. 1, Aug. 14, 1829, Avis Cummings, m. 2, March 18, 1849, Thankfull Williams.

He was a farmer living at Rockland, Me.

Children.
131.   I.   Susan A.[8], b 1831, d. Jan. 2, 1902; m. Capt. Burnham Hyler and removed to Thomaston, Me. Children. Emma B[9], b. 1851; Halver[9], b. 1853; Alida D.[9], b. 1855, and Burnham[9], b. 1857.
132.   II. John C.[8], b. 1832; d. 1874.
133.   III. Roxanna[8], b. 1834, d young.
134.   IV. Eli M.[8], b. 1836, d. young.
135.   V.   Avis A.[8], b. 1840, m. Gorham Butler and had: Josephine[9], b. 1860, and Ralph Emery[9], b. 1862. Reside in Rockland, Me.
136.   ‡VI. Ford H.[8], b. 1842; m. Lutheria Reed.
137.   VII. Sarah A.[8], b. 1844; m. Matthias Ulmer of Rockland, Me., and had: Jennie[9], b. Oct. 8, 1863, and Alice[9], b. Sept. 21, 1865.
138.   VIII. Rose C.[8], b. 1845; d. 1871.

46. PRINCE FORD[7] FULLER, (*Isaac*[6], *Isaac*[5], *Isaac*[4], *Isaac*[3], *Samuel*[2], *Samuel*[1]), b. April 5, 1807, in Warren, Me.; d. Nov. 26, 1838, in Warren; m. Miriam B. Hart of Union, Me.

Their children were:
139.   ‡I.   William H.[8], b. June 19, 1831; m. Margaret K. Overlock.
140.   ‡II. Ellis Bethuel[8], b. Jan. 20, 1833; m. Anne M. Eells.
141.   III. Oscar[8], b. Jan., 1835, d. April, 1838.
142.   IV. Nathan W.[8], b. July 17, 1838; d. Jan., 1863; a soldier of the Civil war; member Co. B, 24th Maine; m. Jan., 1863, Laura A. Adams of Thomaston, Me.

48. TISDALE[7] FULLER, (*Barzillai*[6], *Isaac*[5], *Isaac*[4], *Isaac*[3], *Samuel*[2], *Samuel*[1]), b Jan 29, 1796, in Easton, Mass.; d. ———— ; m. 1, April 23, 1822, Harriet Goward, m. 2, March 28, 1837, Betsey Snow.

Children, recorded at Easton.

143.   I.   Harriet[8], b. Nov. 26, 1823.
144.   II.   Caroline T.[8], b. Oct. 12, 1828; m. May 29, 1853, Nelson Drake.
145.   III. Martha W.[8], b. May 30, 1830, m. Dec. 1, 1855, Charles D. Wilcox, who d. Oct. 18, 1900, in Somerville, Mass Children : Charles Arlington[9], b. May 11, 1857, Herbert Augustus[9], b. Aug. 3, 1865, and Emily T.[9], b. Sept. 28, 1871. Mrs. Wilcox resides at Somerville.
146.   ‡IV.   Tisdale Harlow[8], b. Aug. 2, 1832; m. Eliza Ann Drake.
147.   V.   Elizabeth H.[8], b. April 19, 1835 ; d. Sept. 29, 1901, in Easton, m. Dec. 8, 1860, Lemuel Keith Wilbur of Norton, Mass, and had: Marion Elizabeth[9], b. Sept. 11, 1861, m. Dec. 29, 1886, Alfred A. Sisson of Easton; Mabel Fuller[9], b. Aug. 17, 1869, and Herbert Lemuel[9], b. Sept. 2, 1871, in Easton.

51. HARRISON[7] FULLER, (*Alden*[6], *Isaac*[5], *Isaac*[4], *Isaac*[3], *Samuel*[2], *Samuel*[1]), b. March 24, 1810, d April 22, 1856, at Mansfield, Mass.; m. ———— Mary P. Morse.

Children :

148   ‡I.   Henry J.[8], b May 5, 1834, m. Rebecca J. Vincent.
149.   II.   Mary Ellen[8], b. June 10, 1836, m Nov. 30, 1871, Josiah Craig.
150.   III. Gardner A[8], b. 1838; d. April 11, 1898; unmarried.
151.   ‡IV.   William[8], b. 1840; m. Betsey W. LeBaron.

57. WALDO C.[7] FULLER, (*Hosea*[6], *Isaac*[5], *Isaac*[4], *Isaac*[3], *Samuel*[2], *Samuel*[1]), b. Aug 5, 1817 (L. E. Fuller MSS), in Dalton, Mass.; d March 26, 1904, in Becket, Mass. (buried in Dalton) ; m. 1, Henrietta Stocking, who d. Sept 25, 1841, aged 26 years, m. 2, April 17, 1843, Jane C. Hall, who d. April 9, 1897, in Hinsdale, Mass.

Children ·

152.   ‡I.   William Henry⁸, b. Oct. 3, 1839, m. Sarah Jane Pierce.
153.   II.   Clara Maria⁸, b Dec. 22, 1844, at Dalton, Mass.; m. March 26, 1885, Wesley L. Bartlett. Have two children Reside in Hinsdale, Mass.
154.   III.   Emma S.⁸, b. Feb. 9, 1846, at Dalton; d. Aug. 12, 1877, m. William Wilson and had: Minnie⁹, b. March 23, 1874.
155.   IV.   Flora J.⁸, b. Dec. 17, 1847; m. 1886, Frank T. Oggert of Howarth, N. Y.
156.   ‡V.   Edson W.⁸, b. Sept. 14, 1849; m Fanny Smith.
157.   ‡VI.   Frank Byron⁸, b. Dec. 19, 1852; m. Ida M. Kenerson
158.   VII.   Grace M⁸, b Sept. 1, 1855; d. Sept. 13, 1855.
159.   VIII.   Nathan O.⁸, b. Feb. 28, 1859, at Pittsfield, Mass.; d. there Oct. 4, 1861.

63. LINUS FENN⁷ FULLER, (*Rufus⁶, Isaac⁵, Isaac⁴, Isaac³, Samuel², Samuel¹*), b. Feb. 15, 1807, at Rhinebeck, N. Y.; d. Sept. 24, 1865, at Bridgeport, Ct.; m. June 14, 1844, Catherine Sophia Whiteside, who d. March 17, 1902, ae. 77.

Children :

160.   I.   Maria Louisa⁸, b. ———— ; m. Rev. Mr. Sturgess and has one dau., who is also married.
161.   ‡II.   Rufus G.⁸, b. ———— ; m. Ida Thayer.
162.   III.   James⁸, b. ————, d. young.
163.   IV.   Linus⁸, b. ————, d. young.
164.   V.   Wilhemina⁸, b. ———— ; d. young.

65. RUFUS⁷ FULLER, (*Rufus⁶, Isaac⁵, Isaac⁴, Isaac³, Samuel², Samuel¹*), b. Nov. 13, 1810, at Plymouth, Ct.; d. May 11, 1881; m. March 10, 1857, at Plymouth, Ct., ———— .

Children :

165.   I.   Florence A.⁸, b. ———— ; m. Byron Barker of Hempstead, L. I.
166.   II.   Clarence⁸, b. ———— .

71. LORENZO DOW⁷ FULLER, (*Otis⁶, Isaac⁵, Isaac⁴, Isaac³, Samuel², Samuel¹*), b. Aug. 15, 1820, in Naples, N. Y.; m. Nov. 1, 1868, Mary M. Cleveland in Naples.

Children :

167.   I.   Edward⁸, b. ———— .

75. JEROME BONAPARTE[7] FULLER, (*Otis*[6], *Isaac*[5], *Isaac*[4], *Isaac*[3], *Samuel*[2], *Samuel*[1]), b. Jan. 8, 1829, in Naples, N. Y.; d. ———— ; m. May, 1859, Elizabeth Mercy Wells.

Lived at Buchanan, Mich.

Children :

168.   ‡I.   Jay[8], b. ————.
169.   II.   Milton[8], b. ————.
170.   III.   Clara[8], b. ————, m. E M. Colvin. Resides
                Chicago, Ill. Their children are : Jay Austin[9],
                b. Jan 1, 1890; Richard Edwin[9], b. Aug. 31,
                1899, Willard Otis[9], b. April 3, 1901, and Ruth
                Elizabeth[9], b. Feb. 5, 1903.
171.   IV.   Charles[8], b. ————.
172.   V.   Otis M.[8], b. ————, d. ————.
173.   VI.   Nellie[8], b. ———— ; d. ———— ; m. ———— Wakeley.

79. LEONARD ORCUTT[7] FULLER, (*Jacob*[6], *Isaiah*[5], *Isaac*[4], *Isaac*[3], *Samuel*[2], *Samuel*[1]), b. Sept. 18, 1809, at North Bridgewater, Mass.; d. ———— ; m. April 3, 1836, Susan Ann Thayer.

Their children were :

174.   I.   Abby[8], b. Jan. 30, 1837 , m. Henry Frederick Nash
                of New Bedford, Mass.
175.   II.   Lydia Brown[8], b. Sept. 25, 1839 , m. Thomas B.
                Whitney of New Bedford.

88. ARTEMAS BAKER[7] FULLER, (*Henry*[6], *Isaac*[5], *Isaac*[4], *Isaac*[3], *Samuel*[2], *Samuel*[1]), b. about 1815 ; d. ———— ; m. 1, Nov. 28, 1839, Ophelia P. Packard, who d Feb. 4, 1843 ; m. 2, Caroline W. Williams.

Children :

176.   I.   James Henry[8], b. about 1842 , d. July 25, 1864.
177.   II.   William Francis[8], b Feb. 27, 1854 ; m. Nov. 29,
                1888, Carrie G. Leonard.
178.   III.   Sarah Maria[8], b. May 30, 1856.

91. JOSEPH[7] FULLER, (*Seth*[6], *Isaiah*[5], *Isaac*[4], *Isaac*[3], *Samuel*[2], *Samuel*[1]), b. ———— ; d. ———— , m. Mary Hall.

Children :

179.   I.   Joseph L.[8], b. ————, m. Charlotte Peterson.
180.   II.   George Wyman[8], b. ————.

92. SETH WYMAN[7] FULLER, (*Seth*[6], *Isaiah*[5], *Isaac*[4], *Isaac*[3], *Samuel*[2], *Samuel*[1]), b. June 9, 1816, in Boston, Mass.; d. ———; m. June 24, 1840, Ann DeWitt Cross of New York City.

Their children were:

181.   I.   Anna Augusta[8], b. Sept. 8, 1841, in New York City; d. June 22, 1804, in Boston; unmarried.

182.   II.   Elizabeth Almira[8], b. Sept. 7, 1844, m. Dec. 24, 1868, George W. Learnard of Boston and had: Arthur Wyman[9], b. March 10, 1870; Harrington DeWitt[9], b. June 24, 1876, Treasurer and President respectively of the Seth W. Fuller Co., engineers and contractors in electrical construction, Boston, Mass.

183.   ‡III.   George W.[8], b. April 23, 1846, m. Susan H. Learnard.

184.   IV.   Charles Edward[8], b. Dec. 28, 1848; m. Martha E. Jenney of New Bedford, Mass.; no children.

185.   V.   Frank[8], b. Aug 5, 1850, m. Anna C. Hart of Boston.

97. BENJAMIN F[7] FULLER, (*James*[6], *Isaiah*[5], *Isaac*[4], *Isaac*[3], *Samuel*[2], *Samuel*[1]), b. Aug. 26, 1821, in Warwick, Mass.; d. May 8, 1873; m. July 4, 1844, Emeline R. Greene of Warwick, who d. March 7, 1879.

He was Lieutenant in 21st Mass. Regt., and served three years in the Civil war.

Children:

186.   I.   Hattie Laura[8], b. June 10, 1859, d. Nov. 27, 1885; m. Oct. 28, 1880, Alfred Walker of Leominster, Mass.

99. AUGUSTUS[7] FULLER, (*James*[6], *Isaiah*[5], *Isaac*[4], *Isaac*[3], *Samuel*[2], *Samuel*[1]), b. March 7, 1824, in Warwick, Mass.; d. Aug. 4, 1904, in Baldwinsville, Mass.; m. May 12, 1848, Almira Jane Brooks, who resides in Baldwinsville.

Children born to them were:

187.   ‡I.   Eugene L.[8], b. Feb. 24, 1849; m. Abbie Bingham.

188.   ‡II.   George A.[8], b. Oct 21, 1851; m. Ellen Mary Channing.

189.   III.   Frank E.[8], b. April 10, 1862; d. Aug. 16, 1863.

100. HENRY MARTIN[7] FULLER, (*James*[6], *Isaiah*[5], *Isaac*[4], *Isaac*[3], *Samuel*[2], *Samuel*[1]), b. May 3, 1828, in Warwick, Mass., d. March 15, 1884, m. 1, Dec. 1, 1854, Mary B. Wilson of Winchester, N. H., m 2, ———.

Children by first wife :

190.   I.   Herbert[8], b. ———.

By second wife :

191.   II. Marcia[8], b. ———.
192.   III. Waldo[8], b ———.

101. DWIGHT[7] FULLER, (*James*[6], *Isaiah*[5], *Isaac*[4], *Isaac*[3], *Samuel*[2], *Samuel*[1]), b. Dec. 13, 1832, in Warwick, Mass., d. Feb. 5, 1902, in Springfield, Mass.; m ———, Sarah Jane Johnson, who d. Oct. 8, 1903, in Springfield, aged 69 years.

Children :

193.   I.   Winfield[8] ?, b. ———, 1867.
194   II. Bertha[8], b. ———, 1864, in Warwick, Mass., m. Feb. 17, 1885, Allen Webster, b. in Philadelphia, Pa. They have one daughter, and reside in Springfield.

102. JAMES E.[7] FULLER, (*James*[6], *Isaiah*[5], *Isaac*[4], *Isaac*[3], *Samuel*[2], *Samuel*[1]), b. Oct. 5, 1836, in Warwick, Mass.; d. July 31, 1901, in Worcester, Mass., m. Jan. 18, 1859, Clara Delia Gould of Warwick.

He was an architect and builder in Worcester.

Their children were :

195.   I.   Clara Gertrude[8], b. Jan. 13, 1861, at Warwick; m. Feb. 14, 1884, Edgar Stiles Douglas, and their son, Delano Fuller Woodcliffe Douglas, was b. Aug 17, 1887, at Fort Point, Me.
196.   ‡ II. James Edward[8], b. Oct. 28, 1865 ; m. Maud Louise Knowlton.
197.   III. Frederick Lesure[8], b. Jan. 5, 1870, at Worcester; d. Aug 6, 1870.
198.   ‡ IV. Robert Lesure[8], b. June 29, 1871 ; m. Mary Wentworth White.

103. FRANCIS L.[7] FULLER, (*James*[6], *Isaiah*[5], *Isaac*[4], *Isaac*[3], *Samuel*[2], *Samuel*[1]), b. Dec. 9, 1839, in Warwick, Mass.; m. ———, Hattie M. Whitney of Orange, Mass.

Resides in Malden, Mass.

Children

199.   I.   Charles Harrison[8], b. July 13, 1867; m. Oct. 9, 1896, Mabel Homer.

200.   II.   Lottie M.[8], b. 1869, in Athol, d. Aug. 7, 1871, in Orange.

201.   III.   Hoyt Edward[8], b. July 25, 1871, in Orange.

106. EMERY GODDARD[7] FULLER, (*Benjamin*[6], *Benjamin*[5], *Isaac*[4], *Isaac*[3], *Samuel*[2], *Samuel*[1]), b. July 1, 1822, in Winchester, N. H.; d. May 1, 1899, in Hinsdale, N. H., m. April 27, 1858, in Winchester, H. Eliza Hunt of Rindge, N. H.

Children, all b. in Winchester

202.   I.   Charles Emery[8], b. May 20, 1859; d. April 20, 1881, Ashuelot, N. H., unmarried.

203.   II.   Frederick Hale[8], b March 1, 1861; d. March 6, 1893, in Ashuelot, unmarried.

204.   ‡III.   Frank Herbert[8], b. Oct 22, 1866, m. Eva V. Davis.

110. LUCIUS AMES[7] FULLER, (*Benjamin*[6], *Benjamin*[5], *Isaac*[4], *Isaac*[3], *Samuel*[2], *Samuel*[1]), b. Nov 1°, 1833, in Winchester, N. H.; d. Jan. 15, 1886, in Orange, Mass.; m. March 5, 1861, Ellen Calista Bennett.

Their children are .

205.   I.   George Arthur[8], b. Nov. 17, 1863

206.   II.   Nettie Estella[8], b. Feb. 4, 1867, m. April 8, 1890, Frederick H. Chase. Children born to them: Ruth Emily[9], b. July 27, 1891, Edward Lucius[9], b. Nov. 4, 1892; Frederick Arian[9], b. Feb. 17, 1894, Anne Rebecca[9], b. Nov. 15, 1895, Nettie Estella[9], b. Nov. 21, 1896, Jane Evelyn[9], b. Nov. 26, 1900, and Marion Janet[9], b. April 21, 1902, d. Jan 31, 1903.

207.   III.   Addie Maria[8], b. June 14, 1873.

EIGHTH GENERATION.

118. NELSON WILLIAM[8] FULLER, (*William N.*[7], *Lemuel*[6], *Isaac*[5], *Isaac*[4], *Isaac*[3], *Samuel*[2], *Samuel*[1]), b. July 29, 1838, in Dalton, Mass.; d. April 28, 1907, in Kansas City, Mo., m. in Hillsboro, Ill., Sept. 16, 1863, Elizabeth J. Craig.

Their children .

208.   I.   Alberta G.[9], b. Nov. 5, 1865; m. Sept. 20, 1886,

Alexander G. Henkle. Reside in Kansas City, Mo.

209   II.   Ada Maude⁹, b. June 2, 1868; d. June 16, 1888.
210.   III. Harriet E.⁹, b. Feb. 17, 1872; d. March 29, 1872.
211.   IV.   Ola Bell⁹, b. Sept. 25, 1874, in Walchville, Ill.; d. ———.

127. JAMES⁸ FULLER, (*James⁷, Isaac⁶, Isaac⁵, Isaac⁴, Isaac³, Samuel², Samuel¹*), b. in Warren, Me.; m. Int. Pub. Nov. 3, 1855, with Ellen M. Robinson of Alna, Me.
They reside in North Warren, Me.
Children.

212.   I.   Flora J.⁹, b. 1856, m. C. S. Coburn and resides in Warren, Me.
213.   II.   Edward⁹, b. ———, m. Alice J. Lewis and resides at Kittery Me. No children.

129. CHARLES⁸ FULLER, (*Given⁷, Isaac⁶, Isaac⁵, Isaac⁴, Isaac³, Samuel², Samuel¹*), b. ———, m. ——— and removed to Lincolnville, Me.
Children

214.   I.   Charles⁹, b. ———.
215.   II.   Mary⁹, b. ———.
216.   III. Edward⁹, b. ———.

130. GEORGE⁸ FULLER, (*Given⁷, Isaac⁶, Isaac⁵, Isaac⁴, Isaac³, Samuel², Samuel¹*), b. ———; m. Int. Pub. Oct. 14, 1856, with Abbie C. Gould of Belfast, Me.
Children.

217.   I.   Mary⁹, b. ———.
218.   II.   George⁹, b. ———.
219   III. Myrtle⁹, b. ———.
220.   IV.   Edward⁹, b. ———.

136. FORD H.⁸ FULLER, (*Isaac⁷, Isaac⁶, Isaac⁵, Isaac⁴, Isaac³, Samuel², Samuel¹*), b 1842, in Rockland, Me.; d. 1881, in Boston, Mass.; m. 1862, Lutheria Reed.
Children:
221.   I.
222.   II.

139. WILLIAM H.⁸ FULLER, (*Prince Ford⁷, Isaac⁶, Isaac⁵, Isaac⁴, Isaac³, Samuel², Samuel¹*), b. June 19, 1831, in Warren,

Me.; d. there July 1, 1908; m. Oct. 6, 1856, Margaret K. Overlock of Waldoboro, Me., who d. Oct. 12, 1907.

Their children were:

223.   I.   Frances O.[9], b. Nov. 11, 1857; d. Sept. 25, 1883; graduate Warren Free High School, and a teacher.

224.   II.   Frederick O.[9], b. Nov. 19, 1860, m July 6, 1899, Ida E. Jennison of Boston, Mass, where they now (1908) reside, no children.

225.   III.   LeForest[9], b Aug. 26, 1863; m. Jan 4, 1888, Charlotte C. Ames of Rockland, Me. They reside in Boston. Have no children.

226.   IV.   Mabel A.[9], b. Aug. 11, 1865. Resides in Warren, Me.

227.   V.   Laura A.[9], b. Jan. 19, 1869.

140. ELLIS BETHUEL[8] FULLER, (*Prince Ford[7], Isaac[6], Isaac[5], Isaac[4], Isaac[3], Samuel[2], Samuel[1]*), b. Jan. 20, 1833, in Warren, Me., d. March 3, 1892, in Waltham, Mass.; m. in Camden, Me., Aug. 11, 1854, Anne M. Eells, who resides in Camden.

Children:

228.   I.   Emma[9], b. Oct. 14, 1856; m. Sept. 26, 1876, Augustus Knight.

229.   II.   Carrie C.[9], b. Dec. 25, 1860; d. Jan. 15, 1862.

230.   III.   Alice C.[9], b. Feb. 15, 1862, d. Jan. 30, 1876.

231.   IV.   Lucy B.[9], b. Sept. 11, 1865; d. Feb. 6, 1906.

232.   V.   Nellie H.[9], b. Oct 15, 1873.

146. TISDALE HARLOW[8] FULLER, (*Tisdale[7], Barzillai[6], Isaac[5], Isaac[4], Isaac[3], Samuel[2], Samuel[1]*), b. Aug. 2, 1832, in Easton, Mass., m. May 11, 1851, Ann Elizabeth Drake, b. July, 1833, at Norton, Mass.

Children:

233.   ‡I.   Alphonzo Tisdale[9], b. July 9, 1852.

234.   II.   Harriet E.[9], b. June 2, 1854, m. July 24, 1878, Arthur G. Howard.

235.   III.   Frederick A.[9], b. June 20, 1856; d. Oct. 3, 1885.

236.   IV.   Josephine A.[9], b. July 29, 1857; d. Sept. 20, 1857.

237.   V.   Ann Eliza[9], b. March 6, 1859; m. Oct. 28, 1852, Herbert Collins.

238.   VI.   Henry Clay[9], b Oct. 8, 1862. (Drake Genealogy.)

148. HENRY J.[8] FULLER, (*Harrison[7], Alden[6], Isaac[5], Isaac[4], Isaac[3], Samuel[2], Samuel[1]*), b. May 5, 1834, in Mansfield, Mass.; d.

Oct. 17, 1903, in Taunton, Mass ; m. Rebecca J. Vincent, b. 1838, in Edgartown, Mass , d. March 31, 1872, in Taunton.

Children :

239.   I.   Frederick V.9, b. Sept. 9, 1863 ; d. Jan. 14, 1897 ; m. Feb. 2, 1886, Etta Strange, who d. Sept. 24, 1894 ; no children.

240.   II.   Albert9, b. Jan. 29, 1867 ; m. Jan. 19, 1898, Martha W. Crane, b. in Taunton, March 10, 1865. Reside in Taunton.   No children.

241.   III. Henry9, b. 1870, d. 1871.

151. WILLIAM8 FULLER, (Harrison7, Alden6, Isaac5, Isaac4, Isaac3, Samuel2, Samuel1), b. 1840 ; d. Aug. 31, 1902, in Mansfield, Mass.; m. Dec. 31, 1866, Betsey W. LeBaron.

Children, b. in Mansfield :

242.   I.   Evangeline LeBaron9, b. Oct. 14, 1866 ; m. Oct. 18, 1888, Robert E. Parker, b. at Somerville, Mass.

243.   II.   William Henry9, b. Aug. 16, 1868 ; m. Oct. 2, 1889, Bertha Maud Weeks.

244.   III. Alden9, b. June 11, 1873.

152. WILLIAM HENRY8 FULLER, (Waldo C.7, Hosea6, Isaac5, Isaac4, Isaac3, Samuel2, Samuel1), b. 1840, in Pittsfield, Mass.; resides in Becket, Mass., m. 1865, in Williamstown, Sarah J. Pierce, who d. July 16, 1908, in Becket, Mass.

Children ·

245.   I.   A son, b. June 26, 1868, in Pittsfield.
246.   ‡II.   William H.9, b. Oct. 2, 1869 , m. Orpha L. Spring.
247.   III. A son, b. Dec. 28, 1870.
248.   IV.   Everett Ellery9, b. Aug. 6, 1875 ; m. Mary Tollman
249.   V.   A son, b. Dec. 30, 1876.
250.   VI.   David H.9, b. ——— ; m. Mrs. Sadie B. (Richards) Redding.

156. EDSON W.8 FULLER, (Waldo C.7, Hosea6, Isaac5, Isaac4, Isaac3, Samuel2, Samuel1), b. Sept. 14, 1849, in Washington, Mass.; m. Feb. 28, 1873, Fanny Smith.

They reside in Ogden, N. Y.

Children :

251.   I.   Child, b. Sept., 1876.

George A. Fuller.

157. FRANK BYRON[5] FULLER, (*Waldo C.*[7], *Hosea*[6], *Isaac*[5], *Isaac*[4], *Isaac*[3], *Samuel*[2], *Samuel*[1]), b. Dec. 19, 1852, in Pittsfield, Mass.; d. Aug. 5, 1896, in Hinsdale, Mass., m. Dec. 21, 1886, Ida May Kenerson, who d. about March 17, 1896.

Resided in Hinsdale.

Children :

252.   I.   Pearl Bessie[9], b. Feb. 1, 1888. Resides at Haworth, N. J.
253.   II. Earl Waldo[9], b. Aug. 27, 1889. Resides at Alliance, Neb.
254.   III. A child, b. Jan. 10, 1892 ; died young.

161. RUFUS G.[5] FULLER, (*Linus F.*[7], *Rufus*[6], *Isaac*[5], *Isaac*[4], *Isaac*[3], *Samuel*[2], *Samuel*[1]), b. April, 1851? ; d. July, 1902 ; m. Ida Thayer.

Children :

255.   I.   Livingston[9], b. ———— ; d. aged about 12 years.
256.   II. Linus Whiteside[9], b. ———— ; living 1909.

168. JAY[5] FULLER, (*Jerome B.*[7], *Otis*[6], *Isaac*[5], *Isaac*[4], *Isaac*[3], *Samuel*[2], *Samuel*[1]), b. ———— , m. ————.

Children :

257.   ‡I. Ernest M.[9], b April 17, 1880 ; m. Miriam Dow.
258.   ‡II. Jay[9], b. ————.
259.   III. Anna Elizabeth[9], b. ————, in Detroit, Mich.

183. GEORGE W.[5] FULLER, (*Seth W.*[7], *Seth*[6], *Isaiah*[5], *Isaac*[4], *Isaac*[3], *Samuel*[2], *Samuel*[1]), b. April 23, 1846, in Boston, Mass.; m. Susan H. Learnard.

Children .

260.   I.   Blanch DeWitt[9], b. Nov. 17, 1871 ; d. Nov. 18, 1871.
261.   II. Robert Learnard[9], b. Nov. 2, 1876 ; d. May 20, 1885.

187. EUGENE L.[5] FULLER, (*Augustus*[7], *James*[6], *Isaiah*[5], *Isaac*[4], *Isaac*[3], *Samuel*[2], *Samuel*[1]), b. Feb. 24, 1849 , m. ————.

Resides in Mukwanago, Waukesha Co., Wis.

Children :

262.   I.   Frank[9], b. Sept. 27, 1876 , m. June 29, 1897, A. Geraldine Connell at Chicago, Ill.

188. GEORGE A.[8] FULLER, (*Augustus*[7], *James*[6], *Isaiah*[5], *Isaac*[4], *Isaac*[3], *Samuel*[2], *Samuel*[1]), b. Oct. 21, 1851, in Templeton, Mass.;

d. Dec. 14, 1900, in New York City, m. March 4, 1871, Ellen Mary Channing of Worcester, Mass.

Mr. Fuller was the well-known contractor and President of the George A. Fuller Construction Company, which still does business under that name, with offices in the principal cities of the United States He was the originator of the modern steel skeleton sky-scraper building and one of the foremost contractors of the country. He erected many buildings in Chicago, including the Monadnock, New York Life, Kearsarge, Rand–McNally, Tacoma, Marshall Field and Reliance buildings, the Woman's Temple, Masonic Temple, Ashland Block, Chicago Athletic Club, and Great Northern Theatre. He constructed many buildings of the Chicago World's Fair. He was educated at Andover, after which he took a special course in the Boston School of Technology. Making most of his estimates himself he was a master of details, and of rare executive ability.

Their children were .

263   I.   Grace Beatrice⁹, b. Sept. 10, 1873, in Somerville, Mass., d Sept. 22, 1899; m. Horace Chenery and had Fuller Chenery[10], b. March 6, 1897.

264.   II.   Allon May⁹, b. Jan. 26, 1876, m. 1, Harry Blake ; m. 2, Tyler Morse.

196. JAMES EDWARD⁸ FULLER, (*James E.*[7], *James*[6], *Isaiah*[5], *Isaac*[4], *Isaac*[3], *Samuel*[2], *Samuel*[1]), b. Oct. 28, 1865, at Athol, Mass.; m. April 18, 1895, Maude Louise Knowlton of Worcester, Mass.

Their children, both born in Worcester, are :

265.   I.   Francis Allon⁹, b. Feb. 11, 1897.

266.   II.   Virginia Louise⁹, b June 16, 1899.

198. ROBERT LESURE⁸ FULLER. (*James E.*[7], *James*[6], *Isaiah*[5], *Isaac*[4], *Isaac*[3], *Samuel*[2], *Samuel*[1]), b. June 29, 1871, in Worcester, Mass.; m. March 28, 1900, Mary Wentworth White of Worcester.

Children, born in Worcester :

267.   I.   Cecile Wentworth⁹, b. May 25, 1901.

268.   II.   Robert Bradley⁹, b. May 12, 1903.

204. FRANK HERBERT⁸ FULLER, (*Emery G.*[7], *Benjamin*[6], *Benjamin*[5], *Isaac*[4], *Isaac*[3], *Samuel*[2], *Samuel*[1]), b. Oct. 22, 1866, in Winchester, N. H., m. Jan. 1, 1892, in Winchester, Eva V. Davis.

Mr. Fuller is a merchant in Hinsdale, N. H.

Children :

269.	I.	A dau., b. Oct. 2, 1892 , d. April 13, 1893.
270.	II.	Bertha Eliza[9], } Twins, b. Oct. 22, 1908.
271.	III.	Bernice Marietta[9], }

NINTH GENERATION.

233. ALPHONSO TISDALE[9] FULLER, (*Tisdale H.*[8], *Tisdale*[7], *Barzillai*[6], *Isaac*[5], *Isaac*[4], *Isaac*[3], *Samuel*[2], *Samuel*[1]), b. July 9, 1852, in Easton, Mass. , m Nov. 24, 1872, Ruth A. Stearns, b. Feb. 10, 1856, in Mansfield, Mass.

Children :

272.	I.	Adele Augusta[10], b. Nov. 5, 1873 , d. Sept. 26, 1891.
273.	II.	Clinton Linwood[10], b Sept. 3, 1876; d. July 12, 1901.
274.	III.	Blanche Genevieve[10], b. Oct. 4, 1878.
275.	IV.	Leon Elwood[10], b. Sept. 17, 1881.

246. WILLIAM H[9] FULLER, (*William H.*[8], *Waldo C.*[7], *Hosea*[6], *Isaac*[5], *Isaac*[4], *Isaac*[3], *Samuel*[2], *Samuel*[1]), b. Oct. 2, 1869, in Pittsfield, Mass.; m. Orpha L. Spring.

Reside in Becket, Mass.

Children :

| 276. | I. | Etta Inez[10], b. Feb. 18, 1895, in Becket. |

257. ERNEST M.[9] FULLER, (*Jay*[8], *Jerome B.*[7], *Otis*[6], *Isaac*[5], *Isaac*[4], *Isaac*[3], *Samuel*[2], *Samuel*[1]), b. April 17, 1880, in Ann Arbor, Mich., m. Oct. 5, 1903, Miriam Dow, b. Feb. 14, 1881, in Charleston, S. C.

He is a lawyer in New York City, residing in Brooklyn.

Children :

277.	I.	Miriam[10], b. Sept 1, 1904, at Manning, S. C.; d. Jan. 7, 1905 ; buried at Charleston, S. C.
278.	II.	Alexandria[10], b. May 23, 1906, at Manning.
279.	III.	Stephen Dow[10], b. May 10, 1908, at Brooklyn, N. Y.
280.	IV.	Paul Alden[10], b. Oct. 10, 1909, at Brooklyn.

258. JAY[9] FULLER, (*Jay*[8], *Jerome B.*[7], *Otis*[6], *Isaac*[5], *Isaac*[4], *Isaac*[3], *Samuel*[2], *Samuel*[1]), b. ——— , m. Clara Lillian of Boston, Mass.

Children .

| 281. | I. | Ruth A.[10], b. ———. |

THIRTEENTH GROUP.

FOURTH GENERATION.

SAMUEL⁴ FULLER, (*Isaac³*) AND SOME OF HIS DESCENDANTS.

34. SAMUEL⁴ FULLER, (*Isaac³, Samuel², Samuel¹*), b. Jan. 29, 1718, at Halifax, Mass., date of death not found; m. Sept. 30, 1743, Elizabeth Thompson, b. Aug. 7, 1726; a descendant of John Thompson of Plymouth, Mass.

Children, the first three recorded at Halifax, Mass.:

1.	‡I.	Zadock⁵, b. Sept. 19, 1744; m. Alice Porter.	
2.	II.	Elizabeth⁵, b. Dec. 28, 1745.	
3.	III.	John⁵, b. March 30, 1748.	
4.	‡IV.	Lemuel⁵, b. ——, m. 1, Susannah ——, m. 2, Anna Smith.	
5.	‡V.	Samuel⁵, b. ——; m. Sarah Cushman.	

Chipman Fuller MSS., in possession of Mrs. Anna Fuller Bennett of Pittsfield, Mass., states that Zadock, John and Lemuel removed to Berkshire Co., Mass.

FIFTH GENERATION.

1. ZADOCK⁵ FULLER, (*Samuel¹, Isaac³, Samuel², Samuel¹*), b. Sept. 19, 1744, d. Sept. 17, 1818, in Lanesboro, Mass.; m. Dec. 3, 1767, Alice Porter, "both of Halifax," Mass. She d. in Lanesboro, Oct. 26, 1830, aged 84.

Zadock Fuller was a soldier in the Revolutionary war.

Their children were:

6.	I.	Sarah⁶, b. Sept. 27, 1768; m. —— Thompson of Vermont.

7.   II. Elsie[6], b Feb , 1771 ; m. Joseph Platt and **removed** to Lebanon, Ohio.
8.   ‡III. Jabez[6], b. Jan 27, 1773 , m. —— Tuttle.
9.   IV. Abigail[6], b. March 4, 1777 ; m. Joseph Taintor and removed to Lebanon, Ohio. Their children were   Abigail[7], b. Oct. 30, 1799 , Joseph[7], b. April 3, 1803 ; Patty[7], b. June 17, 1805 ; Orsamus[7], b. Feb. 25, 1808 ; Lucy[7], b. Oct. 21, 1812 ; Ira B.[7], b. Sept. 14, 1814 , Erastus P.[7], b. Sept. 19, 1816 ; Cyrus K.[7], b. Dec. 25, 1818, and Rufus H[7], b. jan. 23, 1821.
10.   V. Samuel[6], b. Sept. 27, 1779 ; m. Hannah **Campbell** and removed to Ohio.
11.   VI. Zadock[6], b. Feb. 4, 1781 ; d. unmarried.
12.   ‡VII. Noah[6], b. April 9, 1787 ; m. Lois Goodrich.

4.   LEMUEL[5] FULLER, (*Samuel[4]*, *Isaac[3]*, *Samuel[2]*, *Samuel[1]*), b. —— ; d. after July, 1839, and before July, 1842 ; m. 1, Susanna —— ; m. 2, Anna Smith, b. Sept. 8, 1814.

Mr. Charles H. Fuller of Lanesboro, Mass., grandson of Zadock Fuller, stated that Zadock had a brother Lemuel, who lived in Worthington, Mass., and deeds on record at Northampton, Mass., show that he bought land in Worthington about 1791, and that his wife's name was Susanna. Worthington records give marriage later to Anna Smith. His will on record gives name of wife as Anna and mentions the following named children :

13.   ‡I.   Lemuel S.[6], b. ——.
14.   II. John[6], b. ——.
15.   III. Henry[6], b ——.
16.   ‡IV. Daniel Pomery[6], b. —— .
17.   V. Mary[6], b. ——.
18.   VI. Rachel[6], b ——.
19.   VII. Eliza[6] (Woods), b. —— ; · m. Tabor **Wood**, March 10, 1824. (Worthington Records.)
20.   VIII. Susan Dwight[6] (Jewell), b. ——.
21.   IX. Flavia[6] (Cudworth), b. —— , m. Eben Cudworth, Feb. 2, 1832. (Worthington Records.)
22.   X. Nancy Harker[6] (Atwood), b. ——.

5.   SAMUEL[5] FULLER, (*Samuel[4]*, *Isaac[3]*, *Samuel[2]*, *Samuel[1]*), b. —— , (he was probably the Samuel Fuller who d. in Halifax, Mass., Nov. 10, 1842, aged 79 years, hence b. about 1763) ; m. Dec. 15, 1785, Sarah Cushman of Plympton, Mass.

Children .

23.   ‡I.   Samuel⁶, b. 1793; m Nancy Waterman
24.   ‡II.   Benjamin⁶, b. ———--; m. 1, Mary Perkins, m. 2,
                Anna F. Bosworth
25.   ‡III. Isaac⁶, b. 1799, m Cynthia Porter.
      U. S. census 1790 gives four in the family.

SIXTH GENERATION.

8. JABEZ⁶ FULLER, (*Zadock⁵, Samuel⁴, Isaac³, Samuel²,
Samuel¹*), b. Jan 27, 1773, d. July 31, 1855, in Lanesboro, Mass.,
m. 1798, Hannah Tuttle, who d. Sept. 6, 1846.
      Children, all b in Lanesboro ·

26.   I.   Sarah⁷, b Dec 20, 1799; d March 3, 1852; m.
                 Nov. 10, 1824, Anson Curtis and had : Solomon
                 T.⁸, Edwin O.⁸, George D.⁸, Mary A.⁸ and
                 Julia E⁸
27.   II.   Julia⁷, b. March 20, 1802, d. Sept. 18, 1825; m.
                 Thomas Cone and had a son, Samuel W.⁸
28.   ‡III.   Jabez Tuttle⁷, b July 12, 1804.
29.   IV.   Anna⁷, b. Aug. 18, 1806; d. Aug. 4, 1883; m.
                 Nov. 10, 1824, Adolphus⁸ Fuller (*Daniel⁷,
                 Jonathan⁶, Ebenezer⁵, Barnabas⁴, Samuel³,
                 Samuel², Edward¹*) of Peru, Mass. Their
                 children were · William A.⁸, Amelia⁸, Clara M.⁸,
                 Daniel E.⁸, Emma D.⁸ and Henry Kirk⁸. (See
                 first vol. Fuller Genealogy.)
30.   V.   Hannah Maria⁷, b. Feb. 15, 1809; d. March 9,
                 1826.
31.   VI   Fanny Elizabeth⁷, b. April 21, 1812, d. 1876, m
                 Latham Garlick. Children : Egbert L.⁸, b. Dec. 9,
                 1834, William E.⁸, b Jan. 9, 1837; Lewis⁸,
                 Henry⁸, Julia⁸ and Evelyn A.⁸
32.   ‡VII.   William Augustus⁷, b. April 29, 1815, m. 1, Adelia
                 Weed; m. 2, Mary Cole.
33.   VIII. Appolonia Delight⁷, b. May 11, 1818; d. Nov. 7,
                 1869; m. Capt. Andrew J. Lewis.

12. NOAH⁶ FULLER, (*Zadock⁵, Samuel⁴, Isaac³, Samuel²,
Samuel¹*), b. April 9, 1787, d. Oct. 8, 1866, in Lanesboro, Mass.;
m. Lois Goodrich, b Aug 23 1791, d. Oct. 26, 1846, in Lanesboro.
      Children, all born in Lanesboro .

34.   I.   Eliza⁷, b. Feb. 6, 1809; d. Oct. 11, 1880; m.
                 Jeremiah Hungerford and lived in Antwerp, N. Y.

Children: Maria[8], b. Aug 16, 1829, Ada[8], b.
Dec. 9, 1831, Laura[8], b. May 5, 1833; Thomas
R.[8], b Sept 29, 1840; Lois L.[8], b. Aug. 22,
1843; J. Hiram[8], b. Feb. 24, 1847. Ada m.
Charles O. Cheney and their son, Charles W.,
was father of William D. Cheney of Syracuse,
N. Y.

35.   II.   Lucy Ann[7], b. Jan. 27, 1811; m. Nicholas
O'Meally and resided in Boaz, Wis. They had:
Thomas[8], William[8], Robert[8], George[8], Lucy[8],
Hiram[8] and Lois[8].

36.   ‡III.   Thomas Royce[7], b. April 6, 1813. m. 1, Harriet
M. Goodrich, m. 2, Sarah Backus.

37.   IV.   Laura Ann[7], b. Aug. 27, 1816, d. Aug. 4, 1902;
m. Henry Murphy and lived in Dexter, N. Y.
Their children were: Nathaniel[8], Joanna[8],
William[8], Harriet[8], Sarah[8] and Frank[8].

38.   V.   Adah M.[7], b. Jan 3, 1819, d. April 5, 1877; m.
Alexander Hakes and had, Marion[8] and Henry[8].
Lived in Perryville, N. Y.

39.   VI.   Huldah M.[7], b. March 11, 1821; d. July 11, 1893;
unmarried.

40.   VII.   Ruth[7], b. March 29, 1823; d. Oct. 3, 1859; m.
Charles Ryan and had· Charles[8], Thomas[8],
John[8] and Margaret[8], who m. August Zierath and
became parents of Cora[9], b. Feb. 8, 1874, and
Dr William T. Zierath[9], of Sheboygan, Wis., b.
July 22, 1877.

41.   VIII.   Charlotte[7], b. April 4, 1825, d Jan. 30, 1888; m.
Feb 22, 1843, Pardon Belcher and resided in
Lanesboro. Their children were: Laura Ann[8],
m. Albert Farnam; Sarah[8], m. Alfred Farnam;
Huldah[8], m ——— Farrington; Harriet[8],
William[8], Arthur[8], Mary[8] and Marian.[8]

42.   IX.   A son, b. Oct. 25, 1827; d. Nov. 17, 1827.

43.   ‡X.   Charles Hiram[7], b. June 26, 1829; m. 1, Elmira P.
Beach, m. 2, Doris E. Wood.

44.   XI.   David Porter[7], b. Oct. 25, 1831; d. Dec. 7, 1833.

13. LEMUEL S.[6] FULLER, (*Lemuel[5], Samuel[4], Isaac[3], Samuel[2],
Samuel[1]*), b. ———; d ———; m Oct. 23, 1840, Irene T. Beals
(Ashfield, Mass., Records), who d. March 26, 1852 (Worthington,
Mass., Records), m. 2, Sophronia ———.

Children, recorded in Worthington:

45.   I.   Levi Dwight[7], b Dec. 8, 1844.

46.   II.   Mary Ellen⁷, b. July 7, 1848.
47.   III. Leroy S.7, b. Aug. 16, 1850; d. May 10, 1851.
48.   IV.   Susan M.7, b. Aug. 13, 1854.

16. DANIEL POMFROY⁶ FULLER, (*Lemuel*⁵, *Samuel*⁴, *Isaac*³, *Samuel*², *Samuel*¹), b. in Worthington, Mass., m. ———, Jane ———.

Children :

49.   J.   Major Pomeroy⁷, b. Aug. 27, 1853, in Pittsfield, Mass.
50.   II.   A dau., b. May 16, 1863, in Pittsfield, Mass.

23. SAMUEL⁶ FULLER, (*Samuel*⁵, *Samuel*⁴, *Isaac*³, *Samuel*², *Samuel*¹), b. 1793?; d. May 29, 1882, aged 89 y. 10 m. 8 d. (C. M Thatcher MSS.) ; m. April 28, 1814, Nancy Waterman, who d. May 5, 1868. ("Both of Halifax.")

Children :

51.   I.   Luther⁷, b. in Halifax ; d. Oct. 6, 1842, aged 28.
52.   ‡II. Everett⁷, b. Jan 31, 1817 ; m. Jane S. Williams.
53.   III. Harrison⁷, b. March 6, 1821 ; m. 1, Sophia Rider ; m. 2, ——— Cushing.
54.   IV.   Polly⁷, b. Sept. 22, 1822 ; m. Isaac Soule.
55.   ‡V.   Nathaniel⁷, b 1824, m. 1, Leonice B. Perkins ; m 2, Joanna C. (Crocker) Jackson.
56.   VI.   Marshall⁷, b. May 2, 1828, m. Sept. 28, 1852, at Middleboro, Mass., Huldah C. Perkins.
57.   VII. Eliza⁷, b. June 10, 1833, m. Int. Pub. Nov. 22, 1850, at Halifax, Mass., Edwin Soule.
58.   VIII. Thomas⁷, b. July 6, 1835, m Christiana Cobb. He d. Jan. 14, 1906.
59.   IX.   Eustis William⁷, b. May 3, 1837 ; m. April 11, 1863, Mary Ann Coffin.
60.   X.   Nancy⁷, b. Dec. 31, 1840 ; m. Aug. 16, 1862, Orrin W. Bosworth.

24. BENJAMIN⁶ FULLER, (*Samuel*⁵, *Samuel*⁴, *Isaac*³, *Samuel*², *Samuel*¹), b. ———; d. ———; m 1, March 30, 1820, Mary Perkins, who d. Nov. 11, 1821; m. 2, Sept. 21, 1826, Anna T. Bosworth, who survived him and m. July 11, 1841, Jason Perkins. "Benjamin Fuller of Halifax and Mary Perkins of Plympton, Mass."

Children :

61.   ‡I.   Benjamin Franklin⁷, b. March 28, 1821 ; m. Lucy W. Stone.

Thomas Royce Fuller.
Mrs. Harriet M. (Goodrich) Fuller.

25. ISAAC[6] FULLER, (*Samuel*[5], *Samuel*[4], *Isaac*[3], *Samuel*[2], *Samuel*[1]), b. ——, 1799; d. July 8, 1876; m. June 24, 1824, Cynthia Porter, who d. Oct. 31, 1889. (Halifax Records.)

Children:

62. I. Isaac Porter[7], b Jan. 1, 1826, in Middleboro, Mass. (Plympton Records.)

SEVENTH GENERATION.

28. JABEZ TUTTLE[7] FULLER, (*Jabez*[6], *Zadock*[5], *Samuel*[4], *Isaac*[3], *Samuel*[2], *Samuel*[1]), b. July 12, 1804, in Lanesboro, Mass.; d. Oct. 18, 1875; m. Laura Garlick, b. March 12, 1812, d. Nov. 17, 1875.

Children:

63. I. Harriet M.[8], b. Dec. 3, 1833; d. Feb. 28, 1853; m. Columbus Rider.
64. II. Rufus S.[8], b. March 22, 1836; d. ——.
65. III. Albert V.[8], b. Jan. 9, 1839, d. ——.
66. IV. Elwin G.[8], b July 28, 1841; d. Nov. 30, 1863, at Falmouth, Va. Corporal Co. G, 34th Regt. N. Y. Vols.

32. WILLIAM AUGUSTUS[7] FULLER, (*Jabez*[6], *Zadock*[5], *Samuel*[4], *Isaac*[3], *Samuel*[2], *Samuel*[1]), b. April 29, 1815, in Lanesboro, Mass.; d. June 5, 1897; m 1, Adelia Weed of Lanesboro; m. 2, Oct. 14, 1856, Mary Cole.

Children by first wife ·

67. I. Rose Ella[8], b. 1841, d. Nov. 22, 1848.
68. ‡II. Herbert Augustus[8], b. June 6, 1842, m. 1, Gertrude M. Allen; m. 2, Helen T. Moore.

By second wife:

69. III. Mary Anna[8], b. Dec. 1, 1861; m. Feb. 25, 1896, Henry Bennett of Manistee, Mich. She graduated at Wellesley College, class of 1884, and is at present (1908) a teacher in the high school at Pittsfield, Mass.

36. THOMAS ROYCE[7] FULLER, (*Noah*[6], *Zadock*[5], *Samuel*[4], *Isaac*[3], *Samuel*[2], *Samuel*[1]), b. April 6, 1813, in Lanesboro, Mass.; d. March 30, 1891, at Edmeston, N. Y.; m. 1, Feb. 5, 1837, Harriet M. Goodrich, b. Dec. 15, 1816, in New Berlin, N. Y., d. there Oct. 13, 1843; m. 2, Dec. 25, 1844, Sarah Backus, b. April 27, 1826, in New Berlin, d. March 26, 1896, in Edmeston.

He removed to Pittsfield, Otsego Co., N. Y., thence in 1848 to Watson, Lewis Co., N. Y. In 1867 went back to Pittsfield and thence in 1885 to Edmeston.

Children, all b. in Watson except Ruth M., who was b. in New Berlin ·

70.   ‡I.   Thomas Wesley[8], b May 12, 1838, m. Alvira T. T Morton.
71.   II.   Zadock I.[8], b. Aug. 8, 1841 ; m. Lucinda Thomson. Resides in New Berlin   No children.
72.   III.   Ruth M.[8], b. Aug. 16, 1846; m. April, 1866, Obediah Wormwood and had : Ina May[9], b. March 1, 1868, and Cora Louisa[9], b. Jan. 12, 1872.
73.   IV.   Child, b. Dec. 29, 1848 , died young.
74.   ‡V.   Heman N.[8], b. April 22, 1850, m. 1, Edith F. Burgess , m 2, Ella E. Bevin.
75.   VI.   Charles H.[8], b. June 19, 1852 ; m. 1, Oct. 25, 1876, Belle Telfer, who d. Sept. 25, 1890 ; m. 2, Jan. 26, 1902, Katherine Wheeler. No children.
76.   ‡VII.   Warren B[8], b. Aug 30, 1855 , m. Ella F. Wheeler.
77.   VIII.   Lois Elmira[8], b Oct 28, 1860 , m. Dec. 31, 1879, Edward W. Hatcher. Has son, Charles W.[9], b. March 11, 1881.
78.   IX.   Eva May[8], b. Nov. 23, 1863 ; m. Nov. 1, 1889, Warren W Morton and has : Glenn W.[9], b. Jan 4, 1896, and Ray F.[9], b. Nov. 10, 1899.

43. CHARLES HIRAM[7] FULLER, (*Noah*[6], *Zadock*[5], *Samuel*[4], *Isaac*[3], *Samuel*[2], *Samuel*[1]), b. June 26, 1829, in Lanesboro, Mass., m. 1, Feb. 22, 1851, Elmira P. Beach, b. Feb. 23, 1832, d. May 7, 1881 , m. 2, July 1, 1896, Doris E. Wood, b. Jan. 11, 1852, in Lanesboro.

Mr. Fuller is a farmer residing near Lanesboro.

His children are .

79.   ‡I   Henry H[8], b. Jan. 25, 1854 ; m. Jessie Culver.
80.   ‡II.   Charles C.[8], b. June 10, 1860 ; m. Mary Newton.
81.   ‡III   William P.[8], b Jan. 30, 1862 ; m. Betsey Loretta Wood.

52. EVERETT[7] FULLER, (*Samuel*[6], *Samuel*[5], *Samuel*[4], *Isaac*[3], *Samuel*[2], *Samuel*[1]), b. Jan. 31, 1817, in Halifax, Mass., d. Feb. 17, 1898, in Taunton, Mass.; m. Aug. 4, 1846, James S. Williams, who d. Oct. 31, 1893, in Taunton, aged 70 y. 26 d.

Charles Hiram Fuller.

Children :

82.   I.   George Everett[S], b 1847, in Taunton, d. there
              Dec. 15, 1882, aged 35 y. 6 m. 30 d.; m. ———.

55. NATHANIEL[7] FULLER, (*Samuel*[6], *Samuel*[5], *Samuel*[4], *Isaac*[3], *Samuel*[2], *Samuel*[1]), b. 1824; d. ———; m. 1, Nov. 26, 1846, Leonice B. Perkins, "both of Halifax," Mass., who d. Jan. 5, 1853; m. 2, Feb. 1, 1857, Joanna C. (Crocker) Jackson.

Children :

83.   I.   Rolinda Alden[S], b Sept. 26, 1847, m. April 30,
              1865, James M. Howard.
84.   II. Nathan Henry[S], b. 1851; m. Oct. 4, 1871, Clara
              F. Wilbur. (Taunton Records.)

61. BENJAMIN FRANKLIN[7] FULLER, (*Benjamin*[6], *Samuel*[5], *Samuel*[4], *Isaac*[3], *Samuel*[2], *Samuel*[1]), b. March 28, 1821 ; d. May 6, 1889, in Carver, Mass., m. Nov. 15, 1846, Lucy W. Stone, who d. Aug. 23, 1900, aged 77 y. 3 m. 20 d.

Children, recorded in Carver :

85.   I.   Sylvia C.[S], b. May 24, 1850; m. Nov. 17, 1869,
               Angelo A. Dunham.
86.   ‡II.   James[S], b. Oct., 1852, m. Alberta C. ———.
87.   III. Henry R.[S], b Nov. 11, 1856, d. Aug. 11, 1860.
88.   IV.   Harriet Washburn[S], b. Nov. 11, 1856; d. Sept. 10,
               1857.

EIGHTH GENERATION.

68. HERBERT AUGUSTUS[8] FULLER, (*William A*[7], *Jabez*[6], *Zadock*[5], *Samuel*[4], *Isaac*[3], *Samuel*[2], *Samuel*[1]), b. June 6, 1842, in Lanesboro, Mass., d. April 20, 1893, in Berkshire, Mass., m. 1, Sept. 25, 1864, in Brooklyn, N Y, Gertrude M. Allen, who d. June 16, 1878; m. 2, March 5, 1884, Helen T. Moore of Tyringham, Mass.

Children .

89.   I.   Emma Adelia[9], b. Jan. 11, 1866, in New Jersey.
               Resides at Hoosac Falls, N. Y.
90.   II.   Ella May[9], b. March 6, 1870, at Adams, Mass.; d.
               there March 25, 1873.
91.   III. Eva Lillian[9], b. Aug. 4, 1872, in Adams.
92.   IV.   Katie Belle[9], b. Jan. 8, 1874, in Adams; m. Jan. 1,
               1895, Rollin M. Chamberlain of New Haven, Ct.
               Children : Ruth [10], b. Dec. 20, 1896, and Emma

Lillian[10], b. Sept. 3, 1900, both born at New Haven.

93.   V.   Ninon Letica[9], b. Dec. 22, 1885, at Tyringham; m. Raymond R. Smith of Highland, N. Y., in U. S. naval service. Reside at Tyringham. Daughter, Letica Fuller[10] Smith, b. Feb. 26, 1908, d. Aug. 24, 1908.

70. THOMAS WESLEY[8] FULLER, (*Thomas Royce[7], Noah[6], Zadock[5], Samuel[4], Isaac[3], Samuel[2], Samuel[1]*), b. May 12, 1838, in New Berlin, N. Y.; d. Dec. 30, 1890; m. Oct. 22, 1858, Alvira T. Morton, b. May 6, 1838.

Their children are:

94.   ‡I.   Charles Wesley[9], b. May 18, 1860.
95.   ‡II.   Thomas Leander[9], b Sept. 7, 1862.
96.   III.   Frederick H.[9], b. June 20, 1876, in Pittsfield, N. Y.; m. Nov. 9, 1901, Caroline Crampton of N. Y. Mills, N. Y. They reside at Washington Mills, N. Y., and have no children.
97.   IV.   Floyd Z.[9], b. Dec., 1879, at Pittsfield, N. Y.; m. Jan. 30, 1907, Hattie Hickling, b. April 12, 1879, in Edmeston, N. Y., where they now (1909) reside.

74. HEMAN N.[8] FULLER, (*Thomas R.[7], Noah[6], Zadock[5], Samuel[4], Isaac[3], Samuel[2], Samuel[1]*), b April 22, 1850; m. 1, Aug. 9, 1870, Edith F. Burgess, b Feb. 14, 1854, d. March 17, 1881; m. 2, June 22, 1860, Ellen E. Bevin, b. July 23, 1849.

They reside at West Edmeston, N. Y.

Children:

98.   ‡I.   Chad W.[9], b. May 13, 1872.
99.   ‡II.   Dorr C.[9], b. Dec. 9, 1877.
100.   III.   A son, b. April 1, 1884, died young.
101.   IV.   Carrie Belle[9], b. May 22, 1885, in Edmeston, N. Y.; m. Jan. 27, 1904, Charles R. Due. Reside in Edmeston.

76. WARREN B.[8] FULLER, (*Thomas R.[7], Noah[6], Zadock[5], Samuel[4], Isaac[3], Samuel[2], Samuel[1]*), b. Aug. 30, 1855, in Watson, N. Y., m. Dec. 13, 1876, Ella F. Wheeler and resides in Cooperstown, N. Y.

Children:

102.   I.   John[9], b. March 11, 1881.

79. HENRY HIRAM[8] FULLER, (*Charles H.[7], Noah[6], Zadock[5], Samuel[4], Isaac[3], Samuel[2], Samuel[1]*), b Jan. 25, 1854, in Lanesboro, Mass ; m. Jan. 21, 1882, in Lanesboro, Jessie B. Culver.

They reside in Cheshire, Mass.

Children:

103.   I.   Elmina Phebe[9], b. April 28, 1889, in Lanesboro; m. Feb. 11, 1906, Ralph Leonard Getman.

80. CHARLES C.[8] FULLER, (*Charles H.[7], Noah[6], Zadock[5], Samuel[4], Isaac[3], Samuel[2], Samuel[1]*), b. June 10, 1860, in Lanesboro, Mass.; m. March 1, 1882, Mary Newton.

Reside in Dalton, Mass.

Children:

104.   I.   George Hiram[9], b. March 29, 1883.
105.   II.   Ray Smith[9], b. June 9, 1888
106.   III. Ward Sidney[9], b. April 27, 1889.

81. WILLIAM P.[8] FULLER, (*Charles H.[7], Noah[6], Zadock[5], Samuel[4], Isaac[3], Samuel[2], Samuel[1]*), b Jan. 30, 1862, in Lanesboro, Mass., m. Nov. 21, 1882, Loretta B. Wood, b. July 24, 1862, in Lanesboro, where they now (1909) reside.

Children, all b. in Lanesboro except Martha, b. in Cheshire .

107.   I.   Leon P.[9], b. June 29, 1884.
108.   II.   Edward L.[9], b. May 27, 1889; d. Oct. 10, 1899, at Cheshire.
109.   III. Grace L.[9], b. Oct. 17, 1894.
110.   IV.   Martha E.[9], b. July 18, 1899.

86. JAMES F.[8] FULLER, (*Benjamin F.[7], Benjamin[6], Samuel[5], Samuel[4], Isaac[3], Samuel[2], Samuel[1]*), b. Oct., 1852, in Carver, Mass.; m. ———, Alberta C. ———.

Children:

111.   I.   Harry C.[9], b. April 26, 1886.

NINTH GENERATION.

94. CHARLES WESLEY[9] FULLER, (*Thomas W.[8], Thomas R.[7], Noah[6], Zadock[5], Samuel[4], Isaac[3], Samuel[2], Samuel[1]*), b. May 18, 1860, in Pittsfield, Otsego Co., N. Y.; m. April 27, 1887, Ida Jennings, b. Jan. 12, 1860, in Smyrna, N. Y., and resides in Edmeston, N. Y.

Children :

112.   I.   Herbert Lee[10], b. June 11, 1888.
113.   II.   Grace Alvira[10], b. Nov. 7, 1893.
114.   III.   Martha Louise[10], b. May 18, 1897.
115.   IV.   Ernest Ray[10], b. May 6, 1899.

95.   THOMAS LEANDER[9] FULLER, (*Thomas W.*[8], *Thomas R.*[7], *Noah*[6], *Zadock*[5], *Samuel*[4], *Isaac*[3], *Samuel*[2], *Samuel*[1]), b. Sept. 7, 1862, in Pittsfield, N. Y., m. May 18, 1892, Vesta Green, b. April 6, 1872, in Glendfield, N. Y., and resides in Edmeston, N. Y.
        Children :

116.   I.   Bessie Louisa[10], b. May 23, 1893.
117.   II.   Flossie Mai[10], b. Oct. 3, 1895, d. Jan. 4, 1903, in Lowville, N. Y.
118.   III.   Clarence Eugene[10], b. June 24, 1897.

97.   FLOYD Z.[9] FULLER, (*Thomas W.*[8], *Thomas R.*[7], *Noah*[6], *Zadock*[5], *Samuel*[4], *Isaac*[3], *Samuel*[2], *Samuel*[1]), b. Dec., 1879, at Pittsfield, N. Y., m. Jan 30, 1907, Hattie Hickling, b April 12, 1879, in Edmeston, N. Y., and resides in Edmeston, N. Y.
        Children :

119.   I.   Glenn[10], b. Jan. 21, 1908.
120.   II.   A son, b. Sept. 30, 1909.

98.   CHAD W.[9] FULLER, (*Heman N.*[8], *Thomas R.*[7], *Noah*[6], *Zadock*[5], *Samuel*[4], *Isaac*[3], *Samuel*[2], *Samuel*[1]), b. May 13, 1872, in Edmeston, N. Y., m. Nov. 27, 1893, Maud Moffatt, and resides in New Berlin Center, N. Y.
        Their children are .

121.   I.   Blanch E.[10], b. July 29, 1895, in New Berlin Center.
122.   II.   Hilda[10], b. July 16, 1900, in New Berlin Center.
123.   III.   Margery[10], b. 1905, in West Edmeston, N. Y.

99.   DORR C.[9] FULLER, (*Heman N.*[8], *Thomas R.*[7], *Noah*[6], *Zadock*[5], *Samuel*[4], *Isaac*[3], *Samuel*[2], *Samuel*[1]), b. Dec. 9, 1887, at Burlington Flats, N. Y.; m. Dec. 21, 1896, Nord M. Dye and resides in West Edmeston, N. Y.
        Their children are :

124.   I.   Lisle H.[10], b. July 18, 1899, in Edmeston, N. Y.
125.   II.   Edith L.[10], b. Aug. 5, 1903, in West Edmeston.
126.   III.   Ella M.[10], b. Aug. 30, 1905, in West Edmeston.

FOURTEENTH GROUP.

FOURTH GENERATION.

JABEZ[4] FULLER, (*Isaac*[3]) AND SOME OF HIS DESCENDANTS.

36. JABEZ[4] FULLER, (*Isaac*[3], *Samuel*[2], *Samuel*[1]), b. May 7, 1723, at Middleboro, Mass., d. Oct. 5, 1781, at Medfield, Mass.; m. May 12, 1747, Elizabeth Hilliard of Boston, Mass.

A correspondent quotes as follows from the History of Medfield: "Dr. Jabez Fuller, son of Isaac of Middleboro, b. 1723, was received from Bridgewater church in 1747. Boston records give the marriage of Jabez Fuller of Medfield and Elizabeth Hilliard the same year (1747)."

Dr. Jabez Fuller was a very skillful physician.

Their children, all born in Medfield, were:

1.	‡I.	Jonathan[5], b. Oct. 3, 1748; m. Lucy Eddy.
2.	‡II.	John[5], b. July 28, 1750, m. 1, Martha Fuller; m. 2, Hannah Lovell.
3.	III.	Elizabeth[5], b. April 12, 1752; m. April 4, 1776, Stephen Dexter of Walpole, Mass., and had: Elizabeth[6], b. March 24, 1777; Sarah[6], b. Feb. 13, 1779; Anna[6], b. Sept. 10, 1780, and Lorin[6], b. June 28, 1783.
4.	‡IV.	Jabez[5], b. May 26, 1753; m. Lucy Loring.
5.	‡V.	Thomas[5], b. June 27, 1755.
6.	VI.	Mary[5], b. June 9, 1758; d. June 11, 1822; m. 1783, Phillip Delano.
7.	VII.	Catherine[5], b. April 2, 1760; d. Dec. 2, 1831, aged 71.
8.	VIII.	Sarah[5], b. Feb. 25, 1763; m. ——— Clark.

9.   IX. Experience[5], b. June 1, 1766; published Aug. 16, 1788, to Timothy Dwight.

FIFTH GENERATION.

1.   JONATHAN[5] FULLER, (*Jabez[4], Isaac[3], Samuel[2], Samuel[1]*), b. Oct. 3, 1748, at Medfield, Mass.; d. March 13, 1802, at Middleboro, Mass.; m. Aug. 31, 1744, Lucy Eddy, who d. Sept. 17, 1839, aged 82 years.

He was a physician and resided at Middleboro.
Children:

10.   I.   Lucy Eddy[6], b. April 20, 1776; d. Sept. 21, 1829, aged 53 years, m April 25, 1802, Seth Bryant, who d Sept. 28, 1822, aged 46 years.
11.   II. Jonathan Hylher[6], b. Jan. 9, 1779; d. Nov. 23, 1793.
12.   III Thomas[6], b. ——— ; d. July 16, 1782, in his 20th month. (Charles M. Thatcher's cemetery records.)
13.   IV. Sally[6], b. Nov. 12, 1781, m. ——— Jenney.
14.   ‡V.   Thomas[6], b. Jan. 13, 1785; m. Mary Baxter.
15.   VI. Zachariah[6], b Nov 22, 1787, m. Susan Barstow.
16.   VII. Betsey[6], b. Feb. 19, 1789.
17.   VIII. John[6], b. March 20, 1796; d. Feb. 23, 1797, aged 11 mos. (C. M. T.)
18.   ‡IX Jabez[6], b July 18, 1791; m. Sarah Hudson Churchill. (Churchill Genealogy.)
19.   X.   Seth[6], b. Dec. 10, 1793, d. June 23, 1870. (A Seth Fuller m. March 29, 1835, Clarinda Richmond, who d Nov. 21, 1890, aged 87 y. 2 mo. C. M. Thatcher)
20.   XI. Mercy Freeman[6], b. July 5, 1898.

2.   JOHN[5] FULLER, (*Jabez[4], Isaac[3], Samuel[2], Samuel[1]*), b. July 28, 1750, at Medfield, Mass., d. Sept. 22, 1830, at Medfield; m. 1, Dec. 30, 1784, Martha[6] Fuller (*Barnabas[5], Nathaniel[4], Samuel[3], Samuel[2], Samuel[1]*) of Halifax, Mass., who d. March 20, 1804; m. 2, Nov. 10, 1804, Hannah Lovell, who d. Dec. 31, 1832, at Medfield, aged 67.

John[5] Fuller served in the Continental Army in 1776 and lost an arm.

Children, all born in Medfield:
21.   I.   Martha[6], b. July 25, 1785; d. Sept. 9, 1822.

22. II. Nabby[6] (Abigail), b Oct. 27, 1786; m. Int. Pub.
Nov 1, 1814, with Edmond Longley Peabody.

23. ‡III. Samuel[6], b. Aug. 29, 1788; m. 1, Mary Sparhawk;
m 2, Jemima Cole.

24. ‡IV. John[6], b Oct. 15, 1792, m. Eleanor Hartshorn.

25. V. Charlotte[6], b. Oct. 11, 1796, m. 1819, Benjamin
Colby of Ashley, Mass.

4. JABEZ[5] FULLER, (*Jabez[4], Isaac[3], Samuel[2], Samuel[1]*), b. May
26, 1753, in Medfield, Mass.; d. April 12, 1813, aged 59 years
(Gravestone at Kingston, Mass.); m. Aug, 1781, Lucy Loring of
Duxbury, Mass., who d. Oct. 25, 1847, aged 89 years. (G. S.
record.)

He was a physician; served in the Revolutionary war and after-
ward settled in Kingston.

Children, b. in Kingston:

26. I. Seth[6], b. Aug. 21, 1782; d Sept. 4, 1807; unmarried, was a physician.

27. II. Nancy[6], b. Aug. 9, 1784; m. Feb. 9, 1806, Jesse
Ingles. No children

28. III. Lucy[6], b. May 8, 1786· d. June 6, 1868; m. Dec.
9, 1818, Timothy Davis. No children.

29. IV. Betsey[6], b. Sept. 25, 1789; m. 1, Feb. 26, 1811,
Silas Tobey; m. 2, Phineas Sprague. Children:
Edward S.[7] Tobey, b. April 5, 1813, at Kingston.

30. V. Polly[6], b. Sept. 20, 1791; d. Oct. 24, 1807.

31. VI. Sophia[6], b. Feb. 2, 1793; d. April 10, 1868;
unmarried.

32. VII. Sally[6], b. April 5, 1801, m. Jan. 21, 1827, Ebenezer
Barker of Charlestown, Mass., and had: Caroline
Tufts[7], b Feb. 4, 1830, Eben Francis[7], b. March
8, 1833; Lucy Loring[7], b. March 13, 1835;
Edward Tobey[7], b. April 14, 1840, and Frederick
Alden[7], b. Jan. 5, 1845, all born at Charlestown.

5. THOMAS[5] FULLER, (*Jabez[4], Isaac[3], Samuel[2], Samuel[1]*), b.
June 27, 1755, in Medfield, Mass.; d. ———; m. June 11, 1778,
in Plympton, Mass., Mary Howland.

He was a physician.

Children:

33. I. Thomas[6], b. ———; d. Jan. 11, 1799, aged 17 y.
1 m. 14 d.

34. II. Betsey[6], b. ———; d. Sept. 15, 1788, aged 2 y.
8 m. 3 d. (Medfield, Plympton and Carver
Records.)

SIXTH GENERATION.

11. Thomas[6] Fuller, (*Jonathan*[5], *Jabez*[4], *Isaac*[3], *Samuel*[2], *Samuel*[1]), b. Jan. 13, 1785, in Middleboro, Mass.; d March 24, 1844, near Fayetteville, Pa., m. Mary Baxter, b. April 28, 1789, d. March 29, 1862.

Thomas Fuller was for a time an agent in Charleston, S. C., for a Boston mercantile firm; coming North he settled in Franklin Co., Pa, and taught a subscription school for 15 years, and then turned his attention to farming and lumbering.

Children:

35.	‡I.	Robert Baxter[7], b. Dec. 21, 1815; m. Julia Ann Barbara Fohl.
36.	‡II.	Thomas Eddy[7], b. Feb. 28, 1818; m. Ann Embich.
37.	III.	Lucy[7], b. Dec. 6, 1819, d. Feb. 21, 1828.
38.	IV.	Sally[7], b. May 31, 1822; d. March 2, 1888; m. Nov. 10, 1851, Alexander Clippenger, who d. Dec. 17, 1900. Children: Robert Marion[8], b. Dec. 22, 1852; Jacob[8], b. March 24, 1855, Mary Edith[8], b. Dec. 25, 1857; Bella[8], b. July 22, 1861; Alexander Sharp[8], b. Jan. 31, 1864, and Thomas[8], b. April 22, 1869.

39.   V.   Daughter[7], ⎫
40.   VI.   Daughter[7], ⎬ twins, b. Nov. 4, 1825; d. Nov. 5, 1825.

41.   VII. Mary[7],   ⎫   ⎧ b. Oct. 8, 1827; m. Feb. 18,
                         ⎪   ⎪ 1862, John H. McMullen, and
                         ⎪   ⎪ had · A son, b. Dec. 15, 1862, d.
                         ⎪   ⎪ young; Thomas[8], b. June 29,
                         ⎪   ⎪ 1864; Anna[8], b. Jan. 10, 1867,
                         ⎬ twins ⎨ and Minnie Bell[8], b. Feb. 23,
                         ⎪   ⎩ 1870.
42. VIII. Elizabeth[7], ⎪   ⎧ b. Oct. 8, 1827; d. March 13,
                         ⎪   ⎪ 1888, m. May 22, 1855, Isaac
                         ⎪   ⎨ Reigle, and had: Mary Emma[8],
                         ⎭   ⎪ b. Feb. 23, 1856, and Susan
                                  ⎩ Edith[8], b. Oct. 9, 1858.

18. Jabez[6] Fuller, (*Jonathan*[5], *Jabez*[4], *Isaac*[3], *Samuel*[2], *Samuel*[1]), b. July 18, 1791, in Middleboro, Mass.; d. 1873, in Perkinsville, Vt.; m. Sept. 7, 1815, Sarah Hudson Churchill of Plympton, Mass.

Children ·

43.   I.   Fanny Woodbury[7], b. Feb. 15, 1818; m. Isaac D.

Ryder and had one child, Emily F.[8], b. 1840;
m ——— French.

44. II. Harriet Newell[7], b. May 31, 1820; m. Oren Taylor
and had· Rosannah H.[8], b. 1845; Mylon O.[8],
b. 1849; Ella[8], b. 1855, and Eddy S.[8], b. 1861.

45. ‡III. Flavius Josephus[7], b. July 10, 1822, m. Josephine
(Boyden) Wilson

46. IV. Sarah Delano[7], b March 12, 1829; m. Simon Buck
and had. Warren[8], resides Lewiston, Me.;
George[8], resides Ashville, N. C., Wallace[8],
deceased, Lynn[8], resides Charlotte, N. C., and
Moses[8], also in Charlotte.

47. ‡V. William Eddy[7], b. June 30, 1832; m. Anna M.
Corey.

48. VI. Anna Maria[8], b Nov. 25, 1835; d. Dec. 30, 1904;
m. Sept, 1858, J. Martin Billings and had:
Albert T.[8], b. Aug. 23, 1859, William J.[8] and
Nellie S[8], twins, b. April 2, 1862.

49. VII. Helen Emery[7], b. Feb. 18, 1840; m. Aurelius
Sherwin and had a daughter, Jennie[8].

23. SAMUEL[6] FULLER, (*John[5], Jabez[4], Isaac[3], Samuel[2],
Samuel[1]*), b. Aug. 29, 1788, in Medfield, Mass.; d. ———; m. 1,
Mary Sparhawk of Sherborne, Mass., who d Dec. 3, 1816; m. 2,
June 22, 1817, Jemima Cole.

Removed to Union, Me., about 1824.

Children, born in Medfield :

50 I. Mary Ann[7], b. ——— ; d. July 10, 1894, at Pem-
broke, N. H.; m. John Bachelder and had:
Charles Lucius[8], b. 1833, in Lowell, Mass.;
Mary Ann[8], b 1835, Goffstown, N. H.; Augusta
A.[8], b 1837, at Goffstown; John[8], b. 1839, at
Concord, Mass., Martha Jane[8], b. 1841, at
Concord, Henry S.[8], b. 1843, at Concord;
Rebecca Wentworth[8], b. 1845, James Lewis[8], b.
1848; Samuel Fuller[8], b. 1850, and George
Franklin[8], b. 1852; the last four born at Pem-
broke, N. H.

51. ‡II. Albert[7], b. Oct. 2, 1814; m. Nancy Clarke.

52. ‡III. Samuel[7], b. Oct. 11, 1816; m. Eliza Jane Sidelinger.

By second wife :

53 IV. Abigail[7], b. in Medfield.
54. V. Fisher[7], b. in Union, Me.; d. young.
55. VI. Fisher[7], b. in Union, d. there, m. Orivelle Taylor.
No children.

56.   VII   Sarah Jane[7], b. ———.
57.   VIII.   Rhoda H[7], b. 1829, d. 1888; m. Harris Lenfest
                 of Union, Me.
58.   IX.   Charles B.[7], b. 1836; d. in Rockland, Me.

24. JOHN[6] FULLER, (*John[5], Jabez[4], Isaac[3], Samuel[2], Samuel[1]*),
b. Oct. 15, 1792, in Medfield, Mass., d. ———; m. Eleanor
Hartshorn, b. in Walpole, Mass., who d Nov. 11, 1874, aged 79
years, in Oxford, Mass.

Children :

59.   ‡I.   John Lewis[7], b. 1816; m. Tryphena Brown.
60.   ‡II.   George[7], b Feb. 22, 1819, m. Angenette Ruggles.
61.   ‡III. Henry Augustus[7], b. Aug., 1822; m. ———.
62.   ‡IV   Charles[7], b ———; m. Caroline DeWitt.
63.   V.   Albert[7], b. Dec. 16, 1824; d. Oct. 17, 1847, in
                Woonsocket, R. I.

SEVENTH GENERATION.

35. ROBERT BAXTER[7] FULLER, (*Thomas[6], Jonathan[5], Jabez[4],
Isaac[3], Samuel[2], Samuel[1]*), b. Dec. 21, 1815, in Fayetteville, Pa.;
d. Aug. 15, 1880, near Navarre, O.; m. Feb. 6, 1849, Julia Ann
Barbara Fohl, b. Dec. 15, 1831, d. April 30, 1900.

Mr. Fuller and his brother, Thomas Eddy Fuller, bought several
thousand acres of mountain timber land in Franklin Co., Pa., and
converted the logs into lumber at an old-fashioned jig-saw mill near
by. In 1865 R. B Fuller and family settled in Bethlehem Tp.,
Stark Co., O., and in 1870 he purchased a farm which he occupied
until his decease.

Children .

64.   ‡I.   Thomas[8], b July 11, 1850; m. Sarah Kuhn.
65.   II.   John[8], b. March 26, 1852, d. Sept. 9, 1854.
66.   ‡III. Robert Baxter[8], b. April 28, 1854; m. Lucretia
                Alice Beazell
67.   ‡IV.   William Eddy[8], b. April 30, 1856; m. Elizabeth A.
                Whitmore.
68.   ‡V.   Jacob Ripley[8], b. Oct. 2, 1858; m. Elmira Jane
                Leighter.
69.   VI.   Ann Mary[8], b. Jan. 31, 1867; m. Feb. 24, 1885,
                Franklin Pierce Masters and had: Homer
                Eugene[9], b. Nov. 19, 1888, and Grace Marie[9], b.
                Feb. 16, 1899.

Judge William Eddy Fuller.

36. THOMAS EDDY[7] FULLER, (*Thomas*[6], *Jonathan*[5], *Jabez*[4], *Isaac*[3], *Samuel*[2], *Samuel*[1]), b. Feb. 28, 1818, in Fayetteville, Pa.; d. Nov. 30, 1904, near Shippenberg, Pa.; m. Jan. 6, 1846, Ann Embich, who d. Jan. 11, 1901.

Children:

70.   ‡I.   Flavius Bryant[8], b. March 31, 1850; m. Sarah M. Mains.

45. FLAVIUS JOSEPHUS[7] FULLER, (*Jabez*[6], *Jonathan*[5], *Jabez*[4], *Isaac*[3], *Samuel*[2], *Samuel*[1]), b. July 10, 1822; d. Feb. 14, 1864, in Wethersfield, Vt.; m. Dec. 12, 1857, Josephine (Boyden) Wilson.

Children, b. in Wethersfield:

71.   ‡I.   Frank William[8], b. Sept. 28, 1858; m. Carrie B. Wright.

72.   II.   Frederick Chase[8], b. Dec. 25, 1862.

47. WILLIAM EDDY[7] FULLER, (*Jabez*[6], *Jonathan*[5], *Jabez*[4], *Isaac*[3], *Samuel*[2], *Samuel*[1]), b. June 30, 1832, in Bridgewater, Vt., m. Nov. 21, 1859, Anna M. Corey.

William Eddy Fuller is Judge of Probate and Insolvency for Bristol County, Mass., and resides in Taunton, Mass.

Judge Fuller received his early education in the common school and the academies of South Woodstock and Randolph, Vt. He entered Dartmouth College in 1852, and Harvard College in his Junior year and graduated in 1856. After teaching for several years, five of which were as principal of the Taunton High School, he began the study of law, and was admitted to the Bristol County bar in 1863. From 1868 to 1883 he was Register of Probate and Insolvency for Bristol County, and was then appointed Judge in the same offices by Governor Benjamin F Butler, which offices he continues to hold after 25 years of service Judge Fuller served for many years as member of Taunton School Board, as trustee of Bristol Academy, and member of the Old Colony Historical Society. He has delivered many public addresses on literary and historical occasions. In 1891 he published a book on Massachusetts Probate Laws, now in its second edition, a handbook in use by the legal profession of the state and regarded as one of the most valuable works on the subject. He is vice president of the Taunton Savings Bank and director in Taunton National Bank. His religious

connections have been with the Unitarian church and in politics he
is a Republican.

His children, all born in Taunton, are :

73.   ‡I.   William Eddy[8], b. Aug. 14, 1870; m. Mary
              Newcomb.

74.   II.   Mary C[8], b. Aug. 14, 1873. Resides in Taunton.

51. ALBERT[7] FULLER, (*Samuel[6], John[5], Jabez[4], Isaac[3], Samuel[2], Samuel[1]*), b. Oct. 2, 1814, in Medfield, Mass., d. 1895, in Union, Me., m. 1839, Nancy Clarke

Children, all b. in Union, Me.:

75.   I.   Isaac Flitner[8], b 1840; d. in the battle of
              Williamsburg.

76.   II.   Mary Ellen[8], b. ———; d. 1902; m. Austin
              Jenness.

77.   III.   Lucy E.[8], b. Oct. 6, 1842; m. Oct. 28, 1864,
              William Fessenden Wight of Warren, Me., who
              d. March 5, 1900. Children · Kendrick F.[9], b.
              Dec. 12, 1865, at Cushing, Me.; Austin F.[9], b.
              June 23, 1871, in Warren, Me.; Maurice W.[9], b.
              Aug 31, 1875, d Feb. 4, 1876, and Zenas F.[9], b.
              Sept. 27, 1878

78.   ‡IV.   James Clark[8], b. July 31, 1842; m. 1, Ambeline
              Sidelinger; m. 2, 1874, Diadema Jackson.

79.   V.   Sarah Catherine[8], b. ———; d. young.

80.   VI.   Sarah Catherine[8], b. 1850. Resides in Union.

81.   ‡VII.   Sylvanus[8], b. June 27, 1856; m. ———.

52. SAMUEL[7] FULLER, (*Samuel[6], John[5], Jabez[4], Isaac[3], Samuel[2], Samuel[1]*), b. Oct 11, 1816, in Mansfield, Mass., d. Oct. 31, 1903, in Union, Me., m. April 28, 1844, Eliza Jane Sidelinger.

Children :

82.   ‡I.   William Emerson[8], b. July 22, 1845; m. Lavina
              Burns.

83.   II.   Abbie Augusta[8], b. Oct. 22, 1846, d. Jan. 31,
              1875, at Bath, Me.; m April 9, 1870, Oliver
              Parker Andrews of Warren, Me., and had :
              Florence[9], b. Dec. 1, 1872, at Thomaston, Me.,
              and Alice[9], b. Feb. 11, 1874, at Bath.

84.   III.   Flora Irene[8], b. April 22, 1848; m. Alden
              Farrington and reside in Norway, Me.

85.   IV.   Margaret Adelaide[8], b. March 9, 1850, m. April 10,
              1873, William Hosmer of Camden, Me., and

had : William Austin[9], b. May 20, 1873, and Jessie Blastow[9], b. April 10, 1886.

86.   V.   Bertha Arovyne[S], b. April 4, 1852; d. Nov. 26, 1875.

87.   VI.   Clara Celeste[S], b. July 23, 1854; m. 1884, Leslie Weed. Reside in Norway, Me.

88.   VII.   Joseph Micajah[S], b. June 24, 1856; d. June 4, 1877.

89. ‡VIII.   Samuel Edward[8], b. Aug. 24, 1858; m. Amy E. Payson.

90.   IX.   James Sanford[S], b. Sept. 24, 1860; d. May 26, 1876.

91.   X.   George Frank[8], b. April 13, 1864.

92.   XI.   John Bailey[S], b. Dec. 2, 1866.

93.   XII.   Mary Maude[S], b. Dec. 5, 1868; m. J. F. Bolster of Norway, Me.

59. JOHN LEWIS[7] FULLER, (*John[6], John[5], Jabez[4], Isaac[3], Samuel[2], Samuel[1]*), b. 1816, in Dedham, Mass.; d. ———; m. ——— Tryphena Brown.

Children :

94.   I.   Mary A.[S], b. ———.

95.   ‡II.   Albert L.[S], b. ———; m. ———.

96.   III.   Henry A.[S], b. ———, d. ———; unmarried.

60. GEORGE[7] FULLER, (*John[6], John[5], Jabez[4], Isaac[3], Samuel[2], Samuel[1]*), b. Feb. 22, 1819, in Dedham, Mass.; d. Oct. 12, 1881; m. April 18, 1844, Angenette Ruggles, b. in Andover, Mass. She resides in Wrentham, Mass.

Children :

97.   I.   Ellen Maria[S], b. 1845, d. Aug. 25, 1846.

98.   ‡II.   George O.[S], b. Dec. 1, 1847; m. Ellen J. Miller.

99.   III.   Ella J.[S], b. May 6, 1849; d. Sept. 24, 1850.

100.   IV.   Mary Annette[S], b. Nov. 11, 1850; d. April 28, 1868.

101.   V.   Emma Frances[S], b. Aug. 16, 1852; m. Elman G. Follett and has two daughters, Millie G.[9] and Mary A.[9]

102.   VI.   Ida R.[S], b. Sept. 24, 1854. Resides in Wrentham; unmarried.

103.   VII.   Lizzie M.[S], b. Sept. 14, 1856; d. young.

104.   VIII.   Bertha M.[S], b. Sept. 3, 1859, m. Nov. 1, 1900, Dr. Charles Hamilton. Resides in Wrentham. No children.

105.   ‡IX.   Charles H.[8], b. Sept. 24, 1861; m. Edith I. Cook.
106.   X.   Nellie J.[8], b Aug. 26, 1863; m. Rev. Arthur
               Wadsworth and has one son, Arthur B.[9]
107.   ‡XI.   John A[8], b. Jan. 25, 1865, m. Emilie Rebecca
               Woolson.

61. HENRY AUGUSTUS[7] FULLER, (*John[6], John[5], Jabez[4], Isaac[3], Samuel[2], Samuel[1]*), b. Aug, 1822, at Medfield, Mass.; d. of yellow fever in New Orleans during the Civil war; m. ———. Widow and children reside in New York state.

Children.

108.   I.   A son, b. ———.
109.   II.   A dau., b. ———.

62. CHARLES[7] FULLER, (*John[6], John[5], Jabez[4], Isaac[3], Samuel[2], Samuel[1]*), b. in Medford? d. July 13, 1883; m. Nov. 28, 1844, in Oxford, Mass., Caroline DeWitt.

Children.

110   I.   Charles H[8], b March 6, 1847, d. Aug. 26, 1849.
111.   ‡II.   Charles A.[8], b. Feb. 7, 1857; m. Clara A. Dodge.
112.   III.   Caroline[8], b March 7, 1864; d Jan. 20, 1891.
               Two other children that died young.

EIGHTH GENERATION.

64. THOMAS[8] FULLER, (*Robert B.[7], Thomas[6], Jonathan[5], Jabez[4], Isaac[3], Samuel[2], Samuel[1]*), b. July 11, 1850, in Franklin Co., Pa.; m. Feb. 4, 1878, in Bethlehem Tp., Ohio, Sarah E. Kuhn, b Jan. 20, 1852.

Children :

113.   I.   Susie Amanda[9], b. Nov. 12, 1879.   Graduate of
               Canton, O , Business College and in business in
               Canton (1909).
114.   II.   Elmer Ellsworth[9], b. Dec. 12, 1882.   A farmer in
               Ohio.

66. ROBERT BAXTER[8] FULLER, (*Robert B.[7], Thomas[6], Jonathan[5], Jabez[4], Isaac[3], Samuel[2], Samuel[1]*), b. April 28, 1854, in Franklin Co., Pa.; m. Jan. 26, 1879, in Canton, O., Lucretia Alice Beazell.

He is a farmer near Navarre, O.

Children ·

115.   I.   Edna Grace[9], b. Sept. 19, 1890.

Miss Susie A. Fuller.
Elmer Ellsworth Fuller.

67. WILLIAM EDDY[8] FULLER, (*Robert B.*[7], *Thomas*[6], *Jonathan*[5], *Jabez*[4], *Isaac*[3], *Samuel*[2], *Samuel*[1]), b. April 30, 1856, in Franklin Co., Pa.; m. Oct. 3, 1878, Elizabeth Angeline Whitmore, b. April 6, 1858, in Stark Co., O.

Mr. Fuller is a clergyman.

Their children are:

116. ‡I. Alston[9], b April 26, 1879; m. July 4, 1909, Estyl Verna Redman.
117. II. A son, b. April 5, 1880, d. April 26, 1880.
118. III. Rosa Adella[9], b. May 24, 1881, in Stark Co., O.
119. IV. William Alvertine[9], b July 24, 1883, in Stark Co. Resides New York City.
120. V. Stella May[9], b April 21, 1885, in Geanga Co., O.
121. VI. Robert[9], b. April 27, 1887, in Geanga Co. In U. S. naval service on the battleship Rhode Island (1910).
122. VII Raymond[9], b. Jan. 28, 1889, in Summit Co., O.
123 VIII. Reno B.[9], b. Jan. 21, 1892, in Wayne Co., O.
124. IX. Clara Edith[9], b. Sept. 27, 1894, in Richland Co., O.
125. X. Forney[9], b Jan. 9, 1898, in Fostoria, O.
126. XI. Lowell[9], b. Feb. 9, 1900, in Fostoria.

68. JACOB RIPLEY[8] FULLER, (*Robert B.*[7], *Thomas*[6], *Jonathan*[5], *Jabez*[4], *Isaac*[3], *Samuel*[2], *Samuel*[1]), b. Oct. 2, 1858, in Franklin Co., Pa.; d. April 19, 1907, near Navarre, O.; m. Nov. 11, 1880, in Stark Co., O., Elmira Jane Leighter.

He was engaged in farming near Navarre.

Their children are:

127. I. Augusta[9], b. May 19, 1883.
128. II. Bernice[9], b. Dec. 30, 1891.

70. FLAVIUS BRYANT[8] FULLER, (*Thomas E.*[7], *Thomas*[6], *Jonathan*[5], *Jabez*[4], *Isaac*[3], *Samuel*[2], *Samuel*[1]), b. March 30, 1850; m. Dec. 24, 1872, Sarah M. Mains.

They reside in Shippensburg, Pa.

Children:

129. I. Charles E.[9], b. April 19, 1875. Resides in Harrisburg, Pa.
130. II. Anne B.[9], b. Jan. 13, 1877; m. —— Watson. Resides in Shippensburg.
131. III. Maud A.[9], b. Jan. 9, 1879; m. —— Heider. Resides in Sterling, Ill.

132.   IV. William M. M.9, b. Feb. 9, 1880. Resides in
               Sterling,Ill
133.   V.   Thomas M.9, b. Feb 24, 1882 ; m. ———. Resides
               in Shippensburg.
134.   VI. Clara T.9, b. Jan. 4, 1884 ; d. aged 20 years.
135.   VII. George W.9, b. Feb. 22, 1886 ; d. aged 2 years.

71. FRANK WILLIAM[8] FULLER, (*Flavius J.*[7], *Jabez*[6], *Jonathan*[5],
Jabez[4], *Isaac*[3], *Samuel*[2], *Samuel*[1]), b Sept. 28, 1858, in Wethersfield, Vt.; m. March 22, 1885, Carrie B. Wright, and resides at
Farley, Mass.
   Children :
136.   I.   Hardy9, b Dec. 21, 1886 ; d. Nov. 22, 1899.
137.   II.   Minnie A.9, b June 11, 1888.
138.   III. Daisy B.9, b. Aug. 19, 1893.
139.   IV.   Hazel A.9, b. Sept. 28, 1895.
140.   V.   Harry D 9, b. July 7, 1902.
141.   VI.   Gladys M.9, b. Sept. 25, 1905 ; d. Jan. 11, 1906.
142.   VII. Evelyn M.9, b. July 20, 1907.

73. WILLIAM EDDY[8] FULLER, (*William E.*[7], *Jabez*[6], *Jonathan*[5],
Jabez[4], *Isaac*[3], *Samuel*[2], *Samuel*[1]), b Aug. 14, 1870, in Taunton,
Mass.; m. Sept. 22, 1897, May Newcomb in Detroit, Mich.
   Mr Fuller resides at Fall River, Mass., a member of the firm of
Fuller & Gray, lawyers.
   Children, all born at Fall River :
143.   I.   William Eddy9, b. June 29, 1898.
144.   II.   Newcomb9, b. Sept 22, 1900.
145.   III. Anna Corey9, b. April 27, 1907.

78. JAMES CLARK[8] FULLER, (*Albert*[7], *Samuel*[6], *John*[5], *Jabez*[4],
Isaac[3], *Samuel*[2], *Samuel*[1]), b. July 31, 1842, in Union, Me.; m. 1,
Ambeline Sidelinger ; m. 2, 1874, Diadema Jackson.
   Children :
146.   I.   Leola9, b. 1873 ; m. ——— Rose of Rockland, Me.

81. SYLVANUS[8] FULLER, (*Albert*[7], *Samuel*[6], *John*[5], *Jabez*[4],
Isaac[3], *Samuel*[2], *Samuel*[1]), b. June 27, 1856, in Union, Me.; d.
Oct., 1891 , m. ———.
   Children :
147.   I.   Alexander9, b. ———.
148.   II.   Mary Ellen9, ———.

82. WILLIAM EMERSON[8] FULLER, (*Samuel[7], Samuel[6], John[5], Jabez[4], Isaac[3], Samuel[2], Samuel[1]*), b. July 22, 1845, in Union, Me.; d. 1886 ; m. Lavina Burns.

Children, born to them were :

149.   I.   Frederick[9], b. Jan. 3, 1871 ; d. Feb. 18, 1875.
150.   II.   Mabel[9], b. Feb. 14, 1873.

89. SAMUEL EDWARD[8] FULLER, (*Samuel[7], Samuel[6], John[5], Jabez[4], Isaac[3], Samuel[2], Samuel[1]*), b. Aug. 24, 1858, in Union, Me.; m. March 11, 1890, Amy E. Payson.

Children :

151.   I.   Herbert Harry[9], b. Oct. 28, 1890, d. Dec. 1, 1890.
152.   II.   Ernest Cummings[9], b. June 19, 1892.
153.   III.   Eda Maude[9], b. April 1, 1896.

95. ALBERT L.[8] FULLER, (*John L.[7], John[6], John[5], Jabez[4], Isaac[3], Samuel[2], Samuel[1]*), b. ——— ; d. ——— ; m. ———.

Children ·

154.   I.   A son, b. ———.
155.   II.   A daughter, b. ———.
156.   III.   A daughter, b. ———.

98. GEORGE O.[8] FULLER, (*George[7], John[6], John[5], Jabez[4], Isaac[3], Samuel[2], Samuel[1]*), b Dec. 1, 1847, in Medfield, Mass , m. May 11, 1870, Ellen J. Miller, b Oct 27, 1850, in Franklin, Mass.

They reside in Pawtucket, R. I., where Mr. Fuller is a member of the firm of Fuller Bros., upholsterers.

Children, all born in Franklin, Mass.:

157.   I.   Nettie G.[9], b. Dec. 27, 1872.
158.   II.   Edith M.[9], b. July 8, 1874 ; m. Oct. 29, 1906, George S. Harrison, b. March 18, 1875, in Pawtucket, and had : Earl G.[10], b. Jun. 10, 1908, in Pawtucket.
159.   III.   George A.[9], b. Jan. 3, 1876 ; d. Dec. 30, 1882.
160.   ‡IV.   Ernest G.[9], b. March 29, 1879 ; m. Beatrice Wilcox.
161.   V.   Henry F.[9], b. Feb. 25, 1881.

105. CHARLES H.[8] FULLER, (*George[7], John[6], John[5], Jabez[4], Isaac[3], Samuel[2], Samuel[1]*), b. Sept. 29, 1861, in Wrentham, Mass.; m. June 15, 1898, Edith I. Cook.

He resides in Pawtucket; member of firm of Fuller Bros., upholsterers.

Children ·

162.   I.   Charles H.9, b Dec. 24, 1900.
163.   II. Clara Angenette9, b. Sept. 1, 1903.

107. JOHN A.8 FULLER, (*George*7, *John*6, *John*5, *Jabez*4, *Isaac*3, *Samuel*2, *Samuel*1), b June 25, 1865; m. Oct 5, 1886, Emilie Rebecca Woolson, and resides in Greenland, N. H.

Children :

164.   I.   John A.9, b. Nov. 14, 1887.
165.   II. Howard E 9, b. July 12, 1892.
166.   III. Geraldine E.9, b. May 16, 1900.
167.   IV. Goldena E.9, b. Jan. 21, 1902.

111. CHARLES A 8 FULLER, (*Charles*7, *John*6, *John*5, *Jabez*4, *Isaac*3, *Samuel*2, *Samuel*1), b. Feb. 7, 1857, in Oxford, Mass.; m. 1880, Clara A. Dodge, and resides in Oxford.

Children :

168.   I.   Frank De Witt9, b. Feb. 8, 1881.
169   II. Sarah Edith9, b. Oct. 16, 1882 ; d. Dec. 22, 1882.
170.   III. Mabel Sarah9, b. June 3, 1884 ; d. March 27, 1886.

NINTH GENERATION.

160. ERNEST G.9 FULLER, (*George O.*8, *George*7, *John*6, *John*5, *Jabez*4, *Isaac*3, *Samuel*2, *Samuel*1), b. March 29, 1879, in Franklin, Mass.; m. Nov. 2, 1902, Beatrice Wilcox, b. July 2, 1889, in Providence, R. I.

They reside in Pawtucket, R. I.

Children :

171.   I.   Helen E.10, b. May 14, 1904, in Pawtucket.

APPENDIX.

The following letter from Prof. H. W. Brainard of Hartford, Ct., recently received, is of interest:

HARTFORD, June 28, 1910.

DEAR SIR

The following is important, and may be new to you. It was sent me by my friend, Frank F. Starr, the genealogist, of Middletown. It refers to Elizabeth Fuller, wife of Rev. Samuel Fuller of Plymouth and Middleboro, and she died at Plympton, about 1713. I think you must have the exact date. Whether she was Fuller's only wife, and the mother of his children, I cannot say. She must have married Fuller after April 11, 1663, and was widow then of Thomas Bowen of Marblehead, New London and Rehoboth, who was brother to Richard and Obadiah Bowen of Rehoboth.

New London County Court records, Vol. 2, fifth leaf from the end:

May 2, 1667. Power of attorney. Elizabeth ffuller of Towne of Plimouth in the Jurisdicktion of Plimouth — sometime the wife of Thomas Bowen, Late of Rehoboth in the Jurisdiction Aforesd, Cooper, deceased, and Samuell ffuller of the Towne of Plimouth — to our well beloved Brother-in-lawe John Prentice of New London in new England. Blacksmith, land in New London, sometime the land of said Thomas Bowen. I the sayde Elizabeth ffuller being Exequtrics unto the sd Thomas Bowen,— as by his will dated April 11, 1663. Power to sell the lands

Thomas Cushman, } witnesses.
Bridgett ffuller, }

This also shows that Bridget, widow of Deacon and Dr. Samuel Fuller, was living May 2, 1667.

Very truly yours,

HOMER W. BRAINARD.

Since receiving the above mentioned letter, I find that Savage, in his Genealogical Dictionary, printed 50 years ago, says: "Thomas Bowen, Salem, 1648, was of New London 1657–60, rem. to Rehoboth 1663. His wid. Elizabeth was in 1669 w. of Samuel Fuller of Plymouth. His will of 11 April 1663, made her extrix., names his s. Richard and br. Obadiah. Thomas Bowen of Marblehead 1674 may have been son of Thomas of Salem 1648."

Also, "Samuel Fuller of Plymouth, son of first Samuel had w. Elizabeth, but was not married before 1650"

In Felt's "Annals of Salem," Vol 1, Thomas Bowen is in list of first settlers "mentioned as of this place." No other reference to him found.

In the "Supplementary Vital Records of Marblehead," item from Court Records, Vol 1, page 56, mentions Thomas Bowen "aged abt. 24 y, his wife Elizabeth, 26-10 m. 1646." Also Vol. 6, p. 151, "Thomas Bowen, w. Elizabeth mentioned June 1661"

Also, Vol. 14, p 116, "Thomas Bowen a. abt. 45 y dep June T. 1669." The "History of the First Church of Roxbury, Mass.," says John Prentice came over with his father Valentine in 1631, removed to New London, 1652; blacksmith   Valentine Prentice died 1633 and his widow Alice m. John Watson.

Ellis, in his "History of Roxbury," says Valentine Prentice brought but one child, his son John.

In the matter of dates of birth of Rev. Samuel Fuller's children, I have followed on page 15 those given in the Brainard and F. A Fuller MSS., but I notice on page 20 the birth of John 3 (*Samuel²*, *Samuel¹*) is given as "about 1668," and the Brainard MSS. gives the same year, which is probably an error, as John would be but about 18 years of age when married about 1686-7   I find also that the statement in the Brainard MSS. (which I have given on page 15), that the burial place of Rev. Samuel Fuller was on the "Hill" at Plymouth is incorrect, and on inquiry of Charles M. Thatcher of Middleboro, he says Rev. Samuel Fuller was buried in Nemasket Hill Cemetery, Middleboro, and the gravestone is still standing.

Davis, in his "Ancient Landmarks of Plymouth," 1883, says: "Samuel, son of Samuel of the Mayflower, by w. Elizabeth had Mercy m. Daniel Cole, Samuel 1659, Experience m. James Wood, John, Elizabeth m. Samuel Eaton, Hannah m. Eleazer Lewis, and Isaac." Now Davis, so far as I have noticed in that volume, gives the children in the order of birth in his genealogical record, but Prof. Brainard, in a later letter of July 14, 1910, states that he finds in the Mayflower Descendants, Vol. 8, p. 3, that "Daniel Cole died 15 June 1736 in 70th year," and "Mercy, wife of Daniel, died Sept. 25, 1735, in 63d year"—"Gravestones, Ancient Cemetery, Eastham, Mass." Then Mercy, wife of Daniel Cole, was born in 1672 or 1673.

Was this Mercy, Mercy Fuller, dau. of Rev. Samuel Fuller? This letter of Prof. Brainard's is one in answer to my inquiry as to his authority for the dates of birth of Rev. Samuel Fuller's children given in his MSS., so often quoted This letter contains no other new facts fixing the dates of birth of the other children.

In answer to a letter of inquiry to Mr. F. A. Fuller, he states that "about all his data was furnished by Newton Fuller." (Both Brainard and F. A. Fuller exchanged genealogical information with the late Newton Fuller.)

Weston, in his History of Middleboro, published 1906, says Rev. Samuel Fuller's wife was Elizabeth Brewster. Prof. Brainard says the same in his MSS, and adds, "Tradition says dau. of Elder Brewster, but research does not confirm it." Dr. Sarah E. Crocker of Boston, who has made extended researches in this direction, states in a letter of July 5, 1910, that this tradition has been disproved, and also incidentally that the late Chipman Fuller of Halifax told her that Ebenezer Fuller, his grandfather (?), "when the Middleboro church records were burned, supplied the church with a list of names from his own records, and adds "that it is strange that he should have recorded the maiden name of Samuel Fuller's wife as Brewster."

A Washington, D. C., correspondent finds that the Bowen family genealogies in the library there only relate to the Woodstock, Ct., family and a foreign family of Wales Prof Brainard mentions in his MSS. that the "Elizabeth Brewster, dau. of Jonathan and Lucretia Oldham Brewster, who married Peter Brawley of New London, died in 1654."

I have mentioned these facts in a hurried and irregular way, as it is necessary for me to furnish this MSS. to the printer and close up the work on this volume.

CORRECTIONS IN 5TH GROUP.

Homer Taylor Fuller, number 141, was Principal of St Johnsbury Academy from 1871 instead of 1872, and the degree of Ph. D. was conferred by Dartmouth instead of Iowa college, as stated in the newspaper clipping.

Henry Jones Fuller, number 291, graduated in 1895 from the Worcester Polytechnic Institute and is President of the Canadian Fairbanks Co , whose business has had a marvelous growth under his efficient management.

A correspondent, a relative of John H. Fuller, number 128, has just enclosed to me a newspaper clipping without date, mentioning "the funeral of Mrs Emma Cushman Fuller, wife of John H. Fuller of Rockingham Ave.," "born in Dover, N. H., 82 years ago," "survived by her husband, one son, John S. Fuller, five grand-daughters and two grandsons."

Index to Fullers.

Linus, 149
Linus E , 21, 134, 136, 138, 145
Linus Fenn, 141, 149
Linus Whiteside, 157
Lisle H , 170
Livia, 62
Livingston, 157
Lizzie Augusta, 58
Lizzie Josephine, 39
Lizzie M., 179
Lois, 52, 61, 127, 134, 137
Lois Elmira, 166
Lois Frances, 87
Lois L , 77
Lorenzo Dow, 142, 149
Loring, 63
Lorna, 41
Lottie M., 153
Louis Edward, 43, 48
Louis Ringe, 94
Louis Sturtevant, 87
Louisa, 86, 91, 134
Louisa C , 34, 91
Louisa Jane, 55
Lovicia, 40
Lowell, 181
Lucia Churchill, 113
Lucinda Maria, 29
Lucius, 85
Lucius Ames, 144, 153
Lucy, 53, 69, 140, 173, 174
Lucy Ann, 163
Lucy B , 155
Lucy Bradford, 65
Lucy Delano, 112
Lucy E., 178
Lucy Eddy, 172
Lucy Leonard, 98
Lucy Maria, 143
Lucy P., 145
Lucy Safford, 41
Lucy Sturtevant, 75
Lulu, 60
Luna, 69
Lura M., 42
Luther, 164
Lydia, 20, 24, 62, 64, 68, 70,

77, 120, 128, 140
Lydia Brown, 150
Lydia Florence, 96
Lysander, 77
Lytle Ella, 50
Mabel, 183
Mabel A., 155
Mabel Sarah, 184
Mabel Sylvester, 126
Madison, 53, 55
Major Pomeroy, 164
Malachi, 62
Marcellus, 78
Marcia, 152
Marcus, 119, 122
Margaret, 102
Margaret Adelaide, 178
Margaret Elizabeth, 115, 126
Margaret Kennedy, 106
Margery, 170
Maria, 53
Maria A., 79, 89
Maria Elizabeth, 56
Maria Louisa, 149
Maria Thomas, 86
Maria Washburn, 101
Marie Adel, 102
Marie Louise, 81
Marion, 97
Marion Keith, 109
Marion Lovett, 96
Mark Ingraham, 39
Marshall, 164
Martha, 24, 26, 38, 172
Martha C., 64
Martha E., 169
Martha Louise, 170
Martha Maria, 80, 97
Martha S., 121
Martha W., 148
Mary, 11, 21, 24, 44, 52, 57, 66,
73, 75, 114, 130, 138, 139,
143, 154, 161, 171, 174
Mary A., 103, 179
Mary Alden, 142
Mary Amelia, 38
Mary Ann, 175

Mary Anna, 165
Mary Annette, 179
Mary Asenath, 115
Mary Atwood, 74
Mary Breese, 94
Mary C., 178
Mary Chandler, 112, 113
Mary Churchill, 54
Mary E., 65
Mary Eliza, 33, 101
Mary Elizabeth, 82
Mary Ellen, 121, 148, 164, 178, 182
Mary F., 37
Mary Flagg, 142
Mary Florence, 99
Mary Frances, 86, 123
Mary H., 32
Mary J., 79
Mary Jane, 40, 42, 146
Mary Lathrop, 81, 98
Mary Leslie, 106
Mary Lillian, 122
Mary Louise, 58, 125
Mary Maria, 146
Mary Maude, 179
Mary S., 31
Matena, 105
Matilda, 112
Matthew Herbert, 106
Matthias G L, 146
Maud A., 181
Maybell Doane, 102
May Belle, 95
May Forest, 91
Mehitable, 137
Melvin Luvelle, 38
Mercy, 11, 12, 13, 15, 17, 19, 20, 61, 111, 112, 133, 186
Mercy A., 79
Mercy Freeman, 172
Merle Evans, 49
Micah, 21
Mildred Allen, 48
Milton, 150
Minerva, 141
Minnie A., 182

Miranda, 33, 120
Miranda Elizabeth, 144
Miranda W., 123
Miriam, 159
Molly, 69
Mortimer B., 108, 110
Moses Wendell, 101
Myra, 56
Myron, 53
Myron L., 106
Myrtle, 154
Nabby, 142, 173
N. Bonaparte, 44
Nancy, 30, 55, 129, 130, 161, 164, 173
Nancy A., 30
Nancy Caroline, 78
Nancy D., 77
Nancy High, 39
Nancy Jane, 96
Nancy W, 32
Nathan, 127, 128, 129, 130
Nathan Henry, 167
Nathan O., 149
Nathan Thomas, 86, 102
Nathan Thompson, 74
Nathan W., 147
Nathaniel, 20, 22, 23, 24, 164, 167
Nellie, 98, 150
Nellie Eliza Lovinia, 58
Nellie H., 155
Nellie J., 180
Nellie L., 46
Nelson Haywood 129
Nelson William, 146, 153
Nettie Estelle, 153
Nettie F., 42
Nettie G., 183
Nettie Miller, 125
Newcomb, 182
Newton, 187
Ninon, Letica, 168
Noah 41, 67, 68, 71, 72, 127, 128, 161, 162
Noah Prince, 26, 31
Noel B., 84, 100

Index to other Names than Fullers.

208   INDEX TO OTHER NAMES THAN FULLERS.

Cushman, Mary (Washburn), 24
    Mrs Mercy, 20, 67
    Rebecca, 23, 24
    Sarah, 161
    Thomas, 62, 185
Cutter, Prida, 137, 143
Darling, Alanson, 71
Davis, Mr., 186
    Angelia, 32
    Eva Margaret, 97, 108
    Eva V., 153, 158
    Frank, 32
    Irvin W., 124
    Jabez, 32
    Julia A., 32
    Nicholas, 61
    Ruth, 98
    Samantha, 32
    Timothy, 173
Day, Andrew G., 27
Dean, Clarence W, 39
Dean, Isabel, 39
    Isabella S., 40
    John R, 39
    Ruth, 39
    Walter E, 39
Dearborn, John C., 78
    Mabel F, 78
Delano, Mary, 112
    Phillip, 171
    Polly, 112
Delaplaine, Emily Louise, 119, 122
    John B, 122
Delva, Anna, 143
    Annette, 143
    Bessie, 143
    Calvin W, 143
    Ellen, 143
    Emeline, 143
    Frank, 143
    James, 143
    Nellie, 143
    Susan, 143
Demerritt, Andrew, 86
Dewey, Miss?, 52,
DeWitt, Caroline, 176, 180

Dexter, Mr., 9
Dexter, Anna, 171
    Rev. Elijah, 85
    Elizabeth, 171
    Lorin, 171
    Sarah, 171
    Stephen, 171
Dickson, Alexander W., 81
Dike, Anthony, 134
    Samuel, 134
Dillingham, Helen May, 102, 109
Dimmick, Caroline Eleanor, 73
    George B., 73
Dingley, Jacob, 67
Doane, Mary C., 87
    Mary Cushing, 102
Dodge, Clara A, 180, 184
Doggett, Experience, 21
    Jabez, 21
    Joanna, 21
    John, 21
    Mark, 21
    S. B., 21
    Seth, 21
    Simeon, 21
    Thomas, 21
Donham, Elizabeth, 112
Doolan, Alice, 101, 109
Doten, Elizabeth, 67, 68
Douglas, Cordelia A., 27, 36
    Delano F. W., 152
    Edgar Stiles, 152
Dow, M. Florence, 95
    Miriam, 157, 159
Dowd, Orrin W., 142
Downey, Mary, 88
Drake, Ann Elizabeth, 155
    Charles Hewitt, 136
    Clement Briggs, 135
    Eliza Ann, 148
    Elizabeth, 136, 141
    Eunice Fuller, 135
    Horatio Nelson, 135
    Linus, 74
    Mary Ann W., 136
    Nelson, 148
    Simeon, 135

SUPPLEMENT

TO THE

GENEALOGY

OF

"SOME DESCENDANTS OF EDWARD FULLER
OF THE MAYFLOWER."

PREFACE.

In 1908 I published the above-mentioned volume, and the following pages contain additional information concerning Edward Fuller's descendants gained from correspondents, from research, from other genealogists and those interested in Fuller genealogy. That volume is referred to in these pages as Volume 1. Mr. F. A. Fuller, number 301 of the 6th Group, Vol. 1, formerly of Mt. Vernon, N. Y., now of Buffalo, who published in 1896 a leaflet on "Mayflower Fuller Genealogy," has found much relating to the first and tenth groups; Miss Clara C. Fuller of Holland Patent and Ossining, N. Y., most of that relating to her branch in the first group, and Mrs. Gardner Fuller, wife of number 74 of the twenty-sixth group, has given much aid in tracing the families of that group. In this supplement the individual numbering in the group is discontinued except numbers taken from Vol. 1. The supplement has its own separate index.

WM. H. FULLER.

Palmer, July, 1910.

EXPLANATION FOR THE SUPPLEMENT.

The names of the sons who have families and whose record is extended are printed in heavier type and the use of the symbol ✣ is discontinued.

ILLUSTRATIONS IN THIS SUPPLEMENT.

Portrait of Major Russel Fuller of the First Group.
Portrait of Simeon Russel Fuller of the First Group.

SUPPLEMENT TO VOLUME I OF
FULLER GENEALOGY.

There is no additional information concerning descendants in the earlier generations not grouped in Volume I.

FIRST GROUP.

SOME DESCENDANTS OF SAMUEL⁵ FULLER, (*Barnabas⁴, Samuel³, Samuel², Edward¹*).

SIXTH GENERATION.

7. **LOT⁶ FULLER,** (*Samuel⁵, Barnabas⁴, Samuel³, Samuel², Edward¹*), b. Sept. 18, 1733, in Barnstable, Mass ; d. July 12, 1811, in Sandisfield, Mass. ; m. ———, Rachel ———, probably in Colchester, Ct.? who d. Feb. 28, 1812.

He came to Bolton, Ct, where he and his w. Rachel joined the church April 13, 1760. In 1768 he bought land in Sandisfield, where he and his wife were admitted to the church May 7, 1769. Lot Fuller is mentioned on Conn. French and Indian War Rolls, June 9 to Dec. 1, 1756, 2d Regt.

Children, born in Bolton, Ct. (In preparing the MSS. for Vol. 1, a list of births of these children was overlooked, which contained Simeon's name, and a list of baptisms used, which did not include Simeon) :

    I. Lot⁷, b. May 6, 1760. Lot Fuller was a soldier in the Revolutionary war, and the U. S. Pension Records give following information concerning him . "Born at Bolton, Ct, May 6, 1760, date of death not stated; date of application for pension, Sept 11, 1832; claim allowed; residence at date of application, Floyd, Oneida Co., N. Y.; residence at enlistment, Sandisfield,

Mass , battles engaged in — Taking of Burgoyne , date
of first enlistment, Sept., 1776 ; of last enlistment, July,
1778, length of service, 7 months in all , rank, private.
Soldier's brother Simeon was 70 years old and a resident
of Steuben, N. Y., in 1832. No other data as to family."

Jones' History of Oneida Co., N. Y., mentions Lot Fuller on jury,
1801. The Potter family genealogy mentions the marriage of Eliza
Jane Potter, b. Sept 7, 1804, dau. of John and Hannah Potter, to
Lot Fuller, Dec. 10, 1827, perhaps a son of Lot[7] Fuller.

  II.   SIMEON[7], b Oct. 21, 1762; m. 1, Mary Cook; m. 2,
       Wealthy Woodward Horton.
  III. Judah[7], b Feb. 3, 1765. See Vol. 1.
  IV. Rachel[7], b April 16, 1767. Nothing further found — not
       mentioned by Sandisfield town clerk as on the vital
       records Children, b. in Sandisfield : See Vol. 1. Noth-
       ing additional learned of them.

SEVENTH GENERATION.

13. SAMUEL[7] FULLER, (*Joshua[6]*, *Samuel[5]*, *Barnabas[4]*,
Samuel[3], *Samuel[2]*, *Edward[1]*), b. Dec. 25, 1752, in Bolton, Ct., d.
1841, at Brant, Erie Co., N. Y., m. Esther Flagg and settled in
Burlington, Vt.

He was a private in Col Ashley's Regt. in 1776, and later a sergeant in Col. Moses Nichols' Regt. at Saratoga in 1777, and was
present at the battle of Bennington, Aug. 16, 1777.

His children were :

  I.   Joshua[s], b July 18, 1781 or 1782.
  II. Joanna[s] or Nancy, b. Dec. 28, 1785 ; m. ——— Spear.
  III. Mary Lovisa[s], b. April 16, 1787 , m. Dec. 4, 1805, Enan
       Clark at Burlington, Vt., and had · Lewis[9], Clarissa[9],
       Asa[9], Reuben W.[9] and one other child, a daughter.
  IV. Esther[s], b. June 1, 1789 , m. ——— Flagg.
  V.   DANIEL[s], b. June 9, 1792 , m. Siba Chittenden.
  VI. William[s], b. Oct 5, 1794.
  VII. ASA[s], b. April 27, 1798; m. 1, Abigail ———— ; m. 2,
       Hannah Pierce

SIMEON[7] FULLER, (*Lot[6]*, *Samuel[5]*, *Barnabas[4]*, *Samuel[3]*,
Samuel[2], *Edward[1]*), b. Oct. 21, 1762, in Bolton, Ct.; d. Dec. 7,
1852, in Steuben, N. Y., m. 1, March 31, 1785, Mary Cook; m. 2,
Sept. 23, 1790, Wealthy Woodward Horton.

Captain Simeon Fuller.

Simeon Fuller was a soldier of the Revolution, and the U. S. Pension records show that he enlisted April 17, 1781, from Sandisfield, Mass., and served as private until the fall of 1782 under Captain Fox, Col. Henry Jackson's Regt.; re-enlisted and served until Jan. 4, 1784, under Capt. Fowler, Col. Greaton's Regt.; applied for pension July 4, 1832, from Steuben, Oneida Co, N. Y., and claim was allowed.

"Soldier's age at date of application 70 years, and soldier's brother Lot was 72 years of age and a resident of Floyd, N. Y., in 1832. No other data as to family.

Simeon Fuller is the only soldier of that name in the Mass. or N. Y. service found on the Revolutionary war pension records. On Mass. war rolls described as 5 ft. 7 in., with light complexion and light hair. He resided for a time in Fort Ann, Washington Co., N. Y., where he was a captain of militia, removed to Steuben about 1792; was a pioneer settler there and one of the most highly respected men of the county.

Children, except the first two, all b. in Steuben, N. Y.:

    I.   Mary[8], b. Feb. 17, 1786, d. Jan, 1813; m. Sept. 7, 1807, Daniel Douglas and had Alanson[9], b. Aug. 15, 1808, and George[9], b. Aug. 10, 1811.

    II.   SIMEON[8], b. July 25, 1791, m. Minerva Sprague.

   III. RUSSELL[8], b. Sept. 5, 1795; m. Lydia J. Potter.

   IV. JOHN WOODWARD[8], b. June 29, 1797, m. 1, Mariah Barnes; m. 2, Marietta Shurtleff.

    V.   Catherine[8], b. April 14, 1800; d. Dec. 18, 1886, at Watertown, N. Y.; m. Feb. 7, 1821, John W. Pierce, b. Aug. 15, 1798, in Philadelphia, Pa., d. July 4, 1877. Their children were: John F.[9], b. May 18, 1822, at Remsen, N. Y.; Lydia Ann[9], b. Nov. 24, 1823, at Remsen; William G.[9], b. Sept. 26, 1826, in Floyd, N. Y., where also were born Wealthy[9], Dec. 10, 1829; Simeon F.[9], Sept. 25, 1831; Isaac[9], Aug. 3, 1833; DeWitt C.[9], Sept. 12, 1835, Russell F.[9], Feb. 28, 1838, George[9], April 28, 1840; Charles E.[9], Oct. 11, 1842, and Franklin[9], Oct. 12, 1845.

EIGHTH GENERATION.

33. **DANIEL[8] FULLER,** (*Samuel[7], Joshua[6], Samuel[5], Barnabas[4], Samuel[3], Samuel[2], Edward[1]*), b. June 9, 1792; d. May 11, 1866, in Irving, N. Y.; m. 1816, Siba Chittenden, who d. Oct. 25, 1841, at Brant, Erie Co., N. Y.

Daniel Fuller served in the war of 1812 and in 1816 was keeping
an inn in Burlington, Vt., and removed to Hamburg, or Brant, N. Y.,
about 1828.

Children, the first five b in Burlington, the others in Brant:

I. Lemira[9], b Jan. 16, 1817, d. 1870, in Richmond, Ill, m.
Harmon Hall and had. Sophia[10], b. 1830, Ellen[10],
Albert[10], Mary[10], Harmon[10], Rosetta[10], Lucretia[10] and
Violetta[10]

II. SAMUEL BETHUEL[9], b Feb 25. 1819; m. Eliza Hall.

III. WILLIAM HARRISON[9], b. Sept. 15, 1822; m Mira Pierce.

IV. Caroline[9], b Jan 31, 1824, d March 22, 1889, at Cherry
Hill, Pa., m Horace Clark, b Dec. 25, 1817, and had.
Caroline[10], Rhoda[10], George[10], Flora[10] and Albert[10].

V. Esther[9], b. March 27, 1827, d Dec. 11, 1905, at Irving,
N. Y., m. Francis Tinney and had: Clarissa[10], Dorwin[10]
and Francis Albert[10]

VI. ALBERT CHITTENDEN[9], b. May 4, 1830, m. 1, Lucy
Marsh, m. 2, Sophronia Marsh.

VII. Louisa[9], b. June 6, 1833, d. May 29, 1859; m. Jan. 2,
1851, Amos Clark and had. Caroline Rose[10], b. Feb. 2,
1852, Ellen, b. Dec. 2, 1854, Maryette[10], b. Feb. 2,
1857, and Amos Adelbert[10], b. May 22, 1859.

VIII. Elizabeth[9], b Nov 14, 1838, d. Aug 10, 1866; m. Eleazer
Clark and had Ida F.[10], b 1860, at Collins, N. Y.

IX. Siba[9], b. Oct. 20, 1841, d. Sept 10, 1903, at Rice Lake,
Wis, m. 1, Peter Tinney; m 2, Chester Scott The
children were: Ida[10], Minnie[10], Chauncey[10], Marion[10],
Elmer[10], Ralph[10], Peter[10] and Caroline[10].

35. ASA[8] FULLER, (*Samuel[7], Joshua[6], Samuel[5], Barnabas[4],
Samuel[3], Samuel[2], Edward[1]*), b. April 27, 1798, in Burlington, Vt.,
d. May 6, 1869, in Brant, N. Y., m 1, Abigail ——, m. 2,
Hannah Pierce, who d. at Wonowoc, Wis.

Children.

I. HENRY[9], b. ——, m Margaret Swartout.

II. Esther[9], b. ——, m. George Whitmore, both d. at
Wonowoc, and left one son, who resides there.

III. Delia[9], b. ——; m. —— West.

IV. Sarah[9], b. ——; d. at Wonowoc, m. Israel Colvin and
had Dallas[10], Clarissa[10], Charles[10], Jeannette[10],
Leonard[10] and Delia[10], five of whom are living.

V. Jane[9], b. ——; m. Thomas West and had: George[10],
b. Aug. 12, 1850, and Julia Frances[10], b. ——.

Russell Fuller.

VI.   Rhoda[9], b. ———; m. Nathan Fiske; both dead. Their
        only child, Dode Fisk, is proprietor af the "Dode Fisk
        Circus."
VII.   Charles[9], b. 1829, d Dec. 17, 1851.
VIII. Julia[9], b. 1840; d. Nov. 25, 1852.
IX.   GEORGE[9], b. ———; m Elizabeth Parker.
X.   Leonard[9], b. July, 1848, d. Oct. 21, 1848.

62. JOHN HARVEY[8] FULLER, (*Judah[7], Lot[6], Samuel[5], Barnabas[4], Samuel[3], Samuel[2], Edward[1]*), b. Oct. 18, 1797, in Sandisfield, Mass.; d. ———; m. Elizabeth ———.
Notes from Southwick, Mass, records show that "Henry,
widower," b. Sandisfield, son of Judah and Sarah (Hastings) Fuller,
d. March 15, 1881, aged 84 y. 4 m. 28 d.

SIMEON[8] FULLER, (*Simeon[7], Lot[6], Samuel[5], Barnabas[4],
Samuel[3], Samuel[2], Edward[1]*), b. July 25, 1791, in Westfield, Wash-
ington Co., N. Y.; d. Sept 15, 1862 (also given 1861), in Willoughby,
O.; m. April (also given March) 20, 1820, Minerva Sprague, b. at
Middlefield, N. Y.; d. April 6, 1866, at Willoughby.
The local history says "Simeon Fuller emigrated to Lake Co., O.,
in 1818. He served six years as Associate Judge; three years as
County Commissioner in Cuyahoga Co, six years in the State
Legislature and two years in the Senate.
Their children, all b. at Willoughby, were:
I.   Russell[9], b. April 23, 1821; d. Dec. 5, 1879, at Willoughby;
       m. Amelia Whitney. No issue.
II.   GEORGE[9], b. Sept. 26, 1822, m. Eliza B Ferguson.
III. Louise[9], b. Oct. 5, 1827, m. Dec. 30, 1847, David Law and
        had Malcolm[10], b. Feb. 12, 1849, Myron[10], b. March
        16, 1851; Isabella Minerva[10], b Aug. 4, 1853; Jane
        Alicia[10], b. March 12, 1859, and George Fuller[10], b.
        June 11, 1863.

RUSSELL[8] FULLER, (*Simeon[7], Lot[6], Samuel[5], Barnabas[4],
Samuel[3], Samuel[2], Edward[1]*), b. Sept. 5, 1795, at Steuben, N. Y.;
d. there March 10, 1856; m. Feb. 25, 1821, Lydia J. Potter.
"Major Russell Fuller was one of the oldest and most prominent
residents of Steuben. He twice represented Oneida County in the
Legislature, and held various other offices of trust and honor."
Their children were:
I. SIMEON RUSSELL[9], b. Nov. 1, 1821, m. Martha White.

II   Mary⁹, b July 18, 1823, d. Nov. 29, 1901, at Holland
     Patent, N Y., m. Sept 28, 1853, Henry Stanton of
     Wethersfield, Ct   They resided in Trenton, N Y. Had
     no children.

JOHN WOODWARD⁸ FULLER, (*Simeon⁷, Lot⁶, Samuel⁵,
Barnabas⁴, Samuel³, Samuel², Edward¹*). b. June 29, 1797, in
Steuben, N. Y., d. April 8, 1868, at Alexandria Bay, N. Y.; m. 1,
Feb 7, 1825, Mariah Barnes, who d ———— , m. 2, Jan. 3, 1832,
Marietta Shurtleff, b. Jan. 29, 1808, in Leroy, N. Y.; d. Feb. 20,
1901.
All births and deaths in this family up to 1910 have been at
Alexandria Bay.
     Children :
   I.   Sarah Maria⁹, b. Jan. 23, 1833, d. Feb 6, 1855, unmarried.
  II.   Catherine Amelia⁹, b Dec. 13, 1834, m Jan. 22, 1861,
        William Maxwell Thompson, b. July 24, 1834, at
        Mallorytown, Ontario, Canada, who d. July 19, 1899.
        Children. Marietta¹⁰, b Nov. 11, 1861; John Fuller¹⁰,
        b March 5, 1864, and Frederick William¹⁰, b. Jan. 4,
        1867
 III.   Cornelia Ann¹⁰, b May 28, 1837; d. Sept. 21, 1863,
        unmarried
  IV.   Lucia Ellen¹⁰, b. Oct 1, 1839, d Aug. 31, 1857, unmarried.
   V.   Marietta¹⁰, b. May 15, 1842, m. Oct. 3, 1864, Martin Joy
        Hutchins, b Nov 7, 1825, in Schuyler, N. Y., and had.
        Martin Joy¹⁰, b Jan. 1, 1867, and Frank Fuller¹⁰, b.
        March 4, 1869; both born at Redwood, Jefferson Co,
        N. Y.
  VI.   Juliet⁹, b Feb. 3, 1845; m July 1, 1869, Andrew Calhoun
        Cornwall, b. Jan 2. 1844, at Pultneyville, N. Y., and had :
        Bertha¹⁰, b June 4, 1873; Bessie Cornelia¹⁰, b. April 3,
        1875; Andrew Howard¹⁰, b Dec. 30, 1876; Fuller
        Frederic¹⁰, b. Oct. 13, 1879; Andrew Raymond¹⁰, b.
        April 30, 1882, and Mary Catherine¹⁰, b Oct. 10, 1886.
 VII.   John Taylor⁹, b. Sept. 25, 1847, m. Aug. 19, 1901, Alma
        Bernice Pyne, b. Dec. 27, 1868, in Conracon, Ontario,
        Canada   No children
VIII.   Francis Evelyn⁹, b May 4, 1850, d. Sept. 5, 1863.

NINTH GENERATION.

SAMUEL BETHUEL⁹ FULLER, (*Daniel⁸, Samuel⁷, Joshua⁶,
Samuel⁵, Barnabas⁴, Samuel³, Samuel², Edward¹*), b. Feb. 25,

John Woodward Fuller.

1819, in Burlington, Vt., d Dec. 15, 1881, in Brant, N. Y.; m.
Eliza Hall, b Feb. 2, 1821, d. Feb 12, 1901, at Farnham, N. Y.

He served as a drummer in the Civil war.

Their children were

    I.   Bethuel[10], b. April 7, 1842, d. Dec. 27, 1862 — a soldier in the Civil war, 116th Regt. N Y. Vols.

    II. Villette[10], b. May 22, 1843, d. April 4, 1844.

    III. Harriet H.[10], b. March 24, 1845, d. March 29, 1898; m. Oct. 7, 1871, Robert Wilson and had. Robert[11], Purdy[11] and Elizabeth[11].

    IV. Ellen D.[10], b May 12, 1848; m. 1869, W. T. Ward and had: Samuel[11], b May, 1870, and Harry[11]. Resides in Sylvan Grove, Kan.

    V. Celia[10], b. June 29, 1852, m. Nov. 9, 1870, John Horton, b. April 9, 1842. Resides at Angola, N. Y.

    VI. **DANIEL L.**[10], b. June 24, 1854, m. 1, Emma Francis, m. 2, Kate Andrews

    VII. Susan P.[10], b. Sept. 23, 1856; m Dec. 12, 1875, Aaron Reeves, b. May 20, 1855, and had. Gertrude M.[11], b. July 1, 1876; Grace E[11], b. Jan. 11, 1886, and Daniel[11], b. May 8, 1881. Resides at Evans, N. Y.

    VIII Siba[10], b May 19, 1859; d Jan. 24, 1861.

    IX. Mark B.[10], b. Nov. 23, 1864; d. 1865.

WILLIAM HARRISON[9] **FULLER**, (*Daniel*[8], *Samuel*[7], *Joshua*[6], *Samuel*[5], *Barnabas*[4], *Samuel*[3], *Samuel*[2], *Edward*[1]), b Sept. 15, 1822, at Burlington, Vt., d 1905, m Jan. 25, 1842, Maria Pierce, b. May 21, 1825. He removed to Wonowoc, Wis.. in 1857, where he was Justice of the Peace for 12 years

Children, all born in Brant, N. Y :

    I.   Harry P.[10], b. Nov. 16, 1843; d. Aug. 14, 1859.

    II. Daniel D.[10], b. Aug. 22, 1845, d. Sept. 9, 1850.

    III. **WILLIAM BETHUEL**[10], b. Feb. 27, 1847, m. Lucretia Willard

    IV. **FRANCIS W.**[10], b. Jan. 8, 1849; m. Emily Hayden. Resides at Minot, N. D.

    V. **ALBERT C.**[10], b. March 7, 1851, m. Lina Ide. Resides at Wonowoc.

    VI. **CHARLES D.**[10], b. Dec. 3, 1853; m. Matilda Eaton, who d.

    VII. Mary[10], b. 1857, m. Dec 24, 1879, George H. Jenewein and had Gladys Myrl[11], b. June 6, 1884. Resides at Wilton, Wis.

    VIII. Harry D.[10]? b. June 5, 1870, in Wonowoc; d. Feb. 8, 1875.

ALBERT CHITTENDEN[9] FULLER, (*Daniel*[8], *Samuel*[7], *Joshua*[6], *Samuel*[5], *Barnabas*[4], *Samuel*[3], *Samuel*[2], *Edward*[1]), b. May 4, 1830, in Brant, N. Y., d. June 16, 1885, m. 1, Dec. 25, 1851, Lucy Marsh, who d. Aug 2, 1854, at Irving, N. Y.; m. 2, Feb. 16, 1856, Sophronia Marsh.

Albert C. Fuller served in the Civil war, was Sergeant in the 100th Regt. N. Y. Vols, and was in the battle of Fair Oaks. For 17 years he was an engineer on the Lake Shore and Michigan Southern R. R. and resided at Irving and Silver Creek, N. Y.

Children :

    I. Juliette[10], b. Nov. 3, 1853, at Irving, N. Y., m 1, Oct. 21, 1874, William A. Watt, b. Sept 9, 1848, at Sheridan, N. Y, and had. Lucy[11], b. July 15, 1875, Susan Emelyn[11], b. March 26, 1877, and Juliette[11], b. ———, m. 2, Oct 9, 1901, Albert H. Stebbins. Resides at Bradentown, Fla.

HENRY[9] FULLER, (*Asa*[8], *Samuel*[7], *Joshua*[6], *Samuel*[5], *Barnabas*[4], *Samuel*[3], *Samuel*[2], *Edward*[1]), b ———, d. about 1892, at Brant, N. Y., m. Margaret Swartout.

Children .

    I. Julia[10], b. about 1854, at Brant, m. Frank Vorce and had three children

GEORGE[9] FULLER, (*Asa*[8], *Samuel*[7], *Joshua*[6], *Samuel*[5], *Barnabas*[4], *Samuel*[3], *Samuel*[2], *Edward*[1]), b ———, at Brant, N. Y.; d. Dec. 23, 1900, at Collingwood, O.; m. Elizabeth Parker.

He was a soldier in the 116th Regt. N. Y. Vols. in the Civil war.

Children :

    1. Masie[10], b ———, m. and resides in Cincinnati, O.

GEORGE[9] FULLER, (*Simeon*[8], *Simeon*[7], *Lot*[6], *Samuel*[5], *Barnabas*[4], *Samuel*[3], *Samuel*[2], *Edward*[1]), b. Sept. 26, 1822, at Willoughby, O., d. Dec. 31, 1879, at Houghton, Mich.; m. Feb 26, 1846, Eliza B. Ferguson, b. at Willoughby, Aug 26, 1826. Resides at Warren, O.

Children born to them were :

    I. Alice Helen[10], b. Dec. 13, 1846, at Kirtland, O.; d. May 16, 1876, at Houghton, m. Aug. 11, 1864, Graham Pope

Simeon Russell Fuller.

and had · George Fuller[11], b Aug. 13, 1865; Helen Graham[11], b. July 8, 1866, and Mary Courtney[11], b. July 2, 1870, all b at Houghton, Mich.

II. Flora Ferguson[10], b. March 7, 1851, at Bedford, O.; d. Dec. 13, 1854, at Ottawa, O.

III. GEORGE THEODORE[10], b Dec. 25, 1852; m. Anna Danielson.

IV. Percival Logan[10], b. Nov. 17, 1856, at Ottawa, O.; d. June 20, 1863, at Houghton.

V. Simeon Ferguson[10], b. Oct. 27, 1861, at Houghton; m. Nov. 25, 1902, Bertha Ellen, and resides in the City of Mexico.

VI. JOHN DANA[10], b. Sept 25, 1863; m. Alice Drinkwater.

VII. Marion Lincoln[10], b. April 9, 1867; d. May 9, 1895, at Detroit, Mich.

VIII. Louise[10], b. ———— ; d. aged 26 years, at Detroit.

SIMEON RUSSELL[9] FULLER, (*Russell[8], Simeon[7], Lot[6], Samuel[5], Barnabas[4], Samuel[3], Samuel[2], Edward[1]*), b. Nov. 1, 1821, in Holland Patent, N. Y.; d. there June 5, 1902; m. there Sept. 10, 1851, Martha White, who survives him.

Their children, born in Steuben, N. Y., are:

I. Clara Cornelia[10], b Aug. 26, 1852.

II. Frank Russell[10], b. Nov. 21, 1856.

All residents of Holland Patent, N. Y.

TENTH GENERATION.

DANIEL L.[10] FULLER, (*Samuel B.[9], Daniel[8], Samuel[7], Joshua[6], Samuel[5], Barnabas[4], Samuel[3], Samuel[2], Edward[1]*), b. June 24, 1854, m 1, Emma Francis; m. 2, Kate Andrews.

Resides at Sylvan Grove, Kansas.

Children by first wife ·

I. Jessie[11], b. ———— ; m. Frederick McCahaid. Resides in New York.

WILLIAM BETHUEL[10] FULLER, (*William H[9], Daniel[8], Samuel[7], Joshua[6], Samuel[5], Barnabas[4], Samuel[3], Samuel[2], Edward[1]*), b. Feb. 27, 1847, at Brant, N. Y.; m. 1866, Lucinda Willard.

Resides at Camp Douglas, Wis.

Children :
  I.   Alta M.[11], b. Jan 8, 1868, m. LaFayette Shear and has
       one son, Vern   Lives at Ernfold Sask, Can.
  II. Maria[11], b June 6, 1869; m. Elmer Leach and has Lynn[12],
       Don[12] and an infant. Resides in Minneapolis, Minn.
  III. Arthur Adelbert[11], b. July 31, 1870. Resides at Camp
       Douglas
  IV. George W.[11], b. Jan. 21, 1878. Resides at Pasco, Wash.

FRANCIS W.[10] FULLER, (*William H.*[9], *Daniel*[8], *Samuel*[7],
Joshua[6], *Samuel*[5], *Barnabas*[4], *Samuel*[3], *Samuel*[2], *Edward*[1]), b.
Jan. 8, 1849 ; m. March 4, 1870, Emily Hayden.
They reside at Minot, N. D.
Children ·
  I.   Elgin Ellsworth[11], b. Feb. 2, 1872 , m. Anna R. Greenup
       and has three children living. Romeo L.[12], Wilbur D.[12]
       and Elgin Lee[12]. Resides in Seattle, Wash.
  II   Nellie May[11], b. Aug 1, 1876, m. April 20, 1895, C. W.
       Hurd and has: Elmer[12] and Ethel[12]. Lives at Great
       Falls, Mont
  III. Everett W.[11], b. March 11, 1884; m. June 20, 1906, Otilda
       Larson and has. Rachel[12] and Clarence[12]. Lives at
       Minot, N. D.
  IV. Lucy M.[11], b. Sept. 29, 1889. Resides at Minot.

ALBERT C.[10] FULLER, (*William H.*[9], *Daniel*[8], *Samuel*[7], *Joshua*[6],
Samuel[5], *Barnabas*[4], *Samuel*[3], *Samuel*[2], *Edward*[1]), b. March 7,
1851 ; m. Lina Ide.
Children .
  I.   Ralph[11], b. ——— ; m. Dolores Manning and has two
       children living.
  II. Claude[11], b. ———.
All reside in Wonowoc, Wis.

CHARLES D.[10] FULLER, (*William H.*[9], *Daniel*[8], *Samuel*[7],
Joshua[6], *Samuel*[5], *Barnabas*[4], *Samuel*[3], *Samuel*[2], *Edward*[1]), b.
Dec. 3, 1852 (also given 1853) ; m. Matilda Eaton, who d. ———.
He is with the Dode Fisk Circus
Children .
  I   William[11], b. ——— ; m. and has four children. Resides at
       Couderay, Wis.

II. Carrie[11], b ———— , m Thomas Durkee and has one son. Resides at Willow River, Minn.
III. Ernest[11], b. ———— Lives at Vancouver, B. C. Unmarried.
IV. Edith[11], b. ———— , m. ————.

GEORGE THEODORE[10] FULLER, (*George*[9], *Simeon*[8], *Simeon*[7], *Lot*[6], *Samuel*[5], *Barnabas*[4], *Samuel*[3], *Samuel*[2], *Edward*[1]), b. Dec. 25, 1852, at Bedford, Ohio; d. March 21, 1879, at Akron, O.; m. May 26, 1880, Anna Danielson.

Children, all born at Calumet, Mich :

I. Mary Louise[11], b. June 12, 1881.
II. Anna Elizabeth[11], b. Jan. 28, 1883
III. George Theodore[11], b. May 28, 1886. Resides in Lawrence, Mich.
IV. Russell J.[11], b. March 28, 1889 , d. Feb. 25, 1907.
V. Helen Graham[11], b. Aug. 3, 1902.

JOHN DANA[10] FULLER, (*George*[9], *Simeon*[8], *Simeon*[7], *Lot*[6], *Samuel*[5], *Barnabas*[4], *Samuel*[3], *Samuel*[2], *Edward*[1]), b. Sept. 25, 1863, at Houghton, Mich. , m April 9, 1887, Alice Drinkwater, b. in Bristol, England.

Children, all born in Hancock, Mich. :

I. George Stanley[11], b. Feb. 11, 1888.
II. Glendora May[11], b. Oct. 24, 1890.
III. Alice Helen[11], b. Nov. 5, 1892.
IV. Laura Jean[11], b. June 6, 1895.
V. Dorothy Mildred[11], b. June 14, 1901.

SECOND GROUP.

7. Isaac[6] Fuller, m. April 18, 1754, Susan Wadsworth of Pembroke, Mass. (Pembroke Records.)
49? Edmund D.? b. Middleboro, to David B. and Eunice (Catheart) Fuller , m. May 27, 1893, Mary A. Rogers.

Children .

I. Charles Wesson[11], b. April 8, 1894.
II. Genevieve A.[11], b. March 18, 1896. (Barnstable, Mass., Records.)

SIXTH GROUP.

98. Maria Asenath[9] (Fuller) Paine.   The Second Annual
     Reunion of the Fuller Cousins was held at the home of
     Henry A. Paine in Belchertown, Mass., in Sept., 1909.

125. Adaline Margaret[9].   Her daughter, Clara Adaline[11], m.
     William Andrew *Van* Benthuysen.

136. Anna Maria[9].   It was *Mr. Farr* who died in 1893.

138. George Willard[9], d. Jan. 2, 1909, at his home in Deerfield,
     Mass

172. Erskine A.[9], d Feb 19, 1894, in Clintonville, O.; m. June 17,
     1856, Harriet Maria Stanley, b. Nov. 9, 1831, at West
     Hartford, Ct   Mr. Fuller was extensively engaged in
     stock farming at Clintonville.

Their children were.

   I   Abbie[10], b. May 14, 1860, m. June 17, 1895, Henry M.
        Melchers, a lumber dealer of Saginaw, Mich., and had
        two daus. that d young

   II. Mary[10], b Nov. 26, 1861, d. March 2, 1893, at Columbus,
        O , m. July 8, 1886, Grayson H. Osborn, b. Oct. 14,
        1856, at St. Louis, Mo. She left a dau, Helen Harriet[11],
        b March 8, 1888, at Columbus.

   III Katherine Stanley[10], b. Feb 4, 1870, m. June 17, 1896,
        Earl C Peters and had Dorothy[11], b. July 19, 1897.

   IV. Martha Elizabeth[10], b. Sept. 7, 1874.   (Thomas Hooker
        Genealogy, 1909.)

222 Melville Weston[9], d. July 4, 1910, at his summer home in
     Sorrento, Me.

252. Warren D.[9], d. 1909, at his home in Ludlow, Mass.

433. Burt C.[11]

Children.

   I.   Blanche[12], b. 1891.
   II. Alta Belle[12], b. 1893.
   III. Earl A.[12], b. 1897.

NINTH GROUP.

17   Albert[8].
     Capt. Albert Fuller d. Dec. 3, 1844, aged 42.
     Mary (Chase) Fuller d. Aug. 31, 1846.
     Son Albert[9], d. Jan. 29, 1842.
     Dau Mary Helen[9], d Jan. 30, 1838, aged 4 years 5 months

41. Jehiel[9], b. March 8, 1839.

TENTH GROUP.

SEVENTH GENERATION.

10. EBENEZER[7] FULLER, (*Ebenezer*[6], *Ebenezer*[5], *Thomas*[4], *John*[3], *Samuel*[2], *Edward*[1]), b. Nov. 8, 1772, in Hebron, Ct.; d. May 10, 1858, in Cazenovia, N. Y.; m March, 1801, Hannah House, b. July 25. 1782, d. April 16, 1847. They settled in Cazenovia, about 1802.

He was a man of cheerful disposition, energetic, active, of industrious habits, and at his death was mourned by a large circle of friends.

Their children, all born at Cazenovia, were :

I.   Polly[5], b March 19, 1802 , d Feb 7, 1854.
II. ERASTUS[5], b. Nov. 25, 1803, m Lucretia Gilbert.
III. Harriet[5], b. Oct. 25, 1804; d. Jan. 25, 1876, at Corning, N Y , m. David Smith, who d. 1864, and had son, James, who d. July 18, 1902.
IV. Emily[5], b. July 27, 1806 ; d Feb, 1858, m. Orange Hill and had one daughter
V.   JOHN H.[5], b. Jan 9, 1809 , m. 1, Wilhemina Tucker; m. 2, Susan Garder.
VI. TERRELL[5], b. Aug. 18, 1813; m Charlotte Frizell; m. 2, Jane Card
VII. DWIGHT A.[5], b. Jan. 27, 1815 , m. Jane E. Merrick.
VIII. GEORGE WASHINGTON[5], b. March 11, 1818; m. Adeline Bradley.
IX. RALPH D.[5], b. Feb. 26, 1820; m. Adeline Coney.

EIGHTH GENERATION.

ERASTUS[5] FULLER, (*Ebenezer*[7], *Ebenezer*[6], *Ebenezer*[5], *Thomas*[4], *John*[3], *Samuel*[2], *Edward*[1]), b. Nov. 25, 1803, in Cazenovia, N. Y.; d. March 22, 1873, at New Woodstock, N. Y., m. Oct. 17, 1832, Lucretia Gilbert, b. Feb 6, 1809, d. July 19, 1867.

He was a farmer residing at New Woodstock.

Their children were .

I.   HARRY H.[9], b. Sept. 13, 1833 ; m. 1, Frank? Randall; m. 2, Flora Jones.
II. TRUMAN G.[9], b. May 1, 1835 ; m. Malinda Smith.
III. Emily[9], b. Aug. 8, 1837 ; d. July 2, 1856 ; unmarried.

IV   Helen⁹, b. July 31, 1839, d. Feb. 16, 1859; m. Oct. 15, 1857, Gustavus Bissell.   No children.

JOHN H.⁸ FULLER, (*Ebenezer⁷, Ebenezer⁶, Ebenezer⁵, Thomas⁴, John³, Samuel², Edward¹*), b. Jan. 9, 1809, in Cazenovia, N. Y.; d. June 7, 1890, at New Woodstock, N. Y.; m. 1, Wilhemina Tucker, b. 1814, d. 1845; m. 2, Jan. 27, 1851, Susan Garder, b. Aug. 17, 1827, d. March 15, 1905.

He was a farmer at New Woodstock.

There were three children, all of whom died young.

TERRELL⁸ FULLER, (*Ebenezer⁷, Ebenezer⁶, Ebenezer⁵, Thomas⁴, John³, Samuel², Edward¹*), b. Aug. 18, 1813, in Cazenovia, N. Y., d. Jan. 15, 1871, at Corning, N. Y., m. 1, Charlotte Frizell, m. 2, Jane Card, who d. Dec. 17, 1873.

He was in the boot and shoe business in Corning.

Children

I.   **CHARLES**⁹, b 1844; m. Susan Kimball.
II   Mary⁹, b Feb. 17, 1847; d. Nov. 2, 1909, m. Wallace Reed, who d ———.

DWIGHT A.⁸ FULLER, (*Ebenezer⁷, Ebenezer⁶, Ebenezer⁵, Thomas⁴, John³, Samuel², Edward¹*), b. Jan 27, 1815, in Cazenovia, N Y, d. May 19, 1890, at Corning, N. Y.; m. 1839, Jane E Merrick, b. Oct. 31, 1818, d. Aug. 28, 1902.

He was a farmer at Corning.

The children born to them were :

I.   George Washington⁹, b. July 19, 1841; living (1910) in Corning.
II.   Dwight L.⁹, b. Sept. 5, 1847, d March 9, 1907.
III. Franklin⁹, b. April 2, 1852, d. Aug 7, 1858.
IV.   William⁹, b April, 1856, d. Dec. 27, 1856.
V   Jennie E.⁹, b. June, 1858; d. July 22, 1860.
VI   Samuel D.⁹, b. July 11, 1863, d. Sept. 23, 1876.

(George W and Dwight L. Fuller, bachelors, were for many years proprietors of the Dickinson House at Corning. They took care of their mother, who was blind for many years before her death.—F. A. Fuller.)

GEORGE WASHINGTON⁸ FULLER, (*Ebenezer⁷, Ebenezer⁶, Ebenezer⁵, Thomas⁴, John³, Samuel², Edward¹*), b. March 11,

1818, in Cazenovia, N. Y., d. Dec. 28, 1904, at Pulaski, N. Y.; m. June 15, 1843, Adeline Bradley, b Feb 15, 1822, d. Oct. 8, 1893.

He was a druggist at Pulaski.

Their children were:

    I.   THEODORE B.9, b. Aug 15, 184–, m. Cora Kenyon.
    II. Ann E.9, b. April 11, 1846, d. Sept. 1, 1848.
   III. GEORGE HOUSE9, b. Jan 20, 1848; m. Sarah Beckwith.
   IV. May Elizabeth9, b. Feb. 12, 1850; living 1910.
    V. WILLIAM D.9, b Sept. 16, 1855; m. Sarah Tiff
   VI. Emma Jane9, b March 4, 1861, living 1910.
  VII Alberta9, b. May 2, 1863, d. May 30, 1863.

RALPH D.8 FULLER, (*Ebenezer7, Ebenezer6, Ebenezer5, Thomas4, John3, Samuel2, Edward1*), b. Feb. 26, 1820, in Cazenovia, N. Y.; d. May 21, 1886, at Portland, N. Y.; m. Dec. 22, 1859, Adeline Coney, b. Feb. 12, 1831.

He was a merchant at Portland.

They had one son.

    I. GEORGE WASHINGTON9, b. Nov. 26, 1860; m. Berneda Fary.

NINTH GENERATION.

HARRY H.9 FULLER, (*Erastus8, Ebenezer7, Ebenezer6, Ebenezer5, Thomas4, John3, Samuel2, Edward1*), b. Sept 13, 1833; d. Feb. 22, 1896, at Cazenovia, N. Y.; m. 1, Frank? Randall, b. Oct. 9, 1855, d. ———, m. 2, Flora Jones.

He resided at Cazenovia.

By first wife he had six children. No further record received.

TRUMAN G.9 FULLER, (*Erastus8, Ebenezer7, Ebenezer6, Ebenezer5, Thomas4, John3, Samuel2, Edward1*), b. May 8, 1835; m. Malinda Smith, who d. ———.

He resides at Cazenovia, N. Y.

Children:

    I. Emmett10, b. Nov. 16, 1859; m. Alvira Buxton.
    II. ERNEST10, b Jan. 30, 1861, m. Alice Coats.
   III. Truman G.10, b. Aug. 14, 1863; m. May Jones.
   IV. Bert10, b. Aug. 22, 1872, m. Jessie Magee; resides at Cazenovia.
    V. Delphine10, b. Aug. 9, 1876; m. Arthur Cook.

CHARLES[9] FULLER, (*Terrell*[8], *Ebenezer*[7], *Ebenezer*[6], *Ebenezer*[5], *Thomas*[4], *John*[3], *Samuel*[2], *Edward*[1]), b. 1844, d. June 17, 1895, at Corning, N. Y., m. 1873, Susan Kimball.

He was a merchant at Corning.

Children :
    I. Fanny[10], b. ———.

THEODORE B.[9] FULLER, (*George W.*[8], *Ebenezer*[7], *Ebenezer*[6], *Ebenezer*[5], *Thomas*[4], *John*[3], *Samuel*[2], *Edward*[1]), b. Aug. 15, 1844, d. July 31, 1896, at Batavia, N. Y ; m. Aug. 5, 1882, Cora Kenyon.

He was a clerk at Batavia.

Children :
    I. A daughter, b. Sept. 8, 1887.

GEORGE HOUSE[9] FULLER, (*George W.*[8], *Ebenezer*[7], *Ebenezer*[6], *Ebenezer*[5], *Thomas*[4], *John*[3], *Samuel*[2], *Edward*[1]), b. Jan. 20, 1848, m. Sept 17, 1873, Sarah Beckwith.

He is a druggist at Pulaski, N. Y.

Children ·
    I. Edward Hill[10], b. July 22, 1875
    II. George B.[10], b. June 20, 1877 ; d. Aug. 20, 1878.

WILLIAM D.[9] FULLER, (*George W.*[8], *Ebenezer*[7], *Ebenezer*[6], *Ebenezer*[5], *Thomas*[4], *John*[3], *Samuel*[2], *Edward*[1]), b. Sept. 16, 1855; d. Jan. 25, 1898, at Syracuse, N. Y.; m. Sept. 8, 1880, Sarah Tifft

He was a druggist at Syracuse.

Children .
    I. A. Bradley[10], b March 8, 1883.
    II. R Tifft[10], b July 23, 1889

GEORGE WASHINGTON[9] FULLER, (*Ralph D.*[8], *Ebenezer*[7], *Ebenezer*[6], *Ebenezer*[5], *Thomas*[4], *John*[3], *Samuel*[2], *Edward*[1]), b. Nov. 26, 1860; m. May 5, 1891, Berneda Fay, b. March 1, 1869.

He is engaged in grape culture at Portland, N. Y.

Children :
    I. Beatrice[10], b. March 8, 1893.
    II. Ralph[10], b. Aug. 26, 1897.
    III. Donald[10], b. Feb. 2, 1899.

IV. Gertrude[10], b. Jan. 1, 1903.
V. George Weston[10], b. March 6, 1908.

TENTH GENERATION.

ERNEST[10] **FULLER,** (*Truman G.*[9], *Erastus*[8], *Ebenezer*[7], *Ebenezer*[6], *Ebenezer*[5], *Thomas*[4], *John*[3], *Samuel*[2], *Edward*[1]), **b.** Nov. 16, 1859, m. Dec. 31, 1883, Alice Coats.

He is a farmer at Cazenovia, N. Y.

Children ·

I. Josephine[11], b. ———.

TENTH GROUP---Continued.

SEVENTH GENERATION.

18. FREDERICK AUGUSTUS[7] **FULLER,** (*Roger*[6], *Ebenezer*[5], *Thomas*[4], *John*[3], *Samuel*[2], *Edward*[1]), b March 1, 1775, in Hebron, Ct., is probably the Frederick Augustus Fuller who settled in Rutland, Vt., and d. there in 1832, m. Rachel Gordon.

Children ·

I. **FREDERICK AUGUSTUS**[8], b. May 24, 1813, m. 1, Emeline Rathbone; m. 2, Marcia B. Marsh.
II. Gordon B.[8], b. ———.
III. Francis[8], b ———.
IV. A dau., b. ——— ; d. unmarried.

EIGHTH GENERATION.

FREDERICK AUGUSTUS[8] **FULLER,** (*Frederick A.*[7], *Roger*[6], *Ebenezer*[5], *Thomas*[4], *John*[3], *Samuel*[2], *Edward*[1]), b. May 24, 1813, in Rutland, Vt., d. ———, m. 1, June 19, 1838, Emeline Rathbone, b. May 27, 1815, d Feb. 6, 1886, at Jamestown, N. Y.; m. 2, Oct. 3, 1889, Marcia B Marsh, b Dec. 17, 1814.

Children .

I. **FREDERICK AUGUSTUS**[9], b. April 10, 1839; m. Cornelia Ludlow Benedict.
II. Dudley B.[9], b. March 10, 1843, d. May, 1889, at San Francisco, Cal.
III. William Rathbone[9], b. Feb. 1, 1846; d. June 26, 1873.
IV. Charles Gordon[9], b. Aug. 9, 1856; m. Isabella H. ---———. Resides at Evanston, Ill.

NINTH GENERATION.

FREDERICK AUGUSTUS[9] FULLER, (*Frederick A.[8]*, *Frederick A.[7]*, *Roger[6]*, *Ebenezer[5]*, *Thomas[4]*, *John[3]*, *Samuel[2]*, *Edward[1]*), b. April 10, 1839, in Rutland, Vt , m. May 24, 1866, Cornelia Ludlow Benedict, who d Dec 22, 1891.

He resides in Jamestown, N. Y.

Children ·

  I.   Frederick Augustus[10], b. ———— , d. in infancy.
  II.   Russell Seymour[10], b Aug 1, 1871, in Brooklyn, N. Y.
  III   Clifford Rathbone[10], b. Feb. 17, 1873, in Brooklyn.
  IV.   Gordon Carter[10], b Aug 3, 1884, in Brooklyn.

ELEVENTH GROUP.

15.   Irad[7]; m Jan. 16, 1804, Chloe Mills

41.   Halsey[8], m. May 29, 1822, Lydia Lee.

43.   Gurdon[8], m April 25, 1848 or 1849, Evelina S. Brigham, 2d wife?

48.   Warren[8], m Oct 26, 1814, Vesta Marsh and had : Timothy Mills[9], b. July 22, 1815 ; Alfred[9], b June 15, 1817, twin with Adaline[9]

51.   Jehiel[8], m. Dec. 28, 1822, Betsey Coming.

52.   Thankful[8], m. Jan. 8, 1823, Jacob Newell.

54.   Asenath[8], m. Nov. 21, 1827, Horace White.

76.   Ella[9] ~~Herdan~~ Her dau , Mrs. Brown, d July, 1909 Her son, Alvin Wilson[10] Comstock, m. Nov. 2, 1899, Harriet Young. Children . Phyllis N.[11], b. Aug., 1900, and Alvin Fuller[11], b. May 13, 1903.

79   L Lavinia[9]; m. Aug. 6, 1845, Dr. Stephen Griggs

149.   Frank Revilo[10], m. March 26, 1894, Laura Hayes Fuller.

150.   Charles[10], m. Nov. 10, 1892, Mary Antoinette Hait.

NINETEENTH GROUP.

42.   Page 196, vol. I. Jonathan[8] (called John in newspaper) d. in Adams, Mass , June 4, 1909, aged 78 years, at the home of his sister, Mrs. Hannah Hildreth. He leaves a son, Albert of Concord, a dau., Mrs William Crafts of Springfield, Mass., and a dau., Mrs. Alvin Horton of Pittsfield, Mass He had always lived in Savoy, Mass.

TWENTY-SECOND GROUP.

70.   Fred Henry[9], m. Nov. 7, 1906, in Lee, Mass., Lela M. Wright.

TWENTY-THIRD GROUP.

SEVENTH GENERATION.

10.   SYLVANUS[7], b. Feb. 24, 1778, at Kent, Ct.; d. March 6, 1848, at Carlisle, O.; m. March 2, 1806, in Plymouth, Pa., Betsey Winton, b. Jan. 24, 1780, d. Oct. 19, 1856, at Carlisle, dau. of Ezra Winton of Weston, Ct.

Family moved to Carlisle about 1829 and settled on 400 acres, two miles from Elyria, O. This homestead is still (1910) in the Fuller family.

Children, all b in Pennsylvania ·

    I.   Paulina W.[8], b. March 11, 1807; d. May 1, 1874, m. June 1, 1835, Dr. Benjamin Franklin Robinson of Elyria, Ohio, and had . Charles W [9], b May 18, 1836; Eugene F.[9], b. Jan. 3, 1842. All dead , no descendants of this family living.

    II.   Lydia[8], b Nov. 4, 1809; d. ———, in Cleveland, O.; m. Abner Barber in Pa , about 1828. Had five children, b. in Ohio   Elizabeth[9], Minerva[9], Asa[9], Antoinette[9] and Van Buren[9].

    III.   Bradley[8], b June 8, 1812; d. Aug. 12, 1814.

    IV.   Betsey A.[8], b. Feb. 9, 1815, d. April 25, 1901, m. Feb. 22, 1837, Charles Drakeley of Carlisle, O., and had . Henry C[9], b Oct. 13, 1838, and Pauline[9], b. Feb. 20, 1841, who m. Sept. 19, 1865, at Madison, Wis., H. Levander Farr.

Mrs. Pauline Fuller Drakeley Farr of Madison, Wis., furnished this additional information regarding descendants of Sylvanus[7].

    V.   Charles F.[8], b. June 24, 1818, d Nov. 12, 1839.

    VI.   ABRAM[8], b May 20, 1820, m. Caroline Bassett Hurd.

EIGHTH GENERATION.

ABRAM[8] FULLER, (*Sylvanus[7], Joshua[6], Joseph[5], Joseph[4], John[3], Samuel[2], Edward[1]*), b. May 20, 1820; d. Dec., 1889; m about 1849, Caroline Bassett Hurd.

Children

I.   Metta⁹, b ———— ; d. aged 2 years
II. CHARLES⁹, b. about 1854 , m. Cora V. Garrett.

NINTH GENERATION.

CHARLES⁹ FULLER, (*Abram⁸, Sylvanus⁷, Joshua⁶, Joseph⁵, Joseph⁴, John³, Samuel², Edward¹*), b. about 1854 ; m. Cora V. Garrett of Carlisle, O.

He still owns the Fuller homestead near Elyria, and a large property in Cleveland, O., where he resides.

Children :

I.   Carrie¹⁰, b. ————.

SEVENTH GENERATION.

30. CHAUNCEY⁷. Among the papers on Fuller genealogy belonging to the late Charles Richardson Smith (See No. 319 of Fifth Group— Dr Samuel Fuller descendants) mention is made of Chauncey Day Fuller, b. June 25, 1799, son of Jehiel and Hannah (Hill) Fuller of Centremoreland, Pa.

Chauncey Day Fuller d. 1867, in Freemansburg, Pa., m. Sarah Wheeler.

Children ·

I.   JAMES W.⁸, b. ————, m Clarissa Miller.
II.   Orlando⁸, b. ————.
III. CHARLES DORRANCE⁸, b. ————.
IV.   George W.⁸, b ————.
V.   Abbott⁸, b. ————.

EIGHTH GENERATION.

JAMES W.⁸ FULLER, (*Chauncey D⁷, Jehiel⁶, Joseph⁵, Joseph⁴, John³, Samuel², Edward¹*), b. ————, in Freemansburg, Pa.; d. about 1872, in Catasauqua, Pa.; m. Clarissa Miller.

Children

I.   JAMES W.⁹, b. 1845 , m. Katharine Maria Thomas
II.   Orange M.⁹, b. ————.
'II. Clarissa C.⁹, b. ————.
V.   Abbott F.⁹, b. ————.
      Clinton⁹, b. July 24, 1858.

CHARLES DORRANCE⁵ FULLER, (*Chauncey D.⁷, Jehiel⁶, Joseph⁵, Joseph⁴, John³, Samuel², Edward¹*), b. ——— ; d. ——— ; m. ———.

Children :

> A dau., Irene⁹, b. ——— ; m. Alex N. Ulrich. No reply received to inquiries for information. (A Stephen Fuller is mentioned from Ct., who settled in Plymouth Township, Pa., about 1768–1773.—Wright's Hist. of Plymouth, Pa.)

NINTH GENERATION.

JAMES W.⁹ FULLER, (*James W.⁸, Chauncey D.⁷, Jehiel⁶, Joseph⁵, Joseph⁴, John³, Samuel², Edward¹*), b. 1845, in Beaver Meadow, Pa.; m. Kathrin Maria Thomas.

Children :

I. George Llewelyn ¹⁰, b. ———.
II. Maud Miller ¹⁰, b. ——— ; m. J. S. Elverson.
III. Blanche ¹⁰, b. ——— ; m. Dr. L. A. Slade.
IV. May Louise ¹⁰, b. ———.
V. James W.¹⁰, b. ———.

TWENTY-SIXTH GROUP.

SIXTH GENERATION.

7. ROSWELL⁶ FULLER, (*Abraham⁵, Joseph⁴, John³, Samuel², Edward¹*), b. Sept. 1, 1774, in Kent, Ct.; d. Mar. 20, 1840, in Perrinton, N. Y.; m. Hannah Berry, b. in Kent, 1775, d. at Grand Isle, Lake Champlain, 1819.

He lived at Grand Isle until his wife's death, then removed to Perrinton.

Children :

I. JEREMIAH⁷, b.——— ; m. ———.
II. Ebenezer⁷, b.——— ; d. aged 22 years.
III. WILLIAM ST. PIERRE, b. ——— ; m. ———.
IV. WELLS B.⁷, } twins, b. ——— ; { m. ———.
V. WALES⁷, } { m. ———.
VI. HENRY TOWER⁷, b. April 27, 1825; m. Sarah Percival Strong.

VII.   Lydia[7], b. ——— ; d. aged 72 ; m. James Baker.   No
          issue.
VIII. Hannah[7], b. ———— , d. aged 44 ; unmarried.
 IX.   Mary Ann[7], b. ———— , d. aged 19 ; unmarried.
  X.   Jeannette[7], b. ——— ; d. aged 14

Since daughters are placed last, correspondent has not probably
mentioned the children in order of birth, and says that only one
daughter—Lydia—married.

SEVENTH GENERATION.

10. FREDERICK FOLLETT[7] FULLER, (*Esbon*[6], *Abraham*[5],
Joseph[4], *John*[3], *Samuel*[2], *Edward*[1]), b. Sept. 25, 1783, in Kent,
Ct.; d. Feb. 24, 1867, at Keesville, N. Y., m. July 1, 1806, Sally
Kinney, b. 1780, d. Nov. 3, 1841, at Keesville.
      Children.
          I.   ARMINTUS[8], b. Jan 7, 1825, m. Lurancy Jordan.   A cor-
                respondent, now dead, states there were three sons and
                four daughters in this family. Two besides Armintus[8]
                are mentioned in Vol. 1.

11. ORRIN[7] FULLER, (*Esbon*[6], *Abraham*[5], *Joseph*[4], *John*
Samuel[2], *Edward*[1]), b. Jan. 1, 1785, in Kent, Ct., d. 1827,
Keesville, N. Y.; m. 1, Betsey Turrell, b. Aug. 9, 1786 ; m. 2, Sarah
Wiltsie.

Lived in New York, but removed to Albany about 1820.
Children by first wife.
          I.   Arminta Fidelia Farrar[8], b. March 28, 1808, d. Jan. 17,
                1901, at Keesville, N. Y., m. Nov. 2, 1826, at Ferris-
                burg, Vt., James Hindes of Addison, Vt, and had :
                Orrin F.[9], b. Oct. 11, 1827 ; George Whitney[9], b. July
                18, 1829, William F.[9], b. June 18, 1831 ; Jacob G.[9], b.
                June 13, 1834 ; E. Wiltsey[9], b. Nov. 15, 1839 ; S.
                Elizabeth[9], b. April 25, 1842 ; L. Augusta[9], b. Oct. 21,
                1846, now Mrs. E. R. Baber, Keesville, N. Y., and J.
                Spencer[9], b. May 4, 1850.
         II.   Laura Jeanette[8], b. Dec. 13, 1809 (also given 1810), d.
                May 23, 1861 ; m. April 23, 1834, Frederick James
                Hosford, b. June 9, 1810, in Albany, N. Y., d. May 15,
                1889, in Brooklyn, N Y.   Children: Mary Smith[9], b.
                Feb. 8, 1835, d. July 8, 1836 ; James Spencer[9], b. Dec.
                13, 1836, resides Kinderhook, N. Y.; Henry[9], b. April
                5, 1839, living (1910) ; Frederic[9], b. Nov. 18, 1841, d.
                Feb. 7, 1866, unmarried, Laura Augusta[9], b. Nov. 19,

1846, d. April 19, 1849; Lucy Ella[9], b. May 17, 1852; d. Sept. 13, 1878.

III. Lucy Luzette[8], b. Dec. 3, 1812; d. ———; m. Medad Martin.

By second wife:

IV. Orrin Baxter[8], b. May 22, 1819; m. Phebe Thorn Clark.
V. Joseph Wiltsie[8], b. 1821.
VI. Jacob Evertson[8], b. 1824; d. ———; unmarried.

13. MILO[7] FULLER, (*Esbon*[6], *Abraham*[5], *Joseph*[4], *John*[3], *Samuel*[2], *Edward*[1]), b. Jan. 6, 1791 (also given July 6), in Kent, ., or Ferrisburg, Vt.; d. April 12, 1860, at Charlotte, Vt.; m. Mary (Polly) Marsh, b. March 19, 1790, d. Oct. 3, 1852, at Charlotte.

Children:

I. CHARLES D.[8], b. Dec. 17, 1812; m. 1, Mary Ann Ray; m. 2, Mary A. Weeks; m. 3, Cornelia Fairbanks.
II. Mary M.[8], b. March 4, 1815; d. Aug. 6, 1894; m. 1, Justus A. Southard; m. 2, William H. Southard. No children.
III. Rufus M.[8], b. Feb. 17, 1817; m. ———.
IV. Eliashil A.[8], b. April 2, 1820; m. Cornelia A. Webb.
V. Cynthia T.[8], b. July 11, 1823; d. Sept. 5, 1879; m. William H. Cunningham and had Rufus[9] of Burlington, Vt., and William[9] of Vergennes, Vt.
VI. Henry W.[8], b. July 10, 1827; m. Melissa Wilson.

JEREMIAH[7] FULLER, (*Roswell*[6], *Abraham*[5], *Joseph*[4], *John*[3], *Samuel*[2], *Edward*[1]), b. ———; d. ———, aged 65 years; m. ———.

Children:

I. Polly Ann[8] *Baker*, b. ———; dead. (Probably m. ——— Baker.)
II. Jennette[8] *Harkness*, b. ———. (Perhaps m. ——— Harkness.)
III. John[8], b. ———; dead.
IV. Christopher[8], b. ———.
V. Winfield[8], b. ———; dead.

WILLIAM ST. PIERRE[7] FULLER, (*Roswell*[6], *Abraham*[5], *Joseph*[4], *John*[3], *Samuel*[2], *Edward*[1]), b. ———; d. ———, aged 71; m. ———, Mira L. ———.

Children :

    I. LEGRAND⁵, b. Feb. 12, 1839; dead; m. Louisa? M
        Merryman.

    II. Frances? Southmayd⁵, b. ———.

WELLS B.⁷ FULLER, (*Roswell⁶, Abraham⁵, Joseph⁴, John³
Samuel², Edward¹*), b. ———, d. aged 79; m. ———.

Children :

    I. Roswell⁵, b. ———.

WALES⁷ FULLER, (*Roswell⁶, Abraham⁵, Joseph⁴, John³
Samuel², Edward¹*), b. ———; d. May 15, 1900, at Webster
N. H., aged 85; m. 1, Jane Voorhes; m 2, Mrs. John Schermerhorn.

Children by first wife :

    I. Henry P.⁵, b. ———.

    II. Charles W.⁵, b. ———.

EIGHTH GENERATION.

LEGRAND⁸ FULLER, (*William St. P.⁷, Roswell⁶, Abraham⁵,
Joseph⁴, John³, Samuel², Edward¹*), b. Feb. 12, 1839, at Ausable
Forks, N. Y., d. ———; m. Dec. 25, 1866, Louisa? M. Merryman,
b. Nov. 27, 1837.

Dr. LeGrand Fuller resided 5 ? Elliot Place, Brooklyn, N. Y.

Children :

    I. Dr. Zenas Preston⁹ Fuller, b. July 4, 1868, a dentist at
        Brooklyn, N. Y. (Walter Merryman Genealogy, 1905.)

ARMINTUS⁸ FULLER, (*Frederick F.⁷, Esbon⁶, Abraham⁵,
Joseph⁴, John³, Samuel², Edward¹*), b. Jan. 7, 1825, at Keesville,
N. Y., d. Dec. 19, 1899, at Leadville, Colo.; m. July 25, 1847, at
Jay, N. Y., Lurancy Jordan, b. Dec. 15, 1828, at Jay, d. Dec. 16,
1862, at Keesville.

Children :

    I. SPENCER HOSFORD⁹, b. ———.

ORRIN BAXTER⁸ FULLER, (*Orrin⁷, Esbon⁶, Abraham⁵,
Joseph⁴, John³, Samuel², Edward¹*), b. May 22, 1819, in New
York; d. April 7, 1896, in Albany; m. Oct. 6, 1840, Phebe Thorn
Clark, b. Sept. 1, 1819, d May 26, 1894.

Children :

I.   Orrin Augustus[9], b. Aug. 15, 1841. Living in Albany. Unmarried (1910). In State Comptroller's office.
II. Edward James[9] 1st, b. Dec. 11, 1843; d. March 30, 1845.
III. Sarah Wiltsie[9], b. Nov. 30, 1846; d. May 5, 1855.
IV. Edward James[9] 2d, b. Dec. 19, 1848; d. May 22, 1851.
V.   Elizabeth Hilton[9], b. Oct. 13, 1851; d. Sept. 30, 1852.
VI. Anna James[9], b. Feb. 9, 1854; d. Aug. 12, 1887; m. Augustus J. Phillips. She left a dau., Cecile K., who m. Joseph Boyd.
VII. JOSEPH WILTSIE[9], b. Aug. 6, 1858; m. Margaret Jane Grant.
VIII. Edward James[9] 3d, b. Nov. 29, 1860; d. Nov. 29, 1864.

JOSEPH WILTSIE[8] FULLER, (*Orrin[7], Esbon[6], Abraham[5], Joseph[4], John[3], Samuel[2], Edward[1]*), b. Oct. 26, 1821, in Albany, N. Y.,; d. May 15, 1889, in Troy, N. Y.; m. Nov. 21, 1844, Mary Elizabeth Wolfe.

He was a member of the firm of Fuller, Warren & Co., stove manufacturers, of Troy.

Children :

I.   Helen[9], b. Aug. 18, 1848, in Troy; m. April 28, 1870, Eliphalet Nott Potter and had: Mary Josepha[10], b. Dec. 22, 1871; Helen[10], b. Dec. 7, 1872; Maria Nott[10], b. May 4, 1874; Eliphalet Nott[10], b. Aug. 9, 1878; J. W. Fuller[10], b. Feb. 7, 1882; Howard[10], b. Feb. 23, 1886. Resides in New York City.
II. Jessie[9], b. 1855, in Brooklyn, N. Y.; m. 1878, Walter Thompson and had: Joseph Wiltsie[10], b. 1881; Walter[10], b. 1882; Jessie[10], b. 1887, and Dorothy Fuller[10], b. 1890. Resides at Tarrytown-on-the-Hudson, N. Y.
III. Mary Wiltsie[9], b. ———. Resides in Troy, N. Y. (1910.)

CHARLES DAY[8] FULLER, (*Milo[7], Esbon[6], Abraham[5], Joseph[4], John[3], Samuel[2], Edward[1]*), b. Dec. 17, 1812, in Ferrisburg, Vt.; d. Aug. 2, 1885, in Brattleboro, Vt.; m. 1, Dec. 8, 1842, Mary Ann Ray; m. 2, Aug. 30, 1857, Mary A. Weeks, who d. Feb. 3, 1870, in Fort Covington, N. Y.; m. 3, 1873, Cornelia Fairbanks, who d. Dec., 1888, in Jay, N. Y.

Charles Day Fuller was in his earlier manhood an iron maker, and also a favorite singing school teacher and a preacher. Later (1857) he was ordained as pastor of the Baptist church in Troy, N. H. Subsequent pastorates were in Westford, West Norwich and

Brookline, Vt., and Nicholville, Ft. Covington, Chateauguay and Jay, N. Y.

Children ·

    I   Charles D'Estaing⁹, b. Aug. 11, 1859, in Westford, Vt.; d. there in 1861.
    II. EDWARD MILO⁹, b. June 10, 1861.
    III Mattie Estelle⁹, b May 17, 1883, in Newfane, Vt.; d. Feb. 28, 1890, in Salem, N. Y.

RUFUS M.⁷ FULLER, (*Milo⁷, Esbon⁶, Abraham⁵, Joseph⁴, John³, Samuel², Edward¹*), b. Feb. 17, 1817; d. Aug. 1, 1849, at Barton's Landing, Vt.; m. March 1, 1848, in Buckingham, Canada East, Eleanor Jane Eaton, b. June 27, 1827, in Brownington, Vt., d. June 27, 1905, in Littleton, N. H.

Children :

    I. Mary⁹, b May 21, 1849, in Burlington, Vt.; m. Sept. 9, 1868, Elbridge Flint of Worcester, Mass., and ha Rufus Frederick¹⁰, b. May 21, 1873, d. Aug. 16, 1873. Resides in Littleton, N. H.

ELIASHIL A.⁸ FULLER, (*Milo⁷, Esbon⁶, Abraham⁵, Joseph⁴, John³, Samuel², Edward¹*), b. April 2, 1820, at Ferrisburg, Vt.; d. Aug. 15, 1908, at Oak Park, Ill.; m. April 13, 1840, at Ferrisburg, Cornelia A. Webb, b. Nov. 5, 1820, who is living (1910) at Oak Park.

He taught school many years, and when about 30 years of age went into the book business in Burlington, Vt.

Children :

    I.   Marion I.⁹, b. Feb. 5, 1843, at Charlotte, Vt.; m. Jan. 1, 1862, at Burlington, Vt., Hampton L. Story. Resides at Oak Park   Has two surviving sons, Edward H.¹⁰ and Frank F¹⁰
    II. Effagene M.⁹, b. Aug. 2, 1844, at Charlotte; m. March 14, 1871, at Burlington, Edward B. Loomis, M. D., and has one surviving daughter, Charlotte C.¹⁰ Resides in Chicago.
    III. JUDSON M.⁹, b. Oct. 10, 1864 ; m. Kate M. Geisinger.

HENRY W.⁸ FULLER, (*Milo⁷, Esbon⁶, Abraham⁵, Joseph⁴, John³, Samuel², Edward¹*), b. July 10, 1827, d. Oct. 20, 1862; m. July 3, 1856, Melissa Wilson.

Henry W. Fuller was a member of Co. I, 5th Regt. Vt. Vols. in the Civil war, and died on board ship Euterpe as he was being removed from Chesapeake Hospital, Fortress Monroe, to New York City hospital.

Children :

I. Burr M.⁹, b. June 4, 1857 ; m. and had four children. Said to reside in Aspen, Colo., but letter of inquiry returned "unclaimed" (July, 1910).

II. Bertha⁹, b. April 18, 1861 ; m. Nov. 29, 1879, Charles Waterman. Their children were : Clayton⁹, b. Feb. 5, 1881 ; Faye⁹, b. Dec. 17, 1886 ; Effie⁹, b. March 29, 1889 ; Charlotte Dell⁹, b. Jan. 24, 1894, and Gerald⁹, b. June 3, 1898. All the children but Charlotte D. are dead.

88. PERCIVAL S.⁸ (See Vol. 1) ; m. Henrietta Case. (D. A. R. Directory.)

NINTH GENERATION.

SPENCER HOSFORD⁹ FULLER, (*Armintus⁸, Frederick F.⁷, Esbon⁶, Abraham⁵, Joseph⁴, John³, Samuel², Edward¹*), b. ———— ; m. ————.

Children :

1. Edith¹⁰, b. ———— ; m. Guy Fuller.

JOSEPH WILTSIE⁹ FULLER, (*Orrin B.⁸, Orrin⁷, Esbon⁶, Abraham⁵, Joseph⁴, John³, Samuel², Edward¹*), b. Aug. 6, 1858 ; m. Sept. 7, 1881, Margaret Jane Grant.

He resides in Albany, N. Y. Is with John G. Myers Co.

Children :

I. Perry Grant¹⁰, b. June 17, 1882 ; m. Jan. 20, 1909, Jessamine Blakeman.

EDWARD MILO⁹ FULLER, (*Charles D.⁸, Milo⁷, Esbon⁶, Abraham⁵, Joseph⁴, John³, Samuel², Edward¹*), b. June 10, 1861, in Westford, Vt. ; m. ————.

He is a Baptist clergyman at Manchester Center, Vt.

Children :

I. Earl¹⁰, b. ————. Residing (1910) in Manchester, Vt.

II. Charles Robert¹⁰, b. Jan. 29, 1906.

JUDSON M.⁹ FULLER, (*Eliashil A.⁸, Milo⁷, Esbon⁶, Abraham⁵, Joseph⁴, John³, Samuel², Edward¹*), b. Oct. 10, 1864, at Burlington, Vt.; m. at Chicago, Ill., Jan. 5, 1887, Kate M. Geisinger.

  Children.

  I.   Judson Earl¹⁰, b. Oct. 13, 1887, in Chicago, Ill.
  II. Doris K.¹⁰, b Oct 31, 1889, in Chicago, Ill.
  III. Margaret¹⁰, b. June 12, 1891, at Oak Park, Ill.
  IV. Eleanor¹⁰, b. March 9, 1904, at Oak Park, Ill.

APPENDIX.

It appears that the Joshua Fuller mentioned in Vol. 1, page 58, who m. Mercy Felt, was born in 1774 in Wrentham, Mass., son of Noah and Esther. (See Wrentham, Mass., Vital Records.) Joshua and Mercy had six children. He died in Waterville, Vt., April 17, 1849. Hence not a descendant of Samuel⁷ Fuller.

Index to Fullers in Supplement.

Index to other Names than Fuller---Supplement.